HITLER'S SECRET
HEADQUARTERS

Franz W. Seidler ✦ Dieter Zeigert

HITLER'S SECRET HEADQUARTERS

The Führer's Wartime Bases, from the Invasion of France to the Berlin Bunker

Translated by Geoffrey Brooks

This Book Club Edition is manufactured under license from
Greenhill Books / Lionel Leventhal Limited - London

Hitler's Secret Headquarters:
The Führer's Wartime Bases, from the Invasion of France to the Berlin Bunker
First published 2004 by
Greenhill Books, Lionel Leventhal Limited, Park House,
1 Russell Gardens, London NW11 9NN
and
Stackpole Books, 5067 Ritter Road, Mechanicsburg, PA 17055, USA

Text © 2000 by Herbig Verlagsbuchhandlung GmbH, Munich
Translation © 2004 by Lionel Leventhal Ltd

ISBN 0-7394-5003-4

Printed and bound in the USA

Contents

Illustrations

Text Figures

Preface

DURING the Second World War the threat of attack by aircraft and other long-range weapons led the principal European belligerents to design and build gas- and bomb-proof structures for the protection of their political and military leaderships. Great Britain and the Soviet Union were forced to do so by reason of their geographical proximity to Germany. The Third Reich, between 1939 and 1945, generated a huge industry in semi-subterranean *Führerhauptquartiere* (*Führer* Headquarters, or FHQ). When defeat came, almost twenty such estates were strewn across Europe with more under construction, their scale increasing beyond all comprehension as time went on.

Whereas Hitler's 'excursions to the front' during the relatively straightforward Polish campaign could be made using his *Sonderzug* (special train) as a base, for the assault on France and the war against the Soviet Union more substantial, fixed headquarters were required. Most of these were located in the occupied territories and extended from Vendôme in the West (for the defence of 'Fortress Europe' against the Allied invasion) to Smolensk on the upper Dnieper (to conduct the battle for Moscow), and from Pleskau, not far from the Russian/Estonian border (to direct Army Group North in the battle for Leningrad), to as far south as the Ukraine (for Stalingrad and the Caucasus).

Hitler's private residence on the Obersalzberg near Berchtesgaden, the 'Berghof', and, from late 1944, the *Reichskanzlei* (Reich Chancellery) in Berlin counted as FHQs even though they had not originally been built for that purpose. During the war they functioned occasionally as headquarters for the *Wehrmacht* High Command, but the air-raid bunkers below ground were not installed until 1943. The *Führerbunker* in the Reich

Chancellery garden served as Hitler's headquarters in the last months of the war; this had been built originally as an air-raid shelter. At the capitulation there were yet more completed FHQs south of Berlin, near Munich and at Berchtesgaden, while still others in Silesia and Thuringia were overrun in the later stages of construction.

The responsibility for the design and construction of the FHQs lay with the *Organisation Todt* (OT), whose virtuosity in bunker-building, street-laying and camouflage had been proved in their construction of the Westwall defences in 1938.

OT took on the architectural planning, assembled a workforce exceeding 20,000 at each location, arranged the transport of material—the bunker surfaces alone required 250,000 cubic metres of steel-reinforced concrete—and supervised each venture. Today, Wolfschanze in East Prussia and Riese in Lower Silesia have become tourist sites, and such vestiges of the remaining headquarters as exist are described in the closing chapters of this book.

The *Chefbaumeister der Führerhauptquartieranlagen* (Senior Construction Engineer of the FHQ Project) was the architect Siegfried Schmelcher, who worked at OT Head Office in Berlin. Born in 1911, after graduating in architecture at the Munich Technical *Akademie* he obtained employment under Dr Fritz Todt, the General Inspector of the German Highways. Although not a member of the Nazi Party or of any of its affiliated organs, in 1937 he was commissioned by the NSDAP's main technical office in Munich to convert the Plassenberg, 'a sixteenth-century pearl of German architecture', from a Bavarian prison into a training establishment for the German *Arbeitsfront* and subsequently the *NS-Bund der Deutschen Technik*. After completing this prestigious project in 1938, he worked into 1939 on plans for rest areas in the framework of the Reich's rapidly expanding programme of *Autobahn* construction. The Bad Eilsen hotel/restaurant complex near Buckeburg is an example of his work.

Schmelcher's work on the Arensburg *Autobahn* complex in Schaumburg-Lippe was interrupted on 8 September 1939 when he was summoned by Dr Todt to the Kaiserhof Hotel in Wiesbaden to receive the commission to plan the new FHQs ordered by Hitler. To his objection that he was not a Party member and was accordingly barred from working on highly secret projects, Todt merely 'shrugged his shoulders'. Schmelcher moved into offices at the Kaiserhof and set about his task ten days later. His wide-ranging authority enabled him to recruit to the OT, on a quasi-military contractual basis, a staff of thirty, most of whom were former fellow graduates. He nominated Leo Müller as his deputy and delegated engineers to take over responsibility for heating, sanitation, water supply, camouflage, land law and so on; in specialised areas, for example ventilation and air-conditioning, he turned to companies such as Dräger GmbH of Lübeck as consultants.

On 1 August 1940 OT set up the *Sondereinsatz Schmelcher* working party and made available to it floor space in their Berlin offices at Pariser Platz 3. OT had a large furniture warehouse in the nearby Moltkestrasse, and articles required to furnish the FHQs were drawn from this store.

Dr Todt was killed in an air crash at Rastenburg in early 1942, and the planning and financial freedoms enjoyed under him by Schmelcher were curtailed following Speer's appointment as Todt's successor. In December 1942 Schmelcher volunteered for military service. He spent ten months with a mountain-troop unit in Mittenwald* before Speer recalled him to OT in October 1943 to plan FHQ Riese in Lower Silesia. By the war's end, all members of *Sondereinsatz Schmelcher* bar Schmelcher himself had been conscripted into infantry regiments.

Schmelcher was probably involved at some stage in the construction of all the FHQs, and he set down his knowledge in a secret report classified '*Geheime Reichssache 91/44*' under the title 'Zusammenstellung der wichtigsten Daten über die von der OT gebauten Quartiere des Führers und der Wehrmachtteile'.† In the subsequent months he dedicated his time to searching for a suitable location for a new bomb-proof FHQ in central or southern Germany. On 7 April 1945 he presented the OT leadership in Berlin with his recommendations in a paper

* Schmelcher was posted to a barracks which just happened to be central to the large group of possible sites for FHQs that were later the subject of his report.—Tr.
† 'A Resumé of the Most Important Data Respecting the HQs Built by the OT for the *Führer* and *Wehrmacht* Arms of Service'.

classified 'Geheime Reichssache 121/45' and entitled 'Bericht über die Erkundung von geeigneten Platzen fur die Neuanlage eines FHQ'.* The capitulation brought an end to these ideas.

After the war Schmelcher practised independently from an architectural office in Munich, examples of his work there being the Children's Wing of the Schwabinger Hospital and several business houses in the Munich inner city. He also restored the bombed-out residence of the Todt family in Franz-Josef Strasse, where he had often stayed as a guest of the General Inspector.

Before his death on 25 June 1991 Schmelcher had given to Professor Franz Seidler, a co-author of this book, copies of the two secret files mentioned above in appreciation of his publications—*Fritz Todt: Baumeister des Dritten Reichs* (Munich, 1986) and *Die Organisation Todt: Bauen für Staat und Wehrmacht, 1939–1945* (Koblenz, 1987)—requesting that means be found for the papers to be published.

This book fulfils his wish; the documents themselves have been passed to the Bundesarchiv for public reference. A further substantial resource has been the diaries of Schmelcher's deputy in the FHQ project, former *Oberbauleiter* Leo Müller. His memoirs, together with additional information obtained during interviews, have enabled a fairly complete picture of the project to be pieced together. A debt of gratitude is owed to him for his assistance.

The authors are also indebted to Professor Franz Remmer of the *Universität der Bundeswehr*, Munich; to Andreas Fels, lecturer in construction practice; to Hans Georg Kampe of Berlin, for his explanation of the telephone system installed for the German High Command; and to all those who in other ways supported this research.

Franz Seidler and Dieter Zeigert

---

* 'Report Regarding the Search for Suitable Locations for a Führer Headquarters'.

Introduction

IN 1735 a 'headquarters' in German parlance was 'that place in the field where the commanding general is lodged with his senior officers. One is also accustomed to call it the General Staff.' In 1828 the definition was broadened to encompass 'the totality of persons belonging to a Corps or Army Command'. Above the lower headquarters stood the *Grosse Hauptquartier*, where one would find 'the General commanding the whole Army' and also, for the avoidance of doubt, 'the officers with charge of the military security service, the messengers, the ordnance and the transport'. This more comprehensive definition prevailed until the Great War, when the officers present at *Grosse Hauptquartier* were known as the *Gefolge des Kaisers* (Kaiser's Entourage) and the lesser headquarters were now called *Stabsquartier* (Staff Headquarters).

It was not unusual, even as late as the mid-nineteenth century, for a military leader to occupy a point in the field known popularly as the *Feldherrnhügel* (literally, 'hill of the warlord'), from where he could survey the battlefield. The position did not always offer a complete panorama, perhaps on account of the terrain or the weather conditions, or because of dust or smoke, and sometimes it would be disadvantaged by exposure to enemy fire. It was thus inevitable that the principal command centre would eventually be sited to the rear and beyond the danger zone, though still in a place to which information about the enemy and other running reports could be delivered expeditiously. For a military commander at any level, information has always been indispensable for proper judgement and decision-making. In the period before the Great War the means of relaying information during battle were manifold and ranged from the despatch rider to the wireless transmitter to telephones and telex machines. Even Morse lamps were used by regular German signals detachments on the Western Front in 1914.

The *Grosse Hauptquartier* met for the first time at Koblenz on 3 August 1914. At its head was the *Kaiser*, the federal warlord, in whom supreme command was vested. At its nucleus, besides the *Kaiser*'s ADCs, were generals of the armies, the heads of telecommunications, the Admiralty Staff and the naval and civilian cabinets and the representative of the Reich Chancellor and the Foreign and Reich Navy Office, together with a series of military service establishments, the Great General Staff composed of the *Militärbevollmächtigten* (military representatives) of Bavaria, Saxony and Württemberg and the representatives of the Military Cabinet and the Imperial Prussian War Ministry, the allied powers and their respective staffs.

The *Grosse Hauptquartier* was never in Berlin. The various locations, according to Cron and Crone, were as follows:

From 3 August 1914	Koblenz
From 30 August 1914	Luxembourg
From September 1914	Charleville-Mezières (between May 1915 and February 1916 parts were at Pless, Upper Silesia)
From 20 September 1916	Pless
From 17 February 1917	Bad Kreuznach (Kurhaus, Hotel Oranienhof, etc.)
From 8 March 1918	Spa (Hotel Britannique), with advanced units from March to the beginning of September 1918 at Avesnes and after wards at Verviers
From November 1918	Kassel (Schloss Wilhelmshohe)
From February 1919	Kolberg until 3 July 1919. (*Grosse Hauptquartier* remained in existence during the Armistice negotiations, the war being terminated by the signing of the Versailles Treaty)

Prescriptively, the *Grosse Hauptquartier* was an institution which exercised supreme political as well as military power from one place, but, as the historian Ritter has pointed out, Bismarck's Second Reich created a defective entity. Although the *Kaiser*, the supreme head of the Reich and the constitutional repository of absolute power, spent more time than anyone at *Grosse Hauptquartier* during the war, he renounced all power of command, assigning it to the Chief of the Field Army General Staff. This officer had the authority to give operational orders to the entire federated Army even though the limits of his power were not clearly delineated— which brought about a situation described by Gorlitz as 'war without a warlord', the military being in a position of unreasonable dominance and the political leadership in a vacuum. The defect in Bismarck's system was *Kaiser* Wilhelm II, whose duty it had been to guarantee the balance.

A comparable situation developed after 1933. Upon Hindenburg's death on 2 August 1934, under the Weimar Constitution Hitler became *Reichskanzler* (Reich Chancellor) and *Reichspräsident* (Reich President) in temporary personal union. Disdainfully ignoring the next stage of the constitutional process, however, he introduced an Enabling Act. This legislation took the function out of the hands of the *Reichstag*, or Parliament, and transferred it to the Reich Government. The Act also abolished the office of *Reichspräsident* in favour of *Führer*, or leader—a title for the Head of State without precedent in German history. The two offices of *Reichskanzler* and *Führer* were then fused and pseudo-legitimised by means of a plebiscite on 19 August 1934.

Under Article 47 of the Weimar Constitution, the *Reichspräsident* was the supreme commander of the *Reichswehr* (armed forces), but by virtue of the 1921 Armed Forces Law, paragraph 8, the practical power of command was vested in the *Oberbefehlshaber der Reichswehr* (Commander-in-Chief of the Armed Forces). Thus, according to Article 50 of the Weimar Constitution, a regulation issued by the *Reichspräsident* in the military sector had to be countersigned by the *Reichskanzler* or *Oberbefehlshaber der Reichswehr*, who thereby assumed the ministerial responsibility for it. The consequence of Hitler's changes—none of which were, under the constitution, legitimate—was that the *Führer*, already in the political driving seat, usurped the rights and duties of the *Oberbefehlshaber der Reichswehr* by introducing an oath of allegiance that had to be sworn to himself personally.

In a second step, in 1935, by virtue of fresh (unpublished) armed forces legislation, the *Reichswehr* became the *Wehrmacht*. Hitler elevated himself to *Oberster Befehlshaber der Wehrmacht* (Supreme Commander of the *Wehrmacht*); the *Reichskriegminister* (Reich War Minister), who had power of command under the constitution, was only *Oberbefehlshaber der Wehrmacht* (C-in-C of the *Wehrmacht*), and so Hitler now outranked him. The *Reichskriegminister* was *Generaloberst* Werner von Blomberg, who had been occupying the office since 1933 as a serving army officer, in breach of the constitution. The *Führer* had no identifiable ministerial responsibility, and as lawmaker-in-chief he had thus cleared the way for his subsequent misuse of military power. Finally, in 1938, by means of the *Erlass über die Führung der Wehrmacht* edict issued on 4 February 1938 and countersigned by Keitel, C-in-C *Wehrmacht*, Hitler deprived the latter of his constitutional power of command over the armed forces in a document which opened thus: 'Henceforth I exercise power of command over the *Wehrmacht* personally. The former *Wehrmacht* Office in the Reich War Ministry, together with its duties, becomes the *Wehrmacht* High Command and is my military Staff immediately under my command.' On this day, Hitler united political and military power in his own person.

The Importance of Communications at Command Level

With the outbreak of the Great War there was an enormous demand at *Grosse Hauptquartier* for adequate and flexible telecommunications. The First Army's Chief of General Staff observed ruefully, 'As carefully as the General Staff might have prepared for war, in 1914 our organisation was not adequate in terms of the technology required to manage an army of millions.' Even though the Prussian headquarters were equipped with wireless telegraphy in 1866, the importance of communications was not recognised and nearly fifty years later little technological progress had been made. The equipment available was insufficient to organise effectively the movements of the eight German armies from one place,

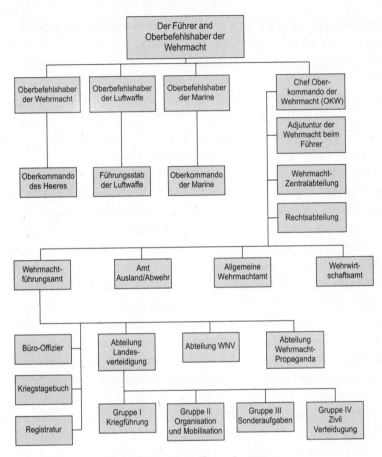

The German command heirarchy, 1939.

and at the Battle of the Marne in 1914 the Germans learned to their cost that their system was inadequate, even over a limited area. Above all, what was lacking was a field-telephone network that would have made possible a link-up at least at divisional level.

In the wake of the Germans' defeat, the provisions of the Versailles Treaty prohibited the use by the *Reichswehr* and its commanders of any means by which troops could be operated offensively or directed in the field. Until 1934, as a result, the German Army had neither wireless transmitters nor field-type telex equipment, and by the spring of 1937 only 30 per cent of *Reichspost* trunk lines had been set aside exclusively for military purposes. Centralisation had been opposed from the early 1930s by the *Luftwaffe* General Staff, which had built up its own private telephone network with the support of the *Reichspost*. It was not until 1937 that the *Wehrmacht-Nachrichtenverbindungswesens* (WNV, or *Wehrmacht* Signals Office) was set up and General Erich Fellgiebel, *Chef des Heeresnachrichtenwesens* (HNW), appointed to run it.

From then on, despite much internal opposition, the lessons of the First World War were finally accepted— although time was now pressing and not all the problems involving personnel and equipment could be overcome. An efficient and flexible telephone network was indispensable for all command structures, especially one which was considering spreading out across most of Europe and into Asia. Despite many difficulties, such a structure evolved, which *General der Nachrichtentruppe* Praun, the last *Chef des Wehrmacht-Nachrichtenverbindungswesens*, described as being 'based on a secure system of *Drehkreuzachsen* [literally, 'turnstile axles']. These were made up of a special system of free circuitry extended, alongside underground trunk cabling, from the Reich borders into the occupied territories by command signals regiments accompanying Army Group front troops.'

By the summer of 1941 there were 1,000 telephone engineer companies—double the number at the outbreak of war. When the tide turned, these units remained with the rearguard in order to ensure that contact between the farthest outposts and their command centres was maintained. *Chef des Heeresnachrichtenwesens* was responsible to the OKW (*Oberkommando der Wehrmacht*, or Wehrmacht High Command) and controlled seven regiments. The implications of the Allied bombing offensive for military communications in Germany had been identified by 1944, because Hans Georg Kampe observed that 'in a few months in 1944, by the use of approximately 15,000 kilometres of *Drehkreuzachsen*, the Command Signals Regiments created a new and valuable closed network within the Reich which worked extremely well right up to the last days of the war.'

'Führer Headquarters' Defined

FHQ in 1939 was composed of the following heterogeneous groups:

1. *Chef des Oberkommandos der Wehrmacht* (C-in-C OKW) (Keitel), with two *Adjutanten* (ADCs);
2. *Chef des Wehrmachtführungsstabes* (C-in-C WFSt, or *Wehrmacht* Command Staff) (Jodl), with one *Generalstabsoffizier* (General Staff officer);
3. *Chefadjutant der Wehrmacht beim Führer* (Senior *Wehrmacht* ADC to the *Führer*) (Schmundt);
4. One *Adjutant* for each *Wehrmachtteil* (*Wehrmacht* arm of service) (Engel, von Below and von Puttkamer);
5. One *Verbingundsoffizier* (liaison officer) for each *Wehrmachtteil*;
6. *Verbingundsoffizier des Oberbefehlshabers der Luftwaffe* (ObdL, or *Luftwaffe* C-in-C);
7. *Verbingundsoffizier des Reichsführer-SS*;
8. *Adjutant der SA* (*Sturmabteilung*, or Stormtroopers) (Brückner);
9. *Chef der Parteikanzlei* (Head of Party Office) (Lammers);
10. *Reichspressechef* (Reich Press Chief) (Dietrich);
11. *Vertreter der Auswärtigen Amtes* (Foreign Office Representative) (Hewel);
12. Two *Ärzte* (doctors);
13. *Reichsbildberichterstatter* (Reich official photographer) (Hoffmann);
14. *SS-Begleitkommando* (Hitler's bodyguard); and
15. *Kommandant FHQu* (FHQ Commandant) (Rommel) with *Sicherungskompanie* (security company), *Nachrichtenzug* (signals troop), *Flakbatterie (mot.)* (motorised anti-aircraft battery) and two *Eisenbahn-Flakzüge* (railway AA wagons).

The idea that Hitler might occupy a headquarters near the battle-lines in the event of war was first expressed in 1938 when *Oberst* Walter Warlimont, *Chef der Abteilung Landesverteidigung in Wehrmachtführungsamt* (Head of the WFSt Land Defence Section), spoke of a *'bewegt Lagerleben'* (mobile camp), but it was not until July 1942 that the term *'Führerhaupt-*

quartier' was first defined in writing, when Hitler authorised his *Wehrmacht* ADC, General Schmundt, to issue the following communiqué:

> The term *'Führerhauptquartier'* is to be used as infrequently as possible. In the narrower sense of the term, it encompasses only the close members of the *Führer's* circle and locally the *Wehrmachtführungsstab*. The other centres associated with it have the following definitions: *Oberkommando des Heeres* [OKH, or Army High Command]; *Feldquartier des Reichsaussenministers* [Reich Foreign Minister's Field Headquarters]; *Befehlsstelle des Reichsführers SS* [SS Command Centre]; and *Feldquartier des Reichsministers Lammers* [Reich Minister Lammers' Field Headquarters]. On grounds of secrecy, the term *'Führerhauptquartier'* should only be used if there is no other way to describe what is meant.

The term *'Führerhauptquartier'* and its telephone/telex address cover name meant Hitler, his inner circle and the WFSt field staff attached quasi-officially to the headquarters. The bulletin requested all 'associated' command centres to adopt their own cover names for the centre and the telephone/telex address.

WFSt (WFA, *Wehrmachtführungsamt*, until 1940, but referred to as WFSt throughout this book for the sake of simplicity) was the work organ of the German Army. The 1939 Service Instructions ruled that it was the sole responsibility of the WFSt C-in-C, 'in questions of command, to ensure that the instructions of the *Führer* and Supreme Commander of the *Wehrmacht* are conveyed to the *Wehrmacht* arms of service and the supreme Reich authorities . . .'

Reduced formally to an executive organ, the WFSt neither prepared nor co-ordinated large-scale operations until 1944. In the OKW *Kriegstagebuch* (KTB, or War Diary) its chief, General Jodl, wrote only of 'preparing', 'informing', 'presenting' and 'working out', tasks which required no exhaustive activity and which were in line with Hitler's decree of 4 February 1938, wherein the activities of OKW even in peacetime lay in 'following his instructions'.

That the WFSt was no more than a hollow façade was clearly displayed during the Polish campaign, when it was left behind in Berlin with no special task to perform; according to Warlimont, WFSt was then little more than a military registry, collating reports and updating situation maps. Hitler's failure to notify WFSt of the demarcation line agreed with

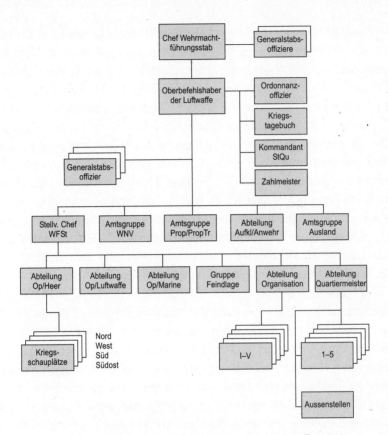

```
┌──────────────────┐        ┌──────────────────┐
│ Chef Wehrmacht-  │────────│ Generalstabs-    │
│ führungsstab     │        │ offiziere        │
└──────────────────┘        └──────────────────┘

        ┌──────────────────┐      ┌──────────────────┐
        │ Oberbefehlshaber │──────│ Ordonnanz-       │
        │ der Luftwaffe    │      │ offizier         │
        └──────────────────┘      ├──────────────────┤
                                  │ Kriegs-          │
                                  │ tagebuch         │
                                  ├──────────────────┤
                                  │ Kommandant       │
                                  │ StQu             │
┌──────────────────┐              ├──────────────────┤
│ Generalstabs-    │              │ Zahlmeister      │
│ offizier         │              └──────────────────┘
└──────────────────┘
```

Stellv. Chef WFSt	Amtsgruppe WNV	Amtsgruppe Prop/PropTr	Abteilung Aufkl/Anwehr	Amtsgruppe Ausland

Abteilung Op/Heer	Abteilung Op/Luftwaffe	Abteilung Op/Marine	Gruppe Feindlage	Abteilung Organisation	Abteilung Quartiermeister

Kriegs-schauplätze — Nord West Süd Südost

I–V   1–5

Aussenstellen

The Wehrmachtführungsstab (Wehrmacht *Command Staff*), 1944–5.

Stalin took its staff aback when the Russians marched into eastern Poland on 17 September 1939. From a political point of view, this created an extraordinarily critical situation, since German troops had suffered losses fighting their way across the demarcation line at various places in order to occupy territory which now had to be ceded to the Soviets. Not until February 1940, after numerous postponements of the proposed attack on France, was WFSt at last invited to join FHQ—but 'keep small'. At the first fixed FHQ no infrastructural preparations were made for it, and the unit had to settle for a requisitioned farmhouse and lodgings in Munstereifel.

Possibly because the *Oberbefehlshaber des Heeres* (Army C-in-C) had expressed reservations regarding the advisability of the operation, the preparations for 'Weserübung' (the occupation of Norway and Denmark in April 1940) were subordinated to Keitel. The OKW thus acted for the first time as a co-ordinating arm of command. The use of a special planning and command unit (the Staff of XXI Army Corps) alienated the *Generalstabs des Heeres* (Army General Staff) from the preparations and demonstrated that WFSt was not considered a planning and command unit independent of the OKH. This line of thinking led Hitler to introduce OKW 'theatres of war' in 1941, followed in 1942 by the instruction that the Army was to concentrate solely on the war against the Soviet Union. For the greater part of the war WFSt was located in the *Sperrkreis II* (Restricted Area II) outer security area at FHQ—an indication of the low regard in which it was held by Hitler.

The pressure to conform was particularly overbearing at FHQ. Jodl, the head of WFSt, was quoted by Warlimont as having described FHQ as 'a cross between a monastery and a concentration camp' which the dominating personality of Hitler had imbued with spirit, shape and expression. The comparison here with a concentration camp presumably referred to the fact that there was no hope of escape until the end of hostilities, since Hitler never approved a transfer request submitted by a competent officer. Professor Hartlaub, then a junior *Unteroffizier* (NCO) assisting the WFSt *Feldstab* (field staff) in the compilation of the OKW War Diary from 1942 to 1945, detected a 'proprietary oppressive atmosphere' with which the FHQ institution seemed to burden its inmates, for 'it moulded one ever more to the pattern, [and] made one into the oiled automaton which it needed.' Frau Schroeder, one of Hitler's personal secretaries and attached to his personal *Adjutantur* throughout the entire National Socialist period, wrote thus to a friend in 1941: 'I think that after this campaign I must make the effort to spend a lot of time amongst really life-affirming people from outside our circle, otherwise in time I will become withdrawn and lose contact with reality.'

The extent of the differences between Hitler and the Army in general is highlighted by the admonition attributed to him that 'the OKH has a task to fulfil and is not to discuss whether the task is right or wrong.' The *Luftwaffe*, on the other hand, under Göring's guidance, had long been regarded as trustworthy and was given a large measure of autonomy throughout the Battle of Britain, for the occupation of Crete in 1941 and for the defence of Italy in 1944. The *Kriegsmarine*, its 300,000 men constituting only 4.4 per cent of the fighting services, fought its own battle on the sea lanes with only rare instances of interference from above. This was probably the implication of Hitler's observation that he possessed 'a Prussian Army, an Imperial Navy and a National Socialist Air Force': Prussia and Austria had a long history of mutual enmity and distrust, and Hitler was Austrian.

General Halder, *Chef der Generalstabs des Heeres* (Chief of the Army General Staff), stated in 1941 that his successor would be 'scarcely more than a postman. The *Führer* deals below me with the individual Army C-in-Cs direct.' Hitler hated the *Generalstabs des Heeres*. Erfurt reports a comment he made to the *ChefGenSt des Heeres* at the beginning of 1945: 'it is intolerable to me that a group of intellectuals should gang up to mouth their opinions to their superior officer. But that is the General Staff system, and I want to get rid of it.'

The Concept of a Mobile FHQ

Hitler's first FHQ was a train. He probably received his first *Staats-sonderzug* (State Special Train) in 1933 or 1934. The Reich Government had two such trains, but, as the number fell short of requirements, every minister was given at least a railway coach, and some became entitled to an entire train. A comprehensive building programme was undertaken, so that, by 1941, 388 coaches had been delivered, these making up 25 *Sonderzüge*, the longest, *Enzian*, operated by the *Chef des Nachrichtenwesens der Luftwaffe* (Head of *Luftwaffe* Signals), having 35 carriages. Another 49 coaches were in the workshops approaching completion.

The frequency of their use—the *Sonderzüge* enjoyed by Hitler, Göring, von Ribbentrop, Himmler and the OKW chiefs in June 1942 alone travelled almost 11,000 kilometres—eventually stretched the capacities of the *Reichsbahn* to such an extent that Hitler's approval had to be obtained by any person below the highest level wishing to operate a private train or acquire new rolling stock.

Hitler's pre-war *Sonderzug* had ten coaches of uniform size, painted dark green and drawn by two locomotives, which from 1944 were armoured. During the occupation of Czechoslovakia and from the outbreak of war onwards, an anti-aircraft wagon was added behind the locomotives and at the rear, making twelve or, depending on the perceived danger of air attack, occasionally up to fourteen wagons. Each AA wagon had two 2cm guns and a crew of 20 to 30 gunners attached to the *Führer-Flak* detachment. In action the AA commander had autonomy.

When not in use the train was kept at Berlin's Anhalter station, which had secure, sheltered sidings. The terminus was on the direct line to Munich and in convenient proximity to the *Reichskanzlei* (Reich Chancellery). Göring's *Sonderzug* was comprehensively furnished. All the coaches were the most modern available, and they included a sleeping car complete with wardrobe and bath. For his comfort whilst using the bath, Göring would have the train brought to a halt, and as a result that section of the railway system came to a standstill too. To assure his safety on the permanent way, Göring's train was always preceded some distance ahead by a locomotive referred to sarcastically as the *Minenräumer* (Minesweeper). One of the carriages was fitted with an installation of unknown type so heavy as to require a six-axle coach unique on the *Reichsbahn* for its transportation.

Sonderzüge were not permitted to exceed a speed of 80kph. Until 1941, when the coach in question was removed, Himmler's train, *Steiermark*, was subject to a unique speed restriction since it was a mixture of old and new coaches and included a royal carriage dating back to the time of the old Mecklenburg Friedrich Wilhelm Railway which could not be used safely in a fast-moving combination.

One carriage of the *Führerzug* (*Führer* Train) was equipped with a Morse telegraphy unit available for signals purposes at any time when travelling on overhead-electrified sections of track, these being found mainly in southern Germany. Radio direction-finding and decryption compromised the use of wireless transmissions in wartime. Telephone

Name(s)	For use by
Brandenburg I and II	Hitler
Westfalen	*Aussenminister* von Ribbentrop
Steiermark, 1944 Transport Nr. 44	*Reichsführer-SS* Himmler
Braunschweig	*Chef OKW*, Keitel
Franken I and II	*Wehrmachtführungsstab*
Ostpreussen, Sachsen, Schwaben, Württemberg	*Oberkommando des Heeres*
Pommern I and II	*Oberbefehlshaber der Luftwaffe*, Göring
Robinson I	*Chef Führungsstab Luftwaffe*
Robinson II	*Chef Generalstab Luftwaffe*
Enzian	*Chef Nachrichtenwesen der Luftwaffe*
Rheinland I and II	*Generalstab der Luftwaffe*
Pommern V	*vermutl. Luftwaffe*
Atlantik	*Oberbefehlshaber der Marine*

Sonderzüge *(Special Trains) for Reich and* Wehrmacht *Leadership, 1943 (extract).*

conversations were therefore considered to be more secure, and every large railway station was linked to the *Reichsbahn* telephone network (BASA), through which the *Wehrmacht* network could be accessed by telephone and telex. The disadvantage was, however, that even the *Führerzug* was subject to the vagaries of railway timetables. Special preparations had to be made for excursions beyond the Reich's borders. As a rule, the various *Sonderzüge* were halted close to tunnels which could be used at short notice for protection, but communication was then difficult if a cable had not been laid in advance.

The inadequacy of a train as an FHQ is highlighted in the following report by *Oberstleutnant* von Vormann, a V*erbindungsoffizier der Heeres* (Army liaison officer) during the Polish campaign:

The *Führerzug* was extremely long. At each end were special wagons with light flak guns under an armoured canopy. I never went into the leading coach, which was occupied by Hitler and his personal staff, and so can say nothing about it. The second wagon was the operations coach, in which life was concentrated over the next few days. The forward half was a room with a large map table, three telephones and some movable easy chairs. The telephone exchange and signals centre were in the rear half. Next came the sleeping car for the SS bodyguard, two more sleeping cars for adjutants, doctors, soldiers and so on, and a dining car. The rest of the train was taken over by the *Reichspressechef* Dietrich. Von Ribbentrop, Lammers and Himmler with their staffs were in the second *Sonderzug, Heinrich*, which always followed the *Führerzug*. Göring directed the *Luftwaffe* from his *Sonderzug* near the Reich capital, [von] Brauchitsch the Army from Zossen, and Raeder the *Kriegsmarine* from Berlin. Warlimont had stayed behind in Berlin with the *Wehrmachtführungsstab*. It was at that time nothing more than a glorified report centre, with no independence or authority to give orders.

As von Vormann understood it, it is doubtful whether the *Führerzug* could really be called the central headquarters because none of Hitler's senior military advisers was aboard. The point has sometimes been made that this lack of preparedness proves that the Polish campaign was not intended but came about through circumstances such as the impending onset of autumn. Be that as it may, for the campaign the train served as the FHQ until 26 September. The main advantage it bestowed was flexibility, for it was easier to arrange visits to front-line troops from a mobile centre than from a fixed one. Since Hitler was expecting France to attack the *Westwall* some time in September, the train would allow him to shuttle his headquarters between the Western and Eastern Fronts if the need arose.

Protecting Hitler and His FHQs

In peacetime the *Reichskanzlei* was protected by units of the SS-*Leibstandarte 'Adolf Hitler'*. Hitler's immediate personal protection was supplied by a special SS bodyguard aided by the *Reichsicherheitsdienst* (RSD, or Security Service), whose large staff of officials looked after internal security in FHQs, at the *Reichskanzlei* and at other sensitive establishments. The bodyguard and RSD normally worked independently but received their instructions from Hitler's personal *Adjutanten* or from Bormann who, as leader of the *Parteikanzlei*, exercised certain control functions. Both services were outside Himmler's jurisdiction. RSD worked only in co-operation with the FHQ Army security body at gates.

Hitler had had bodyguards since 1921. During the reorganisation of the SS into the NSDAP protection force in 1933, a series of local special units such as the *Berlin Stabswache* were set up. These formed human cordons at Hitler's public appearances and guarded significant offices and residences and Hitler's private dwellings. In 1933 they merged into the *SS-Leibstandarte 'Adolf Hitler'*, thus forming a paramilitary special troop of about 1,000 men. Hitler's bodyguard and personal protection force employed his drivers and manservants. It grew from having eight members in 1932 to 140 by 1943, although only a quarter of the latter staff was employed on physical protection, the remainder being engaged on ordnance, motor and courier service and guard duty at other locations as well as forming a personnel reserve.

The duty of the SS bodyguard was to protect Hitler against injury and attack during journeys in mostly open vehicles. Powerful, tall, athletic men were considered most suitable and were chosen without regard to education or work training. Accordingly, some were uncouth and proved an embarrassment at the social level where they were required to mingle. The work alternated between long periods of idleness and service without scheduled rest. Whenever Hitler made public appearances or journeys, including visits to the battle areas, he would have in his immediate vicinity usually six men drawn from the *Sonderkommando* (SKD, or special unit) of SS bodyguards and RSD men. They occupied the second and third vehicles of the usual convoy of six known as '*Kolonne F*' (Convoy F)' and were armed with handguns and machine-pistols. Their uniform was practically indistinguishable from that worn by the *Waffen-SS*.

SS-Leibstandarte 'Adolf Hitler' should have been sufficiently strong to guarantee Hitler's safety in the field, but he was anxious that his escort at the front—and this included the railway system when his FHQ was the *Führerzug*—should not be drawn from SS units. In an instruction to *Chefadjutant der Wehrmacht* General Schmundt on 25 March 1939, Hitler had ordered that, in the event of mobilisation, 'the honour guard for FHQ should be perceived to be the *Wehrmacht* guard regiment formed for the purpose'. An infantry battalion, *Wachbataillon 631*, supplied four companies and a light flak battery for Hitler's protection during 1939. Später, the historian of *Panzerkorps 'Grossdeutschland'*, mentions a unit, *Kommando 'Führerreise'*, established in 1938 and identical to this guard formation. Rommel's report of 3 April 1939, footnoted extensively by Schmundt, spoke of the unit's poor standard of preparation. At the outbreak of war it was, together with *Wachregiment 'Berlin'*, incorporated into the *'Grossdeutschland'* infantry regiment, the latter then being ordered to place at the disposal of the *FHQu-Kommandant* a guard of company strength. Within the terms of the mobilisation measure, the company was formed in two sections from troops of the Krampnitz Cavalry School, the Wunsdorf Panzer training depot and the Halle Army Signals School. Officers were drawn from OKH and various schools and units. In order to generate *esprit de corps* and to advertise their function to the public, the cuff title *'Führerhauptquartier'* was issued to all members of the FHQ guard company on 3 September 1939. This minor force was inadequate for its purpose and confirms that the High Command had not been given reason at that stage to entertain the possibility of fixed field FHQs away from the capital.

The security force assembled for the first time on 23 August 1939 in the *'Grossdeutschland'* barracks at Berlin Tiergarten and two days later, under the command of *Generalmajor* Erwin Rommel, was taken to a training area about 100 kilometres north-east of Stettin. In the expectation of a fluid campaign, the company was divided up on arrival into two guard groups and a front group. Guard Group 1 was responsible for the security and isolation of Bad Polzin station, where Hitler's train would arrive for a short stop; Guard Group 2 was the reserve. As a major security effort was judged unlikely, and in any case the overall ground strength was insufficient if one became necessary, recourse would be had to nearby police or other *Wehrmacht* units if required. The front group was an escort for the *Führerstaffel*, a convoy consisting of a maximum of six vehicles in two columns, 'K' (*Kommandant*), with signals and flak platoons, and 'M' (*Minister*), flanked by Party chiefs together with another signals platoon, luggage and supplies. The front group had no reserve and remained unrelieved from 9 to 27 September. Rommel's extraordinarily detailed order issued at Bad Polzin on 31 August 1939 bears witness to the improvised nature of the operation of which he had control and to the poor degree of readiness of the security company.

On the outbreak of hostilities with Poland, no serious thought had been given to the defence of fixed FHQs against aircraft. The security force was supplemented by a *Luftwaffe* motorised anti-aircraft (AA) battery equipped with twenty 2cm guns and a searchlight battery from the Berlin-based 'General Göring' Regiment. Although these light weapons were useful against low-flying fighters and fighter-bombers, they could not engage high-level bombers. Two *Luftwaffe* AA trains were available to protect the *Führerzug* and the *Ministerzug* used by von Ribbentrop and Himmler.

The Fixed *Führerhauptquartiere*

After war broke out in September 1939, Hitler exercised his role as supreme commander from more or less *ad hoc* mobile or fixed FHQs, two of which were his official residences. There was no planned programme. The project was a new concept in twentieth-century warfare, a revival of the 'field warlord' role as Hitler saw it, linked without doubt to considerations of propaganda. FHQs ranged from the narrow confines of the Führer's *Sonderzug* to the best-known of the concrete complexes, Wolfschanze at Rastenburg in East Prussia, where he spent more time than at any other and which corresponded to his requirement for security to a special degree.

In all, more than twenty FHQ installations of various kinds were either completed or abandoned during construction or in the planning stage. The size to which they had burgeoned in the latter part of the war is clear from the testimony of *Rüstungsminister* (Armaments Minister) Albert Speer, according to which in mid-1944 about 28,000 labourers, plus a large force of concentration-camp inmates, were employed in building work. For the uncompleted Riese project in Silesia, which would allegedly have accommodated over 20,000 staff plus a flak corps of over 6,000, more concrete had been used by the autumn of 1944 than was available for building air-raid cellars in the entire Reich. At that time the work at Riese had already consumed 150 million *Reichsmark*, but the gigantic redoubt could still not have been finished in the foreseeable future 'in sufficient strength'. The appropriation of 3.9 million *Reichsmark* for the conversion of Ziegenberg Castle and land in Hesse for the first fixed FHQ, Adlerhorst, seems almost modest.

Locations of *Führer* Headquarters, 1940–5

0   200   400   600   800   1000km

STO

HAMBURG

BERLIN
Reichsk
Mayba

LONDON

BRUSSELS

Felsennest   Adlerhorst
Wolfsschlucht
S III
PARIS
W 2   Waldwiese
Brunhilde   PRAGUE
W 3

Tannenberg   MUNICH   VI

Siegfried
Obersalzberg   Frühli

BORDEAUX

MILAN

LENINGRAD

OLM

TALLINN

▲ *Wasserburg*

MOSCOW

RIGA

Bärenhöhle

VILNIUS

▲ SMOLENSK

▲
Olga

DANZIG

▲
Wolfschanze

WARSAW

▲ *Anlage Mitte*

KHARKOV

KRAKOW

Wehrwolf

▲

Anlage Süd

VINNITSA

BUDAPEST

rm

BUCHAREST

What lay behind it all? One can only speculate about the reason for the stupendous growth in size of the FHQ complex as the war moved to its end. An impregnable fortress under siege can only endure as long as the available food and water, and FHQ Riese would have been manned by 28,000 people. The matter is not satisfactorily explained by the conclusion recorded in the OKW *Kriegstagebuch* that 'Step by step Hitler transformed himself from political *Führer*, dictator and popular leader into the absolute military dictator and "Greatest Warlord of All Time", who finally made war for the sake of it.'

Chapter 1

From Berlin Zossen
to the Polish Campaign

ZOSSEN, south of Berlin, had been an Army training camp since the epoch of the *Kaisers*. The *Reichswehr* classified it as a *Stammlager* (principal camp), not least because in August 1933 it was designated Army Headquarters in the event of war. It was to Zossen that the Army leaders with their command staffs, the *Chef des Transportwesens* (Head of Transport Command) and the *Chef des Generalquartiermeisters* Head of the Quartermaster-General) were to transfer should the victorious powers of the Great War invade Germany. In August 1933 invasion was considered a possibility should the Geneva Disarmament Conference, which had first convened on 2 February 1932, break down as a result of the German petition for the right to rearm. German rearmament was specifically prohibited by the terms of the Versailles Treaty of 1919, and the signs were that the request would be dismissed; invasion might result if the powers suspected that Hitler was going to rearm irrespective of whether or not they gave their consent. The perceived threat did not materialise, but it highlighted Zossen's shortcomings as a headquarters.

Zossen, however, lacked a proper telephone network. The emergency equipment hastily installed in 1933 became a long-term temporary measure until in August 1936 the *Reichswehrministerium* (Reich Army Ministry) finally took the decision to make Zossen the central control of a modern military communications system. It was to be located in two subterranean bunkers each having 400 square metres of floor space. For the purpose, a tract of virgin woodland, lying to the east of the old structures and known as Jagen 141, was chosen.

There had been many advocates in the *Reichswehrministerium* for an alternative site at the Ohrdruf troop training area in the Harz mountains of central Germany, and it was decided to proceed with a parallel project there. In 1938 a subterranean communications bunker known as 'Amt 10' (Department 10) came into existence. Thus neither Zossen nor Ohrdruf were originally intended as *Führerhauptquartiere*. The Ohrdruf bunker and the mystery surrounding it will loom larger in the reckoning towards the end of this book.

The Zossen scheme was codenamed 'Zeppelin' by the *Allgemein Heeresamt* (General Army Office) and 'Amt 500' by the *Reichspostzentralamt (Reichspost* Central Office). To plans drawn up by the *Heeresbauamt Wunsdorf* (Wunsdorf Army Construction Department), excavation work began in the summer of 1937. While Maybach I, for the *Führungsstab des Heeres*, made rapid progress, Maybach II, for the *Chef des Heerestransportwesen* and his department, was still languishing in the planning stage over a year later.

In 1938 a labour force of between 1,500 and 2,000 was engaged in work on 'Zeppelin'. Concurrently with the construction of the signals bunker and Maybach I, the *Reichspost* was laying connections to the 400-kilometre-long trunk line which encircled Berlin. Eight lines were put down to guarantee continuity should the main ring line be severed.

A few weeks before the outbreak of World War II, at a cost of 30 million *Reichsmark*, the 'Zeppelin' communications centre was ready. The two-metre-thick bunker floor occupied 4,881 square metres of floor space. The thickness of the ceiling was four metres, including the upper concrete anti-shatter layer, and its height varied from 2.75 to 3.25 metres. The outer walls were from 1.6 to 3.2 metres thick.

The Maybach I settlement consisted of twelve four-storey concrete structures each 36.2 metres long by 16.39 metres broad and disguised as dwelling houses. The floor of each was 8.2 metres down, and two bunker levels, divided into seven or eight service rooms, occupied the space below ground. Above ground level were two further storeys, the uppermost being in the roof. Steel, gas-proof communicating doors separated the floors, and ventilation and air supply passed through a filter installation. The air intakes were disguised as chimneys and were designed to allow a supply of fresh air during a gas attack. The central water station was

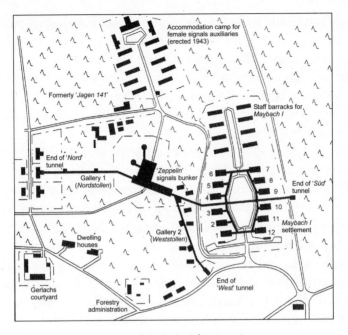

Layout of Maybach I (after Kampe).

fed from eight deep wells. All the buildings were interconnected by a circular, 600-metre long subterranean gallery. Another gallery led from Maybach I to 'Amt 500'.

On 9 August 1939, the three companies from *Nachrichtenabteilung 40* (Signals Detachment 40) transferred from Ohrdruf to Zossen, together with conscripted *Reichspost* specialists, took charge of 'Amt 500'. Telephone proving trials begun on 24 May 1939 were concluded, and the centre was declared operational on 22 August. A total of 400 amplifiers guaranteed the best possible voice quality over long distances, and three diesel generators were on hand to provide current in the event of grid failure. The 42-metre long hall of the 'Zeppelin' signals bunker was lined with 40 trunking boxes able to handle 500 simultaneous connections; the wartime daily average of connections was 120,000. The upper bunker level of 'Zeppelin' contained a monitoring installation enabling all telephone conversations to be eavesdropped, and recorded, by the *Abwehr*.

The technical supervision of the exchange was managed by means of control lamps in the signals bunker. Maintenance of the overall function was the responsibility of the German *Reichspost*.

The underground Morse transmitting station was never operational during the war because of a technical problem associated with the concrete roof. The OKH Morse unit was located in uppermost floor of Maybach I's house No. 12.

From 25 August 1939, OKH personnel began to arrive from the Bendlerstrasse headquarters in Berlin. The *Generalstab des Heeres* (Army General Staff) moved into the Maybach I bunker settlement on 26 August 1939 in readiness for the attack on Poland, scheduled for the next day. At 1900 that evening Hitler rescinded the order and 'Zeppelin' had five hours to inform all units at the front. The task was achieved satisfactorily, although a small number of forward patrols could not be contacted. On 31 August 1939 *Generaloberst* Walter von Brauchitsch, the *Oberbefehlshaber des Heeres* (Army C-in-C), arrived at Zossen: he could now direct all Army operations during the Polish campaign from this one centre. The WFSt remained in central Berlin. At 1700 the same evening Hitler ordered the attack anew for 1 September 1939, and early the following morning the *Wehrmacht* invaded Poland.

Neither the civilian nor the military leadership of the Third Reich was aware that Hitler would exercise his activities as *Führer* from field headquarters rather than from the *Reichskanzlei* (Reich Chancellery), and so it was only at the situation conference that took place during the day following the attack that Warlimont learned of Hitler's intention to travel to the Polish border in the very near future. It was unclear who besides *Chef des OKW* (OKW C-in-C) Keitel would accompany Hitler as 'managing director' of the military command, and apart from the personal and military aides the composition of his entourage was not known, even by Hitler's immediate 'inner circle'.

Two days after German troops invaded Poland on Friday 1 September 1939, the ambassadors of the British and French Governments in Berlin handed to the *Reichsaussenministerium* (German Foreign Ministry) their written declarations of war. At 2100 that evening Hitler and his entourage

Sketch showing side view of bunker house (after Kampe).

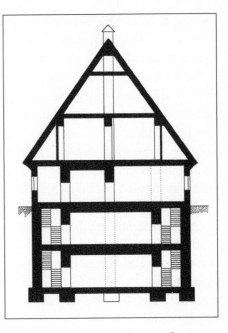

entrained for the 100-kilometre run to Bad Polzin, east of Stettin. One of his secretaries, Gerda Daranowski, recorded that the *Führer* was 'quiet and pale and reflective', while another, Christa Schroeder, recalled in her book that she heard him say to his deputy Rudolf Hess, 'Now all my work is falling apart. My book was written for nothing.' Hitler ordered Heinz Linge, his manservant, to serve him only 'the simplest meals'—nothing more than what the people ate—for he wanted to set a good example. From then on, instead of the brown NSDAP tunic with the swastika armband, he always wore the field-grey jacket which his SS aides had had made for him.

Hitler's *Sonderzug* drew into Bad Polzin at 0156 on 4 September 1939, followed fifteen minutes later by the *Ministerzug* carrying von Ribbentrop and Himmler, and there they remained, on board, until dawn. *FHQu-Kommandant* Rommel had set up headquarters in the station waiting rooms: his '*Grossdeutschland*' field gendarmes had thrown a 500-metre-broad cordon around the station and passengers were obliged to approach and leave by the shortest route along a restricted avenue. Nobody was allowed near Hitler unless accompanied by an RSD official.

The proximity of the railway to the front lines gave Hitler the opportunity to observe *Blitzkrieg* at close quarters. It was his practice to give dictation to Christa Schroeder and brief himself on the war situation before nine, after which he set off for the front, accompanied by his security company. Hitler's aircraft, a four-engined FW 200 registered

D-2600 and flown by his pilot Hans Baur, was always on hand, together with an aircraft of the courier flight, at the nearest military airfield with a suitable airstrip.

On his visits to Army headquarters at the front, Hitler restricted himself to making suggestions and never gave orders. This was the case even when he met von Brauchitsch, in contrast to his attitude towards him later. Hitler enjoyed seeing the reaction of ordinary soldiers who suddenly spotted him unexpectedly, and he would hand round cigarettes. He spent hours inspecting the field kitchens and dining halls and made sure that the officers had no better fare than the men.

Shortly before leaving for his tour of 4 September, Hitler was informed in a telephone message from the *Gauleiter* of Munich that an English art student he had known six years previously, Unity Mitford, had attempted suicide because 'the reconciliation between the British and German peoples had failed'. Hitler ordered that she be treated at his personal expense by the surgeon Professor Magnus at the Universitäts-klinik (University Clinic).

Calling first upon von Kluge's Fourth Army, Hitler was driven in a convoy to the Vistula south of Schwetz and then back to Plietnitz near Schneide-muhl, where his train awaited him. The convoy consisted of 78 vehicles, not counting the scout cars, as *Oberstleutnant* von Vormann related:

> At the head of the column were two armoured scout cars. Next came Hitler with his adjutants and valet, in the second and third cars were the SS bodyguard, and then came the OKW head; in the fifth and sixth cars were the remaining adjutants, photographer and so on. These six vehicles were large, similar, three-axled Mercedes. Then came some more armoured scout cars. Behind these was the motley assortment of 72 other vehicles with von Ribbentrop, Lammers, Bormann, Dietrich and so on.*

The *Chefadjutant der Wehrmacht* had given each vehicle a number to indicate its position in the column. Von Vormann continued: 'The civilian dignitaries degenerated into savages. None was satisfied with the number allotted to his vehicle and a fierce rivalry broke out in which all standards of civilised behaviour were tossed overboard.'

* Unpublished manuscript at the Institut fur Zeitgeschichte, Munich: 'Erinnerungen des Verbindungsoffiziers des Heeres beim Obersten Befehlshaber der Wehrmacht 27.8.–22.9.1939'.

Hitler ignored this unedifying spectacle and at midday stood amidst his entourage to watch German troops cross the Vistula south of Kulm. Later he discovered that the *Reichsaussenministerium* had inadvertently informed foreign diplomats that the *Führersonderzug* would be at Plietnitz that night, and so it was ordered ten kilometres north to the Doberitz Forest. Next day, while he was on his way to Gross Born, near Neustettin, the German Press Agency reported that Hitler had alighted at a small station to speak to wounded soldiers aboard a hospital train.

A horde of 'war tourists' descending upon Army groups at the front line posed intolerable problems for the organisation, and, to nip the problem in the bud, Schmundt, *Chefadjutant der Wehrmacht*, arranged for the security group at the front always to fly to the next landing point, taking up the limited aircraft space available. It was also recognised that the security company was too small in numbers. Before the war it had been thought that a battalion would supply the minimum strength required to guarantee Hitler's safety in the field, but not until the Polish campaign was actually under way were hasty steps taken to adjust the shortage. Thus there came into existence, on paper, the *Führer-Begleit-bataillon*, composed of two Army companies including the existing stretched force, a signals platoon staff and a *Luftwaffe* anti-aircraft battalion.

On 6 September, following a rest day at Gross Born, Hitler toured the banks of the Vistula as far as Graudenz. On 7 September he conferred with Raeder, von Brauchitsch and Halder aboard the *Führersonderzug* about the situation in the West, and on the 8th his train steamed into Ilnau, from where, two days later, he called on von Reichenau's Tenth Army near Konskie in a combined air and road excursion.

On 9 September, when returning from the divisional staff at Tomassov near Lodz, he was again overwhelmed with gifts of flowers from farming people of German stock. During the run with the motor convoy to Graudenz three days previously, deliriously happy farmers had deluged him with bouquets of flowers, and in order to reduce the obvious danger of assassination which this hero-worship engendered, his adjutants now issued an instruction that the *Führer* would not in future accept these

41

gifts and that they should 'be given to the soldiers of the German *Wehrmacht* instead'.

It appears that on 10 September Hitler returned to Munich, where he visited Unity Mitford in hospital, and on the same day he ordered *FHQu-Kommandant* Rommel to begin an immediate search near the western border with France (though beyond the range of French artillery) for a suitable place to build a fixed, short-term FHQ for the impending battles. The organisers of this search, besides Rommel, were the military adjutants Schmundt, Engel, von Below and von Puttkamer; Dr Fritz Todt, *Reichsminister für Bewaffnung und Minition und Generalbevollmächtigte für die Regelung der Bauwirtschaft im Rahmen des Vierjahresplans* (Reich Minister for Armaments and Representative for Construction within the Framework of the Four-Year Plan); and Dr Albert Speer, *Generalbauinspektor für Berlin* (General Building Inspector for Berlin). All wore civilian clothing while scouring the various locations.

On the 12th Hitler talked with Göring in the *Führersonderzug*, and the following afternoon, in company with *General der Infanterie* Blaskowitz, he visited Lodz, which had surrendered without a fight. After another talk with Göring in the train at Gogolin on the 14th, he flew the next day to the San river near Yaroslav and at Ubieszyn climbed a small mound to take the salute of his troops who had crossed the river using an improvised bridge. His entourage on this occasion was so enormous that he frequently vanished from sight in its midst.

By mid-September a platoon of motorcycle despatch riders had arrived and the overall strength of his security company had been augmented by one-third. Although the proposal to incorporate the *Führer-Begleitbataillon* as *IV. Bataillon des Infanterieregiments 'Grossdeutschland'* was not acted upon, its members continued to wear the 'GD' insignia on their shoulder straps because the battalion drew its replacements from *'Grossdeutschland'*. In order to bring in the structural changes with extreme urgency, on 16 September 1939 Rommel was ordered to Berlin to deal directly with the *Chef des Heerespersonalamtes* (Head of the Army Personnel Department) and the *Chef der Stabes des Allgemeinen Heeresamtes* (Chief of Staff of the Army General Office) on an oral basis.

Hitler returned to Berlin on 17 September in order to be well out of the way while the Soviets invaded Poland from the east. The next day the *Führersonderzug* pulled into a stop near Lauenburg, about 65 kilometres north-west of Danzig, whence Hitler travelled to the Polish border to hear a speech by *Gauleiter* Forster welcoming him formally to the 'Freistaat Danzig'. Church bells rang in the 'liberated' villages.

Between 19 and 25 September Hitler set up his FHQ in rooms 251 to 253 of the Casino Hotel on Nordstrasse in Zoppot; the security company arrived on the 21st and was accommodated at the Victoria Hotel. Late during the afternoon of his arrival, Hitler drove in a slow convoy with Keitel, von Ribbentrop, Lammers, Himmler, Dietrich, Bormann and his adjutants along the Langer Markt in Danzig, relishing the people's exuberance. Their jubilation had no limits: Danzig had been a German city for centuries until 1919, and now the injustice of Versailles had been reversed. In his speech, Hitler appealed to Great Britain to accept his offer of peace.

After receiving a deputation of Japanese officers at Zoppot on the 20th, Hitler went by boat next day to Westerplatte to inspect the old battle-ship *Schleswig-Holstein*, which had fired the opening rounds of the war on 1 September: at the renamed Gotenhafen along the coast, he, together with Göring, took the salute at a march-past and then inspected the battlefield on the Oxhoft heights. On the 22nd he flew to Minsk-Mazowiecki, about 40 kilometres east of Warsaw, to hear a situation report from *General der Artillerie* Georg von Küchler, the Commander of the Fourth Army, and at Glinki he looked into the besieged city through artillery scissor-arm binoculars. At his hotel he learned that *Generaloberst* von Fritsch, the OBdH dismissed in 1938 after an intrigue, had died a soldier's death leading his troops on the outskirts of Warsaw. Hitler ordered a State funeral at the Unter den Linden memorial.

After his final journey to the front with von Brauchitsch and senior army officers on 25 September, his train bore him through the night from Lauenburg to the Stettiner Bahnhof in Berlin. That afternoon Rommel returned to the capital with the FHQ security company and posted sentries at the entrances to the *Reichskanzlei*.

In his 1939 propaganda book,* *Reichspressechef* Otto Dietrich dedicated a full chapter to the enthusiasm of the troops for their commander-in-chief:

> Among the many great experiences of the *Führer*'s excursions to the front, the finest were the moments of human bonding with his soldiers . . . in this affirmation of their oath to the *Führer*, one may infer the final secret of their unique victory . . . for us it is the most emotional experience of this war.

The Polish campaign was drawn up by OKH *Generalstab* and carried through without Hitler's interference, although, according to Halder, penning the *Kriegstagebuch* entry of 10 September 1939, there was no strategic plan. What was probably kept from Hitler was knowledge of the major technical problem caused by the superficial destruction of the Polish telephone network by the defending army. This had forced the German Army to call for mobile equipment held in reserve by a single *Nachrichtenregiment* (signals regiment) formed for the purpose—which says much for their long-term preparations and the risks they were running. As the German Army advanced rapidly eastwards, the widening gap quickly gave rise to communications problems, which *Reichspost* military personnel attached to Army units could do little to combat. It was only towards the end of the campaign that the Polish telephone infrastructure was repaired and the situation stabilised. Hitler's train did not cross the Reich frontier and so he remained unaware that the Polish telephone system was not functioning.

At the end of September the *Führer-Begleitbataillon* was formed at the 'General Göring' Regimental Barracks at Doberitz. It was larger than asked for and consisted of the battalion staff, three Army companies, the *Luftwaffe* AA battery, a catering unit and two AA trains.

Following the Polish campaign, the *Führerzug* was not used as an FHQ again until 1941, although Hitler travelled in it for his long journeys to Munich, where he had a flat in the Prinzregentenstrasse or would stop in order to go on to Berchtesgaden for the drive to the Obersalzberg. Later he found it useful for travel between Berlin and his FHQs in East Prussia, and he would often go by rail through the occupied territories.

* *Auf den Strassen des Sieges: Erlebnisse mit dem Führer in Polen*, Munich, 1939.

On 10 October 1939 *FHQu-Kommandant* Rommel was instructed to look for suitable railway stations as temporary resting places for the *Sonderzüge* near the western borders. It was reported that there were twenty in the Soonwald, Westerwald and Black Forest that fitted the requirements, together with a number in Giessen. Thus the mobile option for the FHQ remained, perhaps with an eye to propaganda value: the idea of a permanent, fixed location for the supreme HQ had still not been addressed.

On 8 November 1939, Hitler visited Unity Mitford in hospital and the same day there occurred the assassination attempt by Georg Elser in the *Burgerbraukeller*. When the bomb went off, Hitler was already on the way to his *Sonderzug* at Munich station, Wunsche, his *Adjutant*, having prepared the train too early. At Nuremberg station, Hitler was informed of the bomb attempt. From that moment on, he was certain that Providence 'would allow him to achieve his goal'.

The KTB chronicler wrote of the FHQ as being 'in the process of self-forming'. The 'railway solution' chosen by Hitler for the Polish campaign was acceptable since it was convenient for his visits to the front, while neither the fighting nor the external political situation was giving rise to any concern. It papered over, however, the inadequacies of a rolling establishment which, in the judgement of *Oberst* Warlimont, was rather like 'a wandering camp'. In the spring of 1940 Hitler took his leave of Miss Mitford at Munich railway station prior to her return to England. It had been found too dangerous to remove the bullet from her brain, and she died as a result of her injury in 1948.

Chapter 2

The Western Offensive, 1940

IN order to protect the Reich against invasion from the West, in 1938 Hitler had ordered the immediate construction of fortifications, to be known as the *Westwall* (Atlantic Wall), along a tract of territory 50 kilometres broad, stretching 600 kilometres from the Swiss border to Emden and comprising 22,000 different installations. The *Verteidigungszone des Heeres* (Army Defence Zone) consisted of machine-gun bunkers, observation and artillery emplacements, tank traps, minefields and barbed-wire entanglements. *Luftverteidigungszone West* (Air Defence Zone West) had camouflaged grass airstrips and manned ground fortifications for light and heavy anti-aircraft guns.

Up to a thousand building firms with their own equipment and labour, together with 100,000 men on compulsory *Reichsarbeitsdienst* (RAD, or Reich Work Service) duties and numerous pioneer and infantry battalions, had been co-ordinated for the task under a single supremo, Dr Fritz Todt, *Generalinspektor für das Strassenbauwesen* (Inspector-General of Highways). When Hitler visited the *Westwall* on 18 July 1938 to see how work was progressing, he personally coined the name 'Organisation Todt'. There was never a corporation of this name: it was merely Hitler's pet term for the consortium. At its height on the *Westwall* project, OT employed one-third of a million men. The daily production of concrete was 45,000 cubic metres.

So as to regularise the continuation of the work on the *Westwall* after the outbreak of hostilities, Todt delegated engineer Xaver Dorsch to draw up a military-type constitution. Accordingly, OT workers wore an earth-brown uniform and, under a quasi-military service contract, were subject to the OT code of discipline and to OT courts. When Todt became

Reichsminister für Bewaffnung und Munition (Minister for Arms and Munitions) on 7 March 1940, Dorsch took over as head of OT.

In wartime, OT had exclusive competence over questions of construction in all occupied territories outside the operational areas of the Army groups, but even when contracted by the military it was not bound to follow their instructions in executing the work. Its primary task was the removal of debris and the repair of highways, but improving the general infrastructure and dispensing advice concerning logistics were real contributions by the OT everywhere to the maintenance of the garrisons and the operational freedom of the *Wehrmacht*. The comprehensive achievement of OT, however, was the building of the Atlantic Wall, which was undertaken between August 1940 and June 1944. In all, 10.6 million cubic metres of concrete was used in the construction of 10,206 fortifications and 844 coastal gun emplacements. The U-boat bunkers required 4.4 million cubic metres and *Luftwaffe* buildings (for example, aircraft hangars) one million cubic metres. Special installations such as the various V-1 flying-bomb bunkers and V-2 rocket silos consumed over half a million cubic metres of concrete. For the time, these were almost inconceivably large quantities: 16.5 million cubic metres is sufficient to build six Great Pyramids, or to clad the exterior of 66 large nuclear power stations, or to replicate a 158-kilometre-long stretch of the Wall of China sixteen metres high and tapering from eight metres broad at the base to five metres broad at the top.

OT's achievement in the Second World War is impossible to quantify since the organisation's activities extended beyond fortifications and FHQs. It removed the rubble as the *Wehrmacht* advanced through conquered territory and after Allied air attacks on Germany and elsewhere. It erected blockhouses and barracks for the *Wehrmacht*. The table-sized conical Todt oven of steel plate with iron feet, an invention of the OT's Eska ceramics unit, was delivered by the thousand to the Eastern Front. A study carried out in Great Britain* shortly before the war's end concluded that 'in less than five years, Organisation Todt has carried

* Military Records Branch, Handbook of the Organisation Todt, MIRS London, March 1945, reported in Singer, Hedwig, *Quellen zur Geschichte der Organisation Todt*, Band IV, Osnabrück, 1992.

out the most impressive building programme since the Romans'. In the circumstances, it is not surprising that Hitler should have concluded that OT was 'the greatest building organisation of all time'.

For every planned FHQ, OT set up a management team consisting of employees from the Berlin Head Office in the Pariser Platz. This team had the job of contracting firms, recruiting and caring for personnel at the sites, ordering and transporting materials and drawing up the building plans. The various building firms were grouped into a consortium subordinated to a single large company that functioned as the leading contractor. Thus, for FHQ Adlerhorst, Wayss & Freytag A. G. headed a dozen sub-contractors.

Despite the fact that the operational FHQs would be camouflaged, due regard had to be given to the question of proportion and how the structures blended in with the natural landscape, as had been the case with the autobahn bridges. Hitler's preference for natural stone, as exemplified in autobahn building, was reflected in the design of FHQs. Masons who had revived the old technologies of cutting and laying stone for autobahn bridges could now display their craft in disguising FHQ bunkers. For all his projects Dr Todt demanded the finest craftsmanship:

> In stonemasonry, the treatment of the material, work at the joints, the cut of the stone in curves and at the pillar corners ... require the closest attention to detail and thus the employment of the most skilled masons, if the overall result of a blend with the countryside and architectural perfection is to be obtained.

All new buildings in the Third Reich were to be aesthetically pleasing and architecturally polished monuments in stone to National Socialism, to serve as an example for coming generations.

In every FHQ built by OT there were four basic designs:

1. Bunkers sited above or partially below ground level with fortified entrances for protection against air attack. As a rule, 20 cubic metres of concrete was required for every square metre of surface. Most *Führerbunker* had a useful floor space of 40 square metres. Later in the war, this type of bunker acquired a subterranean gallery. For bunker-building the concrete was pressure-resistant to 300

THE WESTERN OFFENSIVE, 1940

kilograms per square centimetre. It was mixed on site in the ratio of one part cement to three parts sand or stone, the grains not exceeding 63mm in diameter. Three hundred kilograms of cement was required for one cubic metre of concrete. Concrete would not set in temperatures below −2°C. Bunker ceilings were always of concrete reinforced with steel rods 50mm in diameter and set 12cm apart.

2. Bunker houses, i.e. fortified structures often outwardly resembling Alpine chalets with bunkers below ground, in the FHQ grounds and used as dwellings or workplaces.
3. Single-storey, prefabricated, barracks-type housing almost exclusively without a cellar, prepared logs being delivered for assembly on a concrete foundation. One advantage of these huts was the facility with which they could be dismantled and erected elsewhere.
4. Wooden barracks in six different sizes clad with a 30–60cm thick concrete shell within 10–30cm of the walls and having a concrete ceiling. Steel plates 4cm thick could be bolted over the windows for splinter protection. The entrances were generally between 1.8 and 2.5 metres high with two-winged doors of 2cm-thick steel. OT laid only the foundations for barracks. The various sections were delivered by train and could be erected by unskilled labour.

Elsewhere on the FHQ estate, OT was responsible for building garages, flak emplacements, trenches and guard houses, and for putting up wire entanglements and other security systems. The most important camouflage was that against detection from the air. Dr Todt's motto was 'The best camouflage is nature'; only if natural camouflage were unavailable was resort to be had to netting.

All FHQs were linked to the regional highway network. At the outset of the project OT built the necessary access roads and streets, and even laid railway branch lines—work which preceded the first deliveries of equipment and materials. They connected water and electricity, laid drains and sewers and built sewage farms. Although the *Reichspost*, or outside Reich borders generally the *Wehrmacht*, was responsible for telecommunications, OT dug the cable pits.

49

The logistical problems required precise planning by the OT. Barracks were erected in the vicinity of the work being undertaken following the model of the *Autobahn* camps. Dormitories each housed eighteen workers, but kitchens, washrooms, recreation halls, infirmaries, stores, drying rooms and other facilities all had to be laid on. An OT leader from Head Office was responsible for seeing that the workers were fed and clothed, had medical attention and were entertained in their spare time.

It was because of its success at the *Westwall* that Hitler awarded OT the contract to build his fortified FHQs. The search for a site initiated at his request by Rommel on 10 September 1939 had come up with three recommendations: the Schloss estates of Ziegenberg and Kransberg near Bad Nauheim in Hesse; an anti-aircraft emplacement in *Luftverteidigungs-zone West*, near the village of Rodert, Munstereifel, where a bunker was already in place; and a *Westwall* installation on the 1,000-metre high Kniebis near Freudenstadt in the Black Forest. Todt recommended a locality at Wispertal near Lorch-am-Rhein because it was easy to protect and the terrain was favourable for the construction of a bunker complex, but the decision eventually went in favour of Schloss Ziegenberg, presumably because Speer was keen on it. Nevertheless, when work began at Ziegenberg (codenamed 'Adlerhorst') in late September 1939, it got under way at Rodert and Kniebis too, while OT started building a fourth FHQ of their own, Waldwiese, at Glan-Munchweiler in Rhineland-Pfalz.

Schloss Ziegenberg was situated on a mountainside a few hundred metres above the confluence of the Rivers Usa and Forbach and about ten kilometres east of Bad Nauheim in Hesse. In 1939 it was surrounded by agricultural land. Five kilometres to the north lay Schloss Kransberg, which had a cafeteria very popular with day-trippers before the war. The nearby grass airfields at Merzhausen and Kirchgons were earmarked for operational use by the *Luftwaffe*: to enemy air reconnaissance they resembled simple meadows and were ideal for FHQ's Fieseler Storch courier aircraft. At both Ziegenberg and Kransberg, bunkers and signal installations could be excavated into the mountainside. A valley a mile or so north-west of Ziegenberg and known today as Wiesental appeared to offer a good location for Hitler's accommodation bunkers.

Schloss Ziegenberg, including the farmland, was the property of the von Schaffer-Bernstein family but had been confiscated in September 1939 under the *Schutzbereich* (Defence Sphere) law of 11 October 1935. The owners of the Kransberg estate, the Homburg family von Scheidlein, were dispossessed with effect from 1 October 1939 and compensated in the sum of 269,400 *Reichsmark*.

The OT gave the codename 'Mühle' to its work at Ziegenberg and Kransberg, after the disused water mill on the River Usa, where the site supervisors Prädel and Kuhnell lodged. Speer's architectural bureau, whose initial designs for the conversion work were presented within a few days, designated the Ziegenberg/Wiesental project 'Bauvorhaben Z' (Building Plan Z) and Kransberg 'Lager K' (Camp K) or 'Bauvorhaben C'. Later the entire complex was named Adlerhorst.

Furnishings and work on the exterior fabric devolved upon Speer, while OT handled the construction of bunkers and subterranean galleries, OT being the obvious choice following the demonstration at the *Westwall* of their proficiency in working with concrete, building roads and bridges and perfecting camouflage. The largest building firms engaged were Philipp Holzmann A. G. of Frankfurt-am-Main and Wayss & Freytag A. G. of Stuttgart.

The project lasted from September 1939 until August 1940, OT organising three shifts around the clock to get the underground workings completed. The original workforce of 2,000 rose to a maximum of 4,500 in December 1939 and then declined gradually to 1,000 by June 1940. It was accommodated mainly in camps of wooden barracks, although a few workers were provided with lodgings in private rooms and halls. Buses were laid on to transport the men to and from the sites.

OT built the four subterranean work and accommodation bunkers, two air-raid shelters and three air-raid cellars at Ziegenberg/Kransberg and bored 300 metres of running galleries with a combined floor surface of 900 square metres. Spoil amounted to 72,000 cubic metres. A total of 38,000 cubic metres of concrete went into creating 6,960 square metres of floor space. The 3,800 square metres of bunker floor space was split down into living and work space (55 per cent), corridors, gas traps and

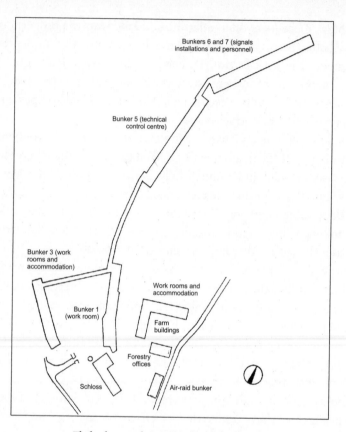

The bunker complex at Ziegenberg (after Bayer).

galleries (24), side rooms (15) and air-raid cellars (6). In all, 4,600 square metres of masonry was used in blending the bunkers, while the landfill amounted to 9,000 cubic metres.

It is difficult to understand what these figures represent, but, for example, the spoil would fill a trench the size of a soccer pitch fifteen metres deep, the concrete could have made a cube with 33-metre long sides, and the masonry was sufficient to erect a six-foot-high wall nearly a mile and a half long.

Speer's architectural plans for the interior redevelopment at Schloss Ziegenberg were revised on several occasions—there are at least four versions—but he finally settled for three rooms totalling 110 square metres on the main floor for Hitler, whose manservants, secretaries and ADCs, together with Keitel and Bormann, would occupy the upper floor while the catering and security staffs inhabited the basement. Twenty-six rooms for other personnel filled the floor immediately below the roof.

Stairways led from the front porch and delivery area to a 100 by 15 metre air-raid bunker with more than twenty fully furnished rooms, each with an average 20 square metres of floor space and arranged like railway compartments beside a through corridor. The bunker ceiling was two metres thick, the outer walls two and a half metres. Artful masonry disguised the exterior. Long subterranean corridors led from this bunker into three further bunkers of similar size, one for guests, the second housing technical equipment (telephone exchange, switching centres, radio and cable rooms, relay station and so forth) and the third a signals bunker with accommodation for personnel comprising fifty mainly four-bed dormitories for 124 persons. The 'farm buildings' in the castle grounds were also a workplace and dormitories for 67 people. A 70 by 15 metre car park with 30 parking places, a workshop and a car wash lay a few hundred metres from the castle. A dormitory for chauffeurs and mechanics was above it, and two air-raid bunkers were located in its basement.

Schloss Kransberg dominated the spur of a mountain and was assigned originally to Himmler. He would have 2,609 square metres. The castle was to remain unaltered, but a two-storey wing would be added, its walls on the courtyard side being disguised with masonry work. In the upper floor of the main property three accommodation/conference rooms and a refectory were planned. The 20-room bunker in the courtyard could sleep 74. A long stairway with gas sluice led from the castle entrance downwards. Three tunnels were designed as escape routes.

At Wiesental near Hilbertborn, on a wedge-shaped, south east-facing slope of the Oberberg two kilometres north of Ziegenberg, seven single-storey fortified houses with air-raid cellars were erected, six on the north side and one on the south. The walls were of 50cm reinforced steel and the ceilings of concrete 20cm thick. The basement walls on the exposed side were overlain with masonry work and the next floor up with planking. The overhanging wooden roofs gave the buildings the appearance of an alpine chalet complex. Except for the 38-metre-long guard house, the buildings averaged 26 to 28 by 11 metres and all were equipped with an air-raid bunker having walls and ceiling two or more metres in thickness. Hitler's personal bunker had a steel-reinforced ceiling 3.2 metres thick. The spoil for this complex amounted to 14,100 cubic metres. OT prepared 10,000 cubic metres of concrete plus 3,800 cubic metres filling and 1,800 cubic metres of masonry in the construction.

The *Führerhaus* had a walnut-panelled, 14-square-metre bedroom, a 24-square-metre study, a bathroom and dressing room, four rooms for ADCs and servants, a 38.5-square-metre map room, a room for the security troops and a toilet block. From the hallway, which was as large as the study, a door led to Hitler's private quarters and a 36-step stairway to the air-raid cellar. The rooms below mirrored the function and layout of the floor above. The neighbouring building was the *Kasino* (Officers' Mess) and had a 60-square-metre dining hall, two lounges of 48 and 60 square metres, a kitchen and cupboards. It was fronted lengthways by a broad terrace from which a roofed walkway led to the *Führerhaus*. The other buildings, in *Landhausstil* (the style of a country house), were for Keitel, Jodl and the *Adjutanten*, the *Reichspressechef* and NSDAP representation, generals' living quarters and the guardhouse. The road to Ziegenberg was closed off with barriers.

The total floor area for the 'Mühle' project, including Wiesental, was 1,360 square metres in blockhouses and protected barracks, 7,740 square metres of bunkers and 900 square metres of underground galleries. The total production of concrete for the period September 1939 to August 1940 of 48,100 cubic metres was enough to build a solid round tower 160 feet tall and 90 feet in diameter. Altogether 854,000 working days (8.5 million man-hours) went into the work, with, on average, 400 men working on the two sites at any one time. At an hourly rate of 70 *pfennig*, the labour cost alone was 5.9 million *Reichsmark*.*

---

* To give some indication of what these cash figures represent, the annual salary of a highly skilled engineer in the Third Reich was 10,000 *Reichsmark* gross. An OT labourer working six days a week earned 2,000 *Reichsmark* gross annually.—Tr.

Berlin NW 7, den 22.April 1941
Sommerstrasse (am Reichstag)
Ruf: 12 7o21
B/V

An die

Wehrkreisverwaltung XII

W i e s b a d e n
Wilhelmstr. 1

Betr.: Bauvorhaben "Mühle",
        Schloss Kransberg und Ziegenberg.

In Beantwortung Ihres Briefes an den Herrn Generalinspektor
für das deutsche Strassenwesen, Abteilung Wiesbaden vom 25.
II.1941 haben wir die Kosten für die Ein- und Umbauten der
beiden Schlösser wie folgt festgestellt:

Schloss Ziegenberg   RM 3.879.745.26

Schloss Kransberg   R M 2.236.680.16

                    Heil Hitler !

                D er Generalinspektor
                      für
                das deutsche Strassenwesen
                  Bauleitung "Mühle"

*A letter signed by Baurat Kuhnell advising of the conversion costs
for the castles at Ziegenberg and Kransberg.*

The conversion work at Ziegenberg cost the budget 3.9 million *Reichsmark* with another 2.2 million for Kransberg, and these figures do not include OT salaries, the labour costs of the *Reichspost* and signals units, the hundreds of kilometres of cables and the best telephonic installations money could buy. The costs for Wiesental are not quantified. Also costly would have been 52.4 kilometres of new or expanded highways and roads required for the complex.

To create gardens, and for camouflage purposes, 2,000 trees and 33,000 bushes were planted, 32,000 square metres of turf laid and 142,000 square metres of land sown with grass seed. The countryside around Wiesental was newly forested, and camouflage netting was placed over buildings and stretched across roads in order to deceive enemy air reconnaissance. The whole area was supposed to be mistaken for a ten-year stand of spruce, but USAAF aerial photographs taken in March 1945 show that these measures were not particularly successful. The Ziegenberg farm and buildings were left as they were, to give the impression of rural land under cultivation.

For the purposes of air defence, two transmitting stations and a series of massive heavy anti-aircraft emplacements with 29 bunkers were installed, together with 85 barrack huts. The AA defence for Adlerhorst was supplied by the five batteries of the *Luftwaffe Reserve-Festungs Flak-abteilung 321* (formed in 1939 but from mid-1940 renumbered 604). Three batteries were equipped with 10.5cm guns, the other two with 3.7cm or 2cm guns. The detachment strength was about 600. In addition, the '*Gross-deutschland*' *Führer-Begleitbataillon* had six motorised anti-aircraft units.

The fitting-out of the two castles was Speer's responsibility. Believing that he ought to provide a standard of living for Hitler similar to that which he had observed at Obersalzberg, he spared nothing at Schloss Ziegenberg—wall panelling, walnut doors and window frames, 'designer' furniture supplied by the Vereinigte Werkstatten of Munich, wallpaper and carpets, and artistic wrought ironwork, paintings, carvings and sculpture for Hitler's living rooms.

The building work at FHQ Adlerhorst took longer than anticipated and both Speer and OT found themselves behind schedule. Even though OT pressed ahead to the standards set at the *Westwall*, the bunkers, gas baffles and armoured doors could not have been made ready by November 1939, Hitler's initial date for the attack on France. When *Oberstleutnant* Kurt Thomas, the new *FHQu-Kommandant*, inspected the work with Rommel on 22 January 1940, both men agreed that considerably more time was required, and when the campaign opened on 10 May 1940 FHQ Adlerhorst was still not ready. In any case, on being shown photographs of Schloss Ziegenberg some time previously, Hitler had declared that the HQ was too luxurious. As supreme commander of the *Wehrmacht* he could not live other than as his soldiers did: his reputation as *Führer* would be on the line, and the people at large, when they visited the earlier HQs after victory, would not be able to understand such luxury. Besides, he would not live in proximity to farm equipment and cattle sheds or be thought of as a *'pferdeliebenden Adeligen'* (horse-loving nobleman). On being shown the designs, Hitler had allegedly responded, 'You have fitted out this field headquarters—and that is what it is supposed to be—with wood carvings and wrought-iron ornamentation. You have put down thick pile carpets. You are surely not thinking that I would actually move into it, are you?' In a later (26 February 1942) monologue on the subject of Schloss Ziegenberg, Hitler said, 'They did what I didn't want, and made a castle out of it. For that reason I wouldn't go there.'

These sentiments cannot be dismissed lightly, for they are in keeping with the spartan lifestyle pursued by Hitler since the outbreak of war, although possibly other, more important reasons were behind them— for example, the fact that the telephone exchange would not have been operational until June 1940. Moreover, the FHQ was not particularly close to the front he had in mind to visit, as he had during the Polish adventure.

After Hitler decided against FHQ Adlerhorst in February 1940, he was offered as other alternatives the three complexes just rearward of the *Westwall*—Waldwiese near Landstuhl in the Pfalz, Tannenberg in the Black Forest near Kniebis and Felsennest in the northern sector at Rodert near Bad Munstereifel. According to *General der Artillerie* Halder's *Kriegstagebuch* (Vol. 1, entries for 24 February to 27 April 1940), the decision in favour of Rodert was taken much earlier than February 1940 since officers of the *Führer-Begleitbataillon* had already moved in and taken charge of the existing infrastructure there by November 1939.

The first of the alternatives, FHQ Waldwiese, centred on the Pfalz village of Glan-Munchweiler, was the only project of the four never used as an FHQ during the war. Work began there in early October 1939, 38,750 days' labour went into the construction and the maximum OT workforce on site was 500 in December 1939. One assumes from the entry dated 25 March 1940 in Halder's KTB that Waldwiese was intended to be a forward command post for Adlerhorst.

By April 1940, OT had manufactured 285 square metres of bunker area and 96 square metres of barracks, together with access roads and camouflaging. The *Führerbunker* was in woodland on the 300-metre contour east of the village. The communications bunker, located in the centre of the village, had the outward appearance of a dwelling house with a slated roof, although the windows were painted on the fabric of the outer walls. In an upland area—'Rosengarten', to the south-west of Glan Munchweiler—garaging for cars and lorries, a bunker for about 60 men, a blockhouse and a wooden observation tower were erected.

Waldwiese was never used by Hitler, who preferred FHQ Felsennest, which was closer to the starting point for the planned invasion of France through the Ardennes. As a result of the order of 1 June 1940, Warlimont's *Abteilung Landesverteidigung des WFSt* (WFSt Land Defence Section) moved into the installation and established a courier run from there to FHQ Felsennest and, later in the campaign, to FHQ Wolfsschlucht, which had also been codenamed 'Waldwiese' during its construction for the purposes of deception.

Felsennest, a *Führerhauptquartier* from 10 May to 6 June 1940, took its name from a 400-metre high wooded hilltop overlooking the hamlet of Rodert, one kilometre south of the small town of Munstereifel, 30 kilometres south of Bonn and 35 kilometres from the Belgian border. Situated in *Luftverteidigungszone West*, the enclosure of 30 hectares boasted a bunker and anti-aircraft emplacements with barracks erected by OT during the construction of the *Westwall* in 1938–9. Euskirchen airfield was twelve kilometres away, and Reichsstrasse 51 offered good highway connections. Todt had suggested the location during the second week of September 1939 and submitted plans for the construction of a *Führer* command centre there.

On 14 November 1939, *Hauptmann* Bertram and *Oberleutnant* Spenge-mann, officers at the *Stab des Kommandantur FHQu* (FHQu-Kommandant's Staff), arrived in the Eifel to look over the site. On 16 December they assumed overall charge of the project from the Bonn OT supervision and arranged for two platoons, each of a sergeant and ten men, for guard purposes from local *Wehrmacht* units. The construction plans were code-named 'Anlage F' and included the upgrading of the local *Westwall*, although this was not specifically ordered by Hitler.

Work began in October 1939 with 200 labourers, rapidly increasing to 700 in January 1940. Despite the bitter cold that winter, work proceeded with the construction of air-raid cellars, improvements to the roads, camouflaging, the laying of water-pipes and generally stockpiling the inventory of materials. On 5 January Dr Todt cast an eye over progress prior to the visit two days later by *Chefadjutant der Wehrmacht* Schmundt, *Heeresadjutant bei Hitler* Engel and the *FHQu-Kommandant*, *Oberstleutnant* Kurt Thomas, when orders were issued to accelerate the conversion of an AA supply dump below the FHQ into offices and three barracks.

On 22 February 1940, Hitler decided in favour of Rodert for his French campaign FHQ because the communications unit at Adlerhorst could not be made ready before mid-June, at the same time ordering OKW and OKH to set up their headquarters nearby. The *Luftwaffe* was left to choose its own location. On the 23rd Schmundt and Todt discussed the remaining work, particularly the inclusion of OKH, with Schmelcher, *Einsatzleiter* (Head of Operations) Henne and the two Bonn OT overseers, and next day the *FHQu-Kommandant* came to Rodert to issue orders to the effect that the completion of the OKH air-raid cellars north of Münstereifel should become a priority.

Felsennest consisted of four bunkers with a 250-square-metre floor area and 430 square metres occupied by two fortified blockhouses and three barracks huts. Three thousand cubic metres of concrete were used in the preparations. Surrounding this terrain was a fixed security fence with wooden watch towers. The compound was named *Sperrkreis I* (Restricted Area I). For Warlimont's *Abteilung Landesverteidigung des WFSt*, five houses in Rodert had been commandeered, while access roads had been laid and camouflaged. The hamlet and surrounding countryside was designated *Sperrkreis II*.

On 4 March 1940, an advance guard of 1. *Kompanie des Führer-Begleit-bataillon* took over the responsibility for security. On 12 March, *Reserve-*

Festungs-Flakabteilung 321 and the rest of *1. Kompanie* arrived, and on 15 March the remainder of the *Führer-Begleitbataillon* moved into the Siegburg–Weyerbusch–Altenkirchen area, the *Stab* (staff) and signals troops following two days later.

Work on the OKH accommodation at Hulloch, about ten kilometres east of Rodert, had started on 1 December 1939. Over a period of four months 5,500 cubic metres of concrete had been manufactured to build seven bunkers of 800 square metres and lay the foundations for 30 barracks huts. The Haniel forestry house was renovated for the use of Army C-in-C von Brauchitsch, with the usual road-laying and camouflage.

During the late afternoon of 31 March, the *Chef der Generalstabs des Heeres*, Halder, spent an hour looking over the OKH quarters and mentioned his reservations regarding the communications installations. On 4 April, *General* Erich Fellgiebel, *Chef des Heeresnachrichtenwesens* (Head of Army Signals), reported that Felsennest would be fully operational on 12 April, but Halder was nevertheless worried about the possibility of enemy interference with communications, having regard to the close proximity of FHQ Felsennest to the lines.

A sharp controversy arose between OT and the military. Although the site was scheduled for completion on 31 March 1940, a few days beforehand many bunkers and buildings still lacked sanitation, air conditioning, ovens, furnishings, blackout curtains and door plaques. The delay had been caused by work having stopped when temperatures fell to −25°C. On 30 March, *Bauassessor* Classen from OT Bonn advised the military that the work would be concluded within a few weeks, but the military did not consider his tempo brisk enough and the *Führer-Begleitbataillon* took over the supervision of the men working on the fixtures and fittings. In the end, the *FHQu-Kommandant* made his final inspection on 6 May.

Felsennest consumed 850,000 man-hours and involved about 400 labourers working a ten-hour day for seven and a half months, each earning an average of 70 *pfennig* an hour. No forced labour nor prisoners of war were used at this time on secret projects.

The *Wehrmacht* installed the communications equipment. For the needs of OKH, Fellgiebel promised 50 telephone lines, to which another 20 were added later, together with a direct-dial facility.

Compared to Adlerhorst, the structural work at Felsennest was modest. The FHQ had only 680 square metres of bunkers, fortified houses and barracks, and OKH was allocated 800 square metres of bunkers and 8,000 square metres for outbuildings—equivalent to thirty large barracks huts. Hitler's personal domain was half a concrete bunker of modest proportions, containing a study, a bedroom and two other small rooms for his manservant Linge and personal *Adjutant* Schaub, plus a kitchen and a bathroom. Keitel, Jodl, Schmundt and Brandt lived in the other half. The bunker was air-conditioned but had no windows. On the other hand, it had extraordinary acoustics, for Keitel stated that he could hear Hitler turning the pages of a newspaper on the other side of the bunker wall.

In addition to this accommodation bunker, there were two barracks huts on a slope some distance away. The dining hut had a long table that could seat twenty, and all meals were served here. A map of France decorated the windowless longer wall. *Hauptmann* Deyhle, Jodl's *Generalstabsoffizier*, and a number of *Feldwebel* clerks inhabited the other hut. It was said to occupy the best spot on the hilltop, 'with an especially beautiful panorama over the afforested heights', as Keitel recorded with envy.

Fortified structures—stronghouses and bunkers—were characteristic of fixed FHQs. Hoffmann observed that Hitler had not been backward 'in giving eloquent expression to his mental state of a fortress-dweller.' Initially this aspiration was limited to single, surface-built or semi-subterranean bunkers often uninhabitable because of damp. This was particularly true of the 'front-line' FHQs of the 1940 Western campaign. Later, bunkers were constructed for other uses, and wall thicknesses grew from two to five metres (and, in the case of the three-storey bunker at Strub barracks, Berchtesgaden, to seven metres). Hitler's obsession with air attack in the second half of the war was the cause: in turning down plans for an expensive development of the site at Felsennest early in 1943, he pointed to the ruins of Euskirchen fifteen kilometres away.

The size of the plot for an FHQ varied according to the length of time it was thought necessary to occupy it. While Felsennest was only 30 hectares, Wolfschanze in East Prussia, even without OKH headquarters, sprawled across 250 hectares, and in the closing months of the war FHQ Riese near Breslau was designed to occupy an area of at least ten square kilometres.

Hitler's journey to FHQ Felsennest, codenamed 'Pfingsturlaub genehmigt' (Whitsun Holiday Approved) proceeded under the tightest security. He boarded the *Führersonderzug* with his entourage at Berlin-Finkenkrug station at 1700 on 9 May 1940; not even his secretaries knew the destination. The train set off to the north-west as if heading for Denmark, but by dawn on 10 May it had pulled into Euskirchen, where the party alighted. The *Sonderzug* then steamed off through Bonn, Mainz and Frankfurt to sidings at Heusenstamm near Offenbach.

Hitler was driven under escort in a motor convoy from Euskirchen to Rodert, Bormann, Keitel and von Below, his *Luftwaffe* ADC, accompanying him as passengers in the three-axle Mercedes. Five minutes behind came the vehicles bearing *Reichspressechef* Dietrich, photographer Hoffmann, Schmundt and the female secretaries. A third convoy carried the luggage.

The German attack on France began at 0535 that morning, thirty minutes after Hitler's arrival at Felsennest, OKW announcing over the wireless that the *Führer* was 'at the front to lead the overall *Wehrmacht* operation'. Hitler inspected the two guest blockhouses and OKW barracks and during the late afternoon of 11 May spent two hours with the OKH at Hulloch briefing himself on the operational plans for the morrow.

Oberst Warlimont reached Rodert with about 40 signallers, clerks and sketch artists who had come part way by air or rail. The *Verbindungs-offiziere* (liaison officers) attached to the *Abteiling Wehrmacht-Propaganda* (*Wehrmacht* Propaganda Section), *Amt Wehrwirtschaft* (Military Economy Department) and *Amt Ausland/Abwehr* (Foreign/Defence Department) were stationed in Munstereifel. Von Ribbentrop, Himmler and Lammers, whose *Ministerzug, Heinrich*, lay in sidings at Altenkirchen east of the Rhine, visited FHQ from there on several occasions over the next few days. The *Feldstaffel* (Field Squadron) of the *Führungsstab der Luftwaffe* (Luftwaffe Command Staff) was quartered about ten kilometres north-west of Munstereifel, and Göring's train was near the tunnel at Trimbs/Polch between Koblenz and Mayen, about 50 kilometres away, while elements of the *Generalstab des Heeres* (Army General Staff) were located in Godesberg and Giessen.

The setting for Felsennest was the most beautiful of all the FHQ settings, Hitler's secretary Christa Schroeder describing it thus in her book:

> The woods, fresh with spring, were filled with birdsong. Hitler called it 'the bird paradise'. He felt very well in these rural surroundings, and as his bunker was very small he held most of his conversations in the open air. He never spent as much time outdoors as he did here. He was enraptured by the beautiful scenery and said he wanted to make an annual commemorative visit here after the war with the same people.

In one of his evening monologues at the end of February 1942 Hitler referred to Felsennest as his 'nicest FHQ', perhaps thinking of the little nook built for him by OT where there was a stone bench set into the remains of a Roman wall beside a fountain.

The daily routine at FHQ revolved around two situation conferences. The WFSt *Feldstaffel* numbered no more than twenty officers and had been set up to bridge the physical gap between the FHQ and various *Wehrmacht* command centres. It consisted of operations groups for the three arms of service, its own operational and quartermaster group and a *Kriegstagebuch* chronicler. Its job was to receive and collate reports on both friendly and hostile activities, from which would be pieced together a situation report, the focus of the daily decision-making process. The communication channels along which information was transmitted at that time were quite simple, and so as not to clog the system a regulated flow in and out was essential. This spacing out required particular means of sending in reports and timetabling, and the bulk of the material was transmitted during the night when the fighting at the fronts generally fell quiet. The OKH and OKM (*Oberkommando der Marine*, or Navy High Command), and the *Führungsstab der Luftwaffe*, tried to have compiled by

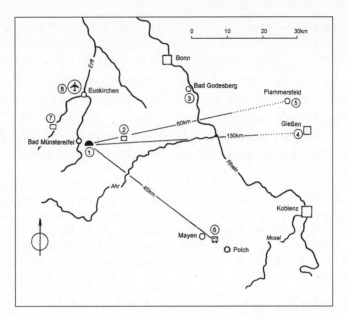

FHQ *Felsennest and its satellite centres (1940): 1. FHQ Felsennest; 2.*
Oberbefehlshaber des Heeres *(Army C-in-C) and* Chef des
Generalstabs; *3, 4. Parts of OKH; 5.* Reichsaussenminister *(Foreign
Minister),* Reichsführer-SS *and Head of* Reichskanzlei; *6. Göring's
headquarters; 7.* Luftwaffe *operations group; 8. Airfield.*

the following morning an summary of how things had stood the previous
evening, and from these morning reports the WFSt *Feldstab* would put
together a situation report not infrequently thirty pages in length, complete with appendices, file notes, short observations on special aspects,
statistics and reports from independent commanders. From this comprehensive document Jodl prepared a shorter report for Hitler. From
the beginning of the Western offensive in 1940, it became the custom to
hold the principal situation conference at midday, followed by a shorter
session of updates in the evening. Between the two sessions, Hitler would
hold talks mainly with Government and NSDAP civilians, essentially
on questions affecting war policy.

Jodl's influence was such that he gradually assumed a role approxi-
mating that of Chief of Hitler's General Staff. Keitel maintained that it

was his responsibility to present the situation report, but he had delegated the job to Jodl at the outset of the Polish campaign. As Keitel saw it, the situation conferences at FHQ were the heart of the whole leadership mechanism but had degenerated into meetings at which orders were issued. Moreover, the agenda was not restricted to operational questions but, more broadly,

> to all areas whatsoever in some way connected with military policy. I, who had been briefed previously about the midday and evening conference, could not escape these time-consuming affairs, and every time Hitler put questions about arrangements or measures which had nothing to do with strategy or politics they had to be followed up and he would then rely on me as C-in-C of the military staff for an answer, although the OKW had no kind of competence to give one.

Keitel may have retained the function voluntarily until the Polish campaign, but, if he did so, he was acting in defiance of standing orders, which specified perfectly clearly that as from 1 March 1939 it was the responsibility of WFSt.*

The C-in-Cs of the three services played no special part in operational planning, meeting with Hitler only when he summoned them to an FHQ—which was not often. Only Göring, by reason of his personal standing in State and *Wehrmacht*, had for a long period a significant effect on Hitler's policymaking. Jodl kept his position from first to last and exercised the greatest influence on Hitler's operational decisions, although after 1942 Schmundt played an equally important role when he combined the duties of *Chef des Heerespersonalamtes* (Head of the Army Personnel Office) with his duties as Hitler's *Wehrmacht* ADC. It was possibly as a result of Schmundt having brought to the *Führer*'s attention the information that OKH was playing down *Generalfeldmarschall* Erich von Manstein's plan for a Panzer attack through the Ardennes (which coincided with Hitler's own ideas) that Hitler now began to intervene more frequently in military operations planned by OKH.

The lesser, 'silent' influence of the Army, Navy and *Luftwaffe* ADCs must not be overlooked. As few others did, they had the opportunity to speak

---

* See OKW KTB 2, *Halbband I/1*, pp. 877 *et seq.*, for a reproduction of the *Kriegsspitzengliederung des Oberkommando der Wehrmacht* standing order dated 1 March 1939 (paras 3 and 4 refer).

privately with Hitler and thereby impart information which had come their way outside the normal channels. The same applied in reverse, and they were expected in the course of their duties within the innermost FHQ circle to keep their respective General Staffs informed regarding tendencies, intentions and occurrences.*

On 13 May 1940, at FHQ Felsennest, Hitler received *Luftwaffe* paratroop officers involved in the capture of Fort Eben Emael near Liége. After decorating them with the Knight's Cross, he posed in their midst for photographers. On the 17th Hitler flew from Odendorf, north-east of Münstereifel, to visit *Generalfeldmarschall* Kurt von Rundstedt, *Oberbefehlshaber* (C-in-C) Army Group A, at his Bastogne headquarters; and on the 18th the new Italian ambassador, Alfieri, presented his credentials at FHQ, the day that Hitler also signed the decree annexing into the Reich the Belgian towns of Eupen, Malmédy and Moresnet (of which Germany had been deprived under the terms of the Treaty of Versailles).

The *Wehrmacht* advanced without a hitch during the opening days of the Western offensive, and this prompted Hitler to order that a new FHQ be established further west to enable him to keep up with the front. As none of the scheduled locations was either ready or suitable, on 19 May Todt, *FHQu-Kommandant* Thomas and ADCs Schmundt and Engel inspected a number of bunkers along the Maginot Line east of Avesnes and south of Maubeuge on the Franco/Belgian border. These were rejected, even though the sites had historical significance for the Germans (the German Army Chief of Staff's advance headquarters having been at Avesnes during the 1918 spring offensive). On 22 May the search party was flown by Hans Baur, Hitler's pilot, to Philippeville. The town lies close to where the Belgian border in the south-east meets the French frontier, and here they discovered what they were looking for—the small village of Brûly-de-Pesche, 25 kilometres north-west of Charleville and consisting of ten farmhouses, a school and a church. All the inhabitants

---

* The three military ADCs had been scouting for suitable FHQ sites in western Germany in early September 1939. It seems likely that they were under Hitler's strictest instructions not to divulge the information to their respective senior command staffs; indeed, according to Warlimont, Halder only learned of the fixed FHQ project when Rommel rang him from the Felsennest site to ask what arrangements he wanted to be made for the telephone exchange there.—Tr.

had fled. The nearest airfield was only a few kilometres distant, at Gros-Caillou.

On 22 May also, the *Führer-Begleitbataillon* formed a *Frontgruppe* (literally, 'front group') to escort Hitler on his tours to the front. Its fighting strength was 30 officers, 192 NCOs and 912 men conveyed in VW Kübel-wagens and motorcycle combinations. Next day the security battalion occupied Brûly-de-Pesche.

Discussions were held at this time by Todt, *FHQu-Kommandant* Thomas and OT *Bauassessor* Classen to agree how the village would be converted, and Classen undertook to complete the work in the shortest possible time.

On 24 May, Hitler flew with Jodl and Schmundt to Charleville for a second call upon Army Group A and, so as to leave open 'the way for an understanding with Britain', gave von Rundstedt orders not to attack the remnant of the British Expeditionary Force at Dunkirk. Von Rund-stedt himself did not argue the point since he wanted to spare his Panzers for the next encounter with the French. As the *Luftwaffe* was not in a position to mount a major operation of this nature, the BEF escaped.

OT began the work at Brûly-de-Pesche on 25 May. In dense woodland immediately north of the village, a pit three metres deep was excavated for the 25-square-metre concrete *Führerbunker* along with five barracks of 1,500 square metres, one of these for Hitler, one for dining and a third for the WFSt. The village houses provided a further 800 square metres of space, the village school being appropriated for the *Lageraum* (situation room) and a number of anterooms. The nave of the church was freshly painted and used as a newsreel cinema once the area behind the altar steps had been partitioned off.

In Brûly-de-Pesche the structures were only for the inner FHQ: OKH was to have its own headquarters at nearby Chimay, where 25 houses were requisitioned and renovated. In all, new surface structures totalled 1,500 square metres in the village and 800 square metres of blockhouses at Chimay for the OKH, together with the usual access roads and camou-flage work. Over the twelve days from 25 May to 6 June, an 600-strong OT workforce laboured from 0600 through to 2230 each day, the last

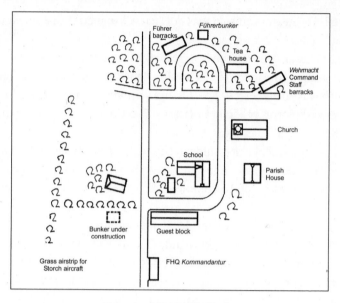

Diagram of FHQ Wolfsschlucht,
drawn by Hitler's Marineadjutant (Naval ADC) von Puttkamer.

man leaving the site on the day Hitler arrived. The *Wehrmacht* installed the communications structure, although nothing is known of how the telephone lines from FHQ were rigged into the *Wehrmacht* network.

On 27 May 2. and 3. *Kompanie* of the *Führer-Begleitbataillon* moved from Rodert to Brûly-de-Pesche to work on the physical security, particularly the perimeter fencing. They were accompanied by the five batteries from *Reserve-Festungs-Flakabteilung 321.**

To mark the Belgian capitulation on 28 May, Hitler issued two proclamations 'of enormous military significance' from FHQ Felsennest, announcing the end of the Belgian Army and declaring with annoyance that the Belgian Government had decided to pursue an alliance with Britain and France. The Italian ambassador, Alfieri, stayed at Felsennest for the last two days of May after confirming to Hitler that Italy would soon enter the war on Germany's side.

* The *FHQu KTB* entry for 6 June 1940 states that this detachment was renumbered 604, and it seems to have been merged into 1. *FlakRgt 604*. A year later it was retitled 1. *Abt FlakRgt 604* when taking charge at FHQ Wolfschanze. It proved to be a lasting solution to the problem of FHQ air defence.

The *Frontgruppe* of the *Führer-Begleitbataillon* was called upon to guard Hitler for the first time on 1 June 1940 when he made an excursion from a Brussels airfield to northern France for a visit to a number of commanders in the field. Afterwards he inspected various Great War battlefields on which he had fought, including those at Ghent, Ypres, Messines and Langemarck, where he walked through the military cemetery. After an overnight stop at Château de Brigode at Annappes, east of Lille, the convoy drove to Vimy, and on the famous Ridge Hitler was briefed on the war situation by von Kluge, C-in-C Fourth Army. From there the convoy progressed through Donai and Cambrai to Charleville for Hitler's return flight to FHQ Felsennest.

On 4 June 1940, *Stab/Führer-Begleitbataillon* and the greater part of Jodl's work staff transferred from Felsennest to Brûly-de-Pesche, those not necessary for operations remaining in Rodert despite the inadequate communications installations there. According to French resistance legend in the Rièzes et Sart region, civilian hostages were taken from surrounding villages to Dinant prison, where they were advised that they would be shot 'should anything happen to the *Führer*' during his stay at Brûly-de-Pesche. In the village itself, arriving German Army vehicles were parked in the woods and covered with camouflage netting. The grass airstrip for use by the Fieseler Storch light aircraft always at readiness lay beside the *FHQu-Kommandantur* on the southern edge of the village.

The strength of the security forces at Brûly-de-Pesche totalled 26 officers, 185 NCOs and about 750 men. Sentries patrolled the perimeter of the wire fence, whilst the weaponry of the forces was augmented by six truck-mounted 2cm guns and 35 light and two heavy machine guns following instructions issued on 21 May regarding the possibility of attacks by paratroops and glider-borne infantry. This supplemented the existing arsenal of four 37cm anti-tank guns, and twenty standard 2cm and eight 'railway' 2cm anti-aircraft guns.

Despite the exodus of the over 300,000-strong BEF from Dunkirk, Hitler proclaimed in a radio broadcast to the German people on 5 June 1940 that 'the greatest battle of all time has ended in victory for our soldiers.' The next day he left Felsennest for the new FHQ in Belgium.

Eye-witness accounts state that Hitler spent most of his time in the open air at FHQ Wolfsschlucht because the buildings were infested with midges and the varnish made his eyes swell. In a recorded monologue later, he complained that 'it was also not secure there'. He never used the *Führerbunker*, even though the Royal Air Force regularly overflew the village and on one occasion dropped some incendiaries which fell on the quarters of his SS bodyguard and the RSD. *General der Artillerie* Halder, *Chef der Generalstabs des Heeres*, criticised the twenty minutes it took to drive from OKH to FHQ and described the telephones as 'deafening'. Von Brauchitsch, Army C-in-C, came from Berlin to Wolfsschlucht only twice to attend briefings.

On 10 June 1940 Italy declared war on Britain and France. Hitler issued a proclamation stating that 'At this hour all Germany is filled with jubilation that Fascist Italy, of her own free will, has entered the struggle against the common enemy, France and Great Britain, on our side.'

On 14 June Himmler arrived for a conference at Brûly-de-Pesche in a Schmiesser MP 38. While the driver, *SS-Obersturmführer* Hans Bastians, was waiting for his return, the engine exploded and Bastians was killed. He was buried in the village that day with full military honours—the first fatality at any FHQ. Hitler received an American journalist for the last time on the 15th, when Karl Wiegand was assured of Germany's friendliest attitude towards the United States. Verdun surrendered the same day.

When the second phase of the campaign against France, Operation 'Rot' (Red) began on 5 June, a further FHQ project, codenamed 'Wolfs-schlucht 2', was approved, to enable Hitler to be nearer his front-line troops. Between Rheims and Soissons lies Margival, where, at Rilly-Germaine, north of the town, there is a railway tunnel 650 metres in length, and this seemed to offer a suitable shelter for the *Führerzug*. Guards from a motorcycle detachment were posted at either end of the tunnel on 13 June, and, following his survey with *FHQu-Kommandant* Thomas, Todt gave OT instructions to build a bunker nearby for Hitler. On 15 June an OT motorised column of *Frontarbeiter* (front workers) started the preparations.

On 16 June Hitler travelled by road to meet the Chief of the Spanish General Staff, General Vigon, in Acoz castle, south-east of Charleroi, where the latter was advised of the imminent capitulation of the French armed forces. That day Thomas and Schmundt visited Tannenberg, the new FHQ in the Black Forest, to obtain a report on its readiness. On the 17th it was confirmed that France had requested terms, and Hitler stamped his right foot in a gesture of joy.* Marshal Pétain's request for terms was announced at once to the German public, and the former *Kaiser*, Wilhelm II, sent a congratulatory telegram from exile in Holland. The workforce excavating the new FHQ complex outside the Margival railway tunnel was sent away since 'Wolfsschlucht 2' was no longer required. The site itself was not forgotten, however.

In the afternoon of 17 June Hitler flew to join his *Führerzug* at Frankfurt-am-Main for a conference with Mussolini in Munich to discuss the Armistice arrangements, and on 18 June *1. Kompanie/Führer-Begleitbataillon* was transferred to Compiègne from Laon and set up quarters in the local school: with other *Wehrmacht* units, it was to form the honour guard arranged for the Armistice-signing ceremony. During the afternoon of 19 June Hitler returned by air from Frankfurt to Gros-Caillou, where he ordered FHQ Tannenberg to be readied. The same day a unit of VI Army Corps arrived at Brûly-de-Pesche to guard the installations.

It was at Compiègne that the *Kaiser*'s Reich had had to admit on 9 November 1918 that it could not go on. Hitler ordered OT to restore the surroundings to their condition at that time. The railway saloon coach in which the German delegation under Matthias Erzberger had signed the Armistice Protocol on 12 November 1918 was brought from the local museum and placed in the same siding at Rethondes station.

The terms of the new Armistice treaty with France were worked on in the church at Brûly-de-Pesche and completed early on 21 June. Hitler arrived at Compiègne with his convoy at 1515 on the same day and stood in silent contemplation of the stone plaque at the edge of the wood, its inscription commemorating the event of November 1918 in the following

* The photograph was 'misinterpreted' by the British Press as evidence that Hitler was suffering from St Vitus's Dance.

terms: 'On 11 November 1918 the criminal pride of the German *Kaiserreich* was subjugated here to the free peoples whom it had sought to enslave.' Having taken offence at this text, Hitler issued an order next day to the effect that the historic coach, the memorial plaque and the monument to the Gallic triumph were to be removed to Berlin; the remaining stone-work and foundations were to be destroyed, but the monument to Marshal Foch would remain undisturbed.

Fifteen minutes after the German delegation, consisting of Hitler, Göring, von Brauchitsch, von Ribbentrop and Hess, had taken their seats, the French negotiators, led by *Général* Huntzinger, entered the coach. Hitler and his entourage rose in formal greeting. Keitel then related the conditions of the Armistice, which interpreter Dr Paul Schmidt read out in French, and once this had been accomplished the German party, bar the last two, left the coach, although Hitler was present from time to time to observe the progress of the negotiations. He returned to FHQ Wolfsschlucht at 2000. A few hours later Hitler received a telegram from Moscow in which Soviet Foreign Minister Molotov extended his Govern-ment's 'warmest congratulations on the *Wehrmacht*'s brilliant success'.

On 23 June Hitler spent a few hours in Paris. At 0405 he flew from Gros-Caillou to Le Bourget aerodrome, returning at 1030. Baur piloted him, the party consisting of Hitler, Keitel, Bormann and the ADCs. At Le Bourget the vehicles of the *Führer-Begleitbataillon* were waiting. Speer and the architects Hermann Giesler and Arno Breker led the tour. Paris was as if deserted. Hitler looked over the opera house and the Church of the Madeleine (built to commemorate Napoleon's victories), and visited the Eiffel tower and Napoleon's tomb. Then he went to Montmartre. Surveying the panorama of the city he said, 'I am grateful to Fate that I have now seen this city, the aura of which has always preoccupied me.'

In company with his old comrades Max Amann and Ernst Schmidt, on 25 June Hitler visited battlefields where the trio had fought between 1914 and 1918, returning to Brûly-de-Pesche overnight, and on the 26th, at Lille, he sought the spot where, as a soldier, he had painted a watercolour. Then the veterans visited Armentières, Kemmel and Dun-kirk before returning to Brûly-de-Pesche.

THE WESTERN OFFENSIVE, 1940

Jodl's WFSt convoy had abandoned FHQ Wolfsschlucht for FHQ Tannenberg on the 25th via Sedan, Strasbourg and Kehl. Hitler left during the morning of 27 June 1940, and from Gros-Caillou he flew in his FW Condor, D-2600, to Eutingen airfield, where *1. Kompanie/Führer-Begleit-bataillon* was waiting to escort him to FHQ Tannenberg. On 2 July Brûly-de-Pesche was relinquished to the Organisation Todt.

During preparations for the Western offensive, the construction of FHQ Tannenberg under *Oberbaudirektor* Autenrieth began concurrently with that at Waldwiese on 1 October 1939. The site lay between Baden-Baden and Freudenstadt on the 1,000-metre high Kniebis at the edge of a high moor. It was served by the Black Forest highway built before the war by Todt. The work, which, as with Waldwiese, was the expansion of an existing installation of *Luftverteidigungszone West*, was concluded on 1 July 1940.

Altogether 2,340 cubic metres of concrete went into making two bunkers—one for Hitler, the other for communications—with a total surface area of 275 square metres. Some of the standing structures were developed, and a barracks of 85 square metres was erected. Five hundred labourers worked on the project in November 1939, but over half the eight-month period the number was about 100. The working week was set at 54 hours, and a total of 43,750 working days were expended upon the project.

Hitler stayed at FHQ Tannenberg from 27 June until 5 July 1940, although he and his entourage spent a great deal of time in the open because the bunker had not dried out and was unfit for habitation. They were favoured by good weather. Hitler said later that the FHQ had been built in accordance with his wishes—'simple and nice, but it was too damp, and if we had stayed any length of time there we would all have gone down with something.'

Warlimont's WFSt was more than a kilometre away in the Alexander-schanze *Gasthaus* on the highway, much to Hitler's displeasure because this was outside the *Sperrkreis*. He is supposed to have recommended to WFSt that the hotelier 'be compensated by your frequent recourse to his cellar for the inconvenience of barring his clientele'—advice which was no doubt followed. The landing strip for courier aircraft at FHQ Tannenberg was in frequent use because OKH Headquarters was now at Fontainebleu.

On 28 June, to a jubilant reception, Hitler was driven in convoy through Alsace to battlefields in the Vosges. The left mudguard of his six-wheeled Mercedes staff car bore his personal tactical insignia, a running wolf inside an inverted triangle. (Hitler often referred to himself as 'Herr Wolf'.) Near Kehl he met General der Artillerie Dollmann, C-in-C Seventh Army, who had forced the breach at the southern end of the Maginot Line, then in brilliant sunshine he visited Strasbourg, where Staatsminister Meissner explained to him the architecture of the cathedral. Afterwards he toured Schlettstadt and Colmar to the bunkers along the Lower Rhine at Breisach, from where the German thrust had started. On 30 June Hitler looked over armoured parts of the Maginot Line at Mulhouse and conversed companionably with simple soldiers. In his bright trench coat he made a colourful, civilian-like impression. From Freiburg he took the Führerzug to Oppenau, returning by road to his FHQ.

At Tannenberg Hitler had a string of important military and political conversations—including one with Italian ambassador Alfieri on 1 July, whom he assured that 'in England nobody seriously believes any more that they can win', and another with Goebbels on the subject of his return to Berlin—and received a deputation of young women serving with the Reichsarbeitsdienst (RAD, or German Work Service). On 2 July he edited Jodl's draft of the OKW's final report on the campaign in the West. The same day Jodl and Warlimont presented the Führer with the outline plan for the invasion of Britain. Hitler listened but made no decision, although he accepted with reluctance that the FHQ would have to be at Schloss Ziegenberg, a location contrary to his inclinations.

In the last few days at Tannenberg Hitler worked on the speech that he eventually read to the Reichstag on 16 July. On 4 July Schmundt ordered preparations to be made for departure. That night the luggage was shipped in lorries to the Führersonderzug at Oppenau station. Hitler left Tannenberg at midday on the 5th, and then visited wounded soldiers in the military hospital at Freudenstadt. Two formations of the Führer-

Begleitbataillon protected the approaches to Oppenau station, and at 1300 the *Führerzug* steamed off for Berlin's Anhalter terminus. *Führerzug Atlas* conveyed Jodl's WFSt to Reichenhall and Salzburg, following Hitler's indication that he would soon be spending time at Obersalzberg. The WFSt field staff lived and worked in their train from 5 July until 29 August 1940. Upon their return to Berlin, while the remainder of WFSt were quartered in cavalry and Panzer training barracks at Krampnitz, the *Feldstaffel* spent the next four months aboard the train at Grünewald station, and one assumes that this must have been by choice.

On 5 July, leaving only a small guard detachment at Tannenberg—and despite the opinion of Schmundt, recorded in the KTB the previous day, that the transfer was 'not essential'—the *Führer-Begleitbataillon* at Tannenberg travelled *en masse* to Adlerhorst in anticipation of a five-month stay in connection with Operation 'Seelöwe' (Sealion, i.e. the proposed invasion of Great Britain), the staff and signals troop travelling to Schiefertal OT camp, parts of 1. *Kompanie* to Waldweg OT camp and parts of 2. *Kompanie* to Bad Nauheim.

The *Führersonderzug* arrived in Berlin at 1500 on 6 June after an overnight stop at Münchberg, and on his way to the *Reichskanzlei* huge crowds afforded the *Führer* a rapturous reception. The next day, in a move to uphold the prestige won by the *Wehrmacht* in the occupied territories, Hitler warned his troops of the heaviest sentences, including the death penalty, for the committing there of criminal offences such as rape and looting.

On 16 July, in Instruction No 16 issuing orders for Operation 'Seelöwe', Hitler designated Adlerhorst as his FHQ; the 'inner circle'—the WFSt reduced to its barest minimum—was to locate to within 50 kilometres of FHQ. At the end of July 1940, when the bulk of 1. and 2. *Kompanie* arrived from Paris, where they had been carrying out guard duty, the *Führer-Begleitbataillon*'s total strength in and around Adlerhorst was 1,100 men, to which must be added the 600 or so of the *Luftwaffe* anti-aircraft detachment. They passed the time sharpening up with field exercises.

Concerns about the poor organisation of the FHQ structure prompted *Oberst* Warlimont to express the hope in the OKW War Diary on 5

September 1940 that when the planned invasion of Great Britain went ahead the HQs of all *Wehrmacht* arms of service would by then have been fully co-ordinated into the highest command centre. In the event, 'Seelöwe' was postponed on 12 October 1940 pending a better opportunity the following spring (which never arose). On 25 November 1940 the *Führer-Begleitbataillon*, which had been under the command of *Oberstleutnant* Kurt Thomas since February, returned to its '*General Göring*' regimental barracks at Berlin-Doberitz. Adlerhorst was maintained in readiness for 'Seelöwe' by communications technicians and a guard supplied by *Generalkommando IX*, Kassel. Hitler never used Tannenberg again, and the compound was taken over by *Wehrkreiskommando V* in Stuttgart.

Chapter 3

Berghof and
the Balkans, 1940–1

FROM 10 July 1940 Hitler spent a total of fifty days at the Berghof during the remainder of that year.* With the exception of two houses—'Wachenfeld', the later Berghof, and the 'Kehlsteinhaus', Hitler's private residence—the Obersalzberg near Berchtesgaden at the northern foot of the Hoher Goll was the property of the NSDAP and was never a seat of government: it was, therefore, only an FHQ in the sense that it served as such on the frequent occasions during the Second World War when Hitler was staying there. His periods of residence there tended to be short, and amounted, cumulatively, to a little over a year.

Long before the war several Ministers in the Reich Government had purchased properties on the Obersalzberg. Göring had had a house built there in 1934 to which a *Luftwaffenadjutantur* barracks was added in 1938, the two buildings being connected by a long footpath. Speer occupied the 'Waltenbergerhaus' on the edge of the Obersalzberg, which the Party acquired in 1937. Two years later he erected, a little below it, a study, where it was his custom to discuss architecture with Hitler. In 1937 the Bormann family moved into the 'Villa Seitz', which had come into the possession of the Party early that year. The 'Pension Moritz' was bought by the Party for 260,000 *Reichsmark* and would later become the 'Platterhof' *Volksgasthaus*, where (almost) anybody could spend the night for one mark. The 'Gasthaus zum Turken' on the Eckernbichl, sold compulsorily to the Party for 165,000 *Reichsmark* in 1933, served the dual function of Obersalzberg signals centre and quarters for the SS guard and RSD company following the completion of conversion work in 1937. The 'Villa

---

* The dates of all Hitler's periods of residence here are listed in Appendix I.

Bechstein', which *Frau* Helene Bechstein, a benefactress of Hitler, had sold to the Party in 1935, was modernised into accommodation for prominent visitors such as Goebbels, Mussolini and King Boris of Bulgaria. A new SS barracks was completed there in the summer of 1938.

The multi-purpose *Theaterhalle*, with seating for 2,000, had been opened in 1937. It was occasionally used for meetings but more regularly as a cinema, where free film shows would be screened for Obersalzberg residents and building workers irrespective of their national origins. Between 1936 and 1937 a *Teehaus* (Tea House) was built to Professor Fick's plans on the Mooslahnerkopf. This was a pavilion with a diameter of nine metres and a small hexagonal shop. To supply the Obersalzberg, and replacing agricultural land and pasture compulsorily purchased by the Party, a 170-hectare holding had been equipped for dairy farming and pig-raising in 1938.

Hitler's 'Haus Wachenfeld' was far too small for a head of state, and in 1936 work was begun to convert the property into the 30-room 'Berghof', finance being made available by German industry's *Adolf-Hitler-Spende* (Donation Fund). A lengthy building to house his personal *Adjutanten*, their colleagues' offices and the telephone exchange was erected nearby.

The NSDAP had given Hitler the 'Kehlsteinhaus' as a 50th birthday present. The 6.5-kilometre-long street which led up to it was a masterpiece of highway engineering. It terminated in a parking place at and altitude of 1,710 metres. After leaving the car, one walked 162 metres along a passageway to a lift, which rose 142 metres directly into the 'Kehlsteinhaus'.

The NS estate on the Obersalzberg amounted to almost 1,000 hectares; 78 hectares had been purchased from the private ownership of nineteen residents and eighteen farmers for 6.06 million *Reichsmark* and 716 hectares, mostly woodland and rock, from the Bavarian state for 1.1 million *Reichsmark*.

At the outbreak of war the buildings on the Obersalzberg were designated 'a building programme of the *Führer* important for the war effort'. This enabled Bormann, the building supremo of Obersalzberg, to declare the *Führer* building project to be a reserved occupation, rendering conscripts and reservists so employed ineligible for mobilisation. This explains why there was never a shortage of labour on the Obersalzberg in the first three years of the war: even the youngest and fittest engineers and technical workers on the Obersalzberg were never called up, not even those classified as 'fit for duty at the front', and only after the disaster at Stalingrad did Speer finally manage to persuade Bormann that he had to release the younger men on the mountain for military service. From that point onwards the number of foreign labourers increased, the influx being mainly Czech and Italian, and by the end of the war only one-third of the workforce was German.

Construction work on the Obersalzberg was handled by 'ARGE Obersalzberg', a consortium formed by the Philipp Holzmann A. G. of Frankfurt-am-Main and Held & Franke of Berlin, working in conjunction with Polensky & Zollner of Berlin and Leonhard Moll of Munich. The senior engineer was Georg Grethlein, who was famed for his equal-handed treatment of workers irrespective of their national origins. Bormann's most fanatical assistant, and the least-loved overseer on all projects, was the Obersalzberg administrator, *Dipl. Ing.* Schenk.

Whereas from 1939 onwards in the German Reich restrictions were in force on all requisites and foodstuffs, and building materials could be supplied only with special permission, construction work on the Obersalzberg continued exactly as it had in peacetime. Since everything was 'important for the war effort', heavy lorries made the long journey to Berchtesgaden from the farthest outposts of the Reich without the least concern about fuel. The foreign currencies with which Bormann settled accounts spoke more eloquently than words of the pressing need to speed the building work so that the place should be ready for the *Führer*'s immediate use once victory, which was believed to be impending, had been achieved.

Amongst the buildings important for the war effort on the Obersalzberg were 20 kilometres of highway, settlements for employees, the post office—which stamped letters with the prestigious postmark 'Obersalzberg'—and its kiosk selling picture postcards and souvenirs, Martin

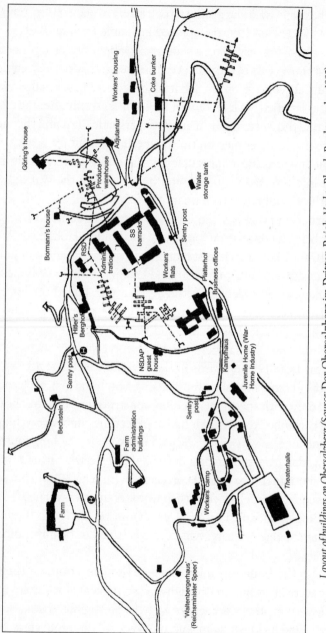

Layout of buildings on Obersalzberg (Source: Der Obersalzberg im Dritten Reich, Verlag Plenck, Berchtesgaden, 1982).

Bormann's apiary in Lenzerfeld and the gigantic produce store 110 metres long by 26 metres broad at the foot of the Eckernbichl which supplied the vegetarian *Führer* with his vegetables and fruit.

Hitler's first stay at Obersalzberg during the war did not occur until 10 July 1940: he spent time there only when military affairs permitted or if it were necessary for his health. The only military men constantly in sttendance were the *Wehrmachtadjutanten*. Keitel and Jodl lived as guests of *Reichsminister* Lammers at the '*Kleine Reichskanzlei*' (Little Reich Chancellery), Berchtesgaden-Steingass, which had been made available in July 1937 so that affairs of state could be continued during Hitler's visits to the Berghof. WFSt personnel worked in the *Sonderzug* at Salzburg station until the end of 1942, when they were found other accommodation at Bischofswiesen-Strub barracks. The *Chef des Generalstabs des Heeres* (Head of the Army General Staff) flew from Berlin, or later from East Prussia, once a week, although it was not uncommon for Hitler to receive commanding generals at the Berghof direct from the Eastern Front.

In contrast to earlier custom, during the war Hitler received only friendly statesmen and allies at the Obersalzberg. In the first phase of the war he urged them to lend more help for victory and in the second phase he strengthened their resolve with details of new weapons and large slices of propaganda.

The first foreign state guest at the Berghof was the Romanian President Gigurtu on 26 July 1940, when Romanian territorial disputes with Hungary, Bulgaria and the Soviet Union, economic matters, the influence of the Jews and the nationalisation of the oil industry were discussed. The next day Hitler received President Filoff of Bulgaria, whom he assured of the Reich's disinterest in the Balkans. On 28 July the Slovakian President, Josef Tiso, thanked him for his 'fatherly care for Slovakia' and received in return an assurance of Germany's enthusiasm for protecting the Carpathians. On 28 August the Italian Foreign Minister, Count Ciano, arrived, to prepare for the Arbitration of Vienna two days later, the conversation revolving around the protection of oil supplies in the event of a conflict in the Balkans. On 17 October, in the *Teehaus* at Obersalzberg, Hitler talked to the Italian Crown Princess, Marie-Jose, who pleaded for the King of Belgium, Leopold III, to be heard regarding the problems of his conquered people.

On 21 October 1940 Hitler made his longest journey in the *Führersonderzug* when he travelled to meet General Franco at Hendaye on the Spanish border. The operation was codenamed 'Herbststurm' (Autumn Storm). Overnight on the 21st, the train sheltered in a tunnel at Yvoir, where, earlier, there had been a furore when Hitler's train was blocked by a sleeping coach uncoupled from von Ribbentrop's train and left outside the tunnel entrance, which caused a serious delay in trunking the *Führerzug*'s telephone network into the circuit boxes that were installed in the tunnel and resulted in a strongly worded complaint being lodged with the *Reichsverkehrsministerium* (Transport Ministry) by Hitler's personal *Adjutantur*. During the afternoon of 22 October, in the *Führerzug* at Montoire station, about 50 kilometres north of Tours, French Vice-President Pierre Laval discussed with Hitler arrangements for the meeting scheduled there for the 24th with Marshal Pétain.

Hitler's train drew into Hendaye station at 1600 on the 23rd for the meeting with Franco. It had been planned that the trains of the respective leaders would arrive in the station from north and south at the same time, but Franco's train was delayed, and Hitler spent an hour strolling the platform with von Ribbentrop. After an inspection of the 11th Infantry Division honour guard, talks were held in the German train, a convoy of vehicles being held in readiness in the station forecourt to take the two leaders four miles to a road tunnel in the event of air attack. Besides von Ribbentrop, Hitler was accompanied by Keitel, Bormann, von Brauchitsch, Dietrich, Generals Dollmann and Bodenschatz and *Unterstaatssecretär* Gauss. Hitler left Hendaye at 0435 the next morning, having failed to persuade Franco to enter the war or allow German troops to attack Gibraltar from Spanish bases. He said later, 'I would rather have three or four teeth extracted than have to go through something like that again.'

Hitler's train steamed into Montoire at 1530 on 24 October. Waiting to meet it was the *Frontgruppe* of *Hauptmann* von Blomberg's *Führer-Begleitbataillon* from Schloss Ziegenberg with orders 'to accompany the *Führerzug* so that, in the event of any mishaps, the *Führer* can continue his journey by car.' Three other groups were detailed to guard the railway tunnels at Yvoir, at Montoire and at Cambo near Hendaye.

The talks with Pétain in Hitler's saloon car in the presence of Laval and von Ribbentrop, which had the objective of luring France into the war against Great Britain, lasted almost two hours but were ultimately fruitless. Pétain was driven back to Tours, escorted by *Führer-Begleit-bataillon* motorcycle outriders, while Hitler headed for home. At Yvoir, Hitler's train was hauled into the tunnel for the night at 2130 after an enemy aircraft was reported over the Meuse valley. The next day Hitler diverted to Munich following the receipt of a report from the German ambassador in Rome that Mussolini was planning to invade Greece from Albania. Von Ribbentrop set up a meeting between Hitler and Mussolini in Florence for the 28th, but three hours before the *Führer*'s arrival the Germans received confirmation that the Italians had already invaded. When he met Mussolini, Hitler made very clear to him his apprehensions regarding *Il Duce*'s decision.

No work was carried out on any new FHQ structure during August and September 1940, the only two months of the war when this was the case. As the initial plans for the attack on the Soviet Union took shape, Hitler demanded a fortified headquarters close to the front so that, as *Oberbefehlshaber der Wehrmacht*, he could involve himself swiftly in opera-tions and also visit his front-line troops without having to make long journeys. Immediately after the visit to Berlin by Soviet Foreign Minister Molotov from 1 to 14 November 1940, Hitler gave orders for a search to be made for suitable locations for three command centres, one of which was to be 'a permanent headquarters' in East Prussia.

One of the most frequent callers to Obersalzberg was the highly re-garded King Boris III of Bulgaria. On 18 November the Spanish Foreign Minister, Suñer, would not budge regarding the decisions made by Franco at Hendaye the previous month; he was followed by Count Ciano, who was obliged to sit through a long session listening to criticism of the Italian invasion of Greece. Hitler received Leopold III at the Berghof on 19 November. The King wanted to know if Belgium would remain an independent monarchy after the war. He also requested more food and the release of all Belgian prisoners of war. At Hitler's invitation, the Yugo-slav Foreign Minister, Cincar-Markovich, visited the Berghof on 28 November and was offered a non-aggression pact.

In their search for a permanent site for the new FHQ in East Prussia, Todt, Schmundt and Engel agreed upon the suitability of a large tract of terrain eight kilometres east of Rastenburg. As a result of their report, on 19 December Hitler ordered the immediate construction of a fortified installation, directing that special attention be paid to its 'camouflage, but also defences against paratroop landings'. Von Ribbentrop and Himmler were to have 'satellite headquarters nearby', and the work was to be completed by April 1941. The same day Hitler ordered a search for two more locations in Poland that would be 'of a more temporary character', but, as OT had already identified two sites in October, the *FHQu-Kommandant* and Todt merely rubber-stamped the recommendation that the additional locations at Tomasov and Krosno be utilised.

Outwardly the work was to give the impression of being an urban-isation scheme linked to new factories being built by the Askania chemical works. The OT head office's building plans were therefore coded 'Askania Nord' for Rastenburg, 'Askania Mitte' for Tomasov and 'Askania Süd' for Krosno. 'Askania Nord' was the largest and finest of the three. The thickly wooded region around Rastenburg offered natural camou-flage against aerial reconnaissance, combined with the scenic beauty of pine forests, meadows and lakes. Transportation links were good, and so construction could proceed unimpeded. *Bauassessor* Friedrich Classen, who had been in charge of FHQ building in the West in 1940, was appointed *Direktor* of the Rastenburg project.

At Christmas 1940 Hitler visited *Wehrmacht* units in the West. On 22 December the *Führersonderzug* left Berlin for Dunkirk and Boulogne via Aachen. Hitler spent the night in the train in a tunnel near Boulogne, and as he was taking supper with his close circle 'bombs came down and the *Flak* barked'. The next day he visited Army long-range batteries and the *Kriegsmarine* at Calais before taking lunch with OT labourers. For the nights of 24 and 25 December the train stood in a tunnel at Beauvais, where Hitler visited two *Luftwaffe Jagdgeschwader* (fighter squadrons) and addressed the crews. He lunched on Christmas Day with a *Bomber-geschwader* (bomber squadron). That afternoon he had talks with the French head of government, Admiral Darlan, in the *Sonderzug* north of Paris, criticising the dismissal of Laval by Pétain on 13 December and warning the French against anti-German plots.

On Boxing Day the train steamed east for Sarrebourg. Hitler alighted at Metz to call in on the *SS-Leibstandarte* and visit the Army infantry regiment that had received the highest number of awards for bravery and had spent the most time in action. In his address he told his soldiers, 'You must understand that my heart beats for you and that I am happy to spend my Christmas with the troops.' At Sarrebourg he travelled by road convoy to Angevillers in Lorraine, there reboarding the *Sonderzug* for Berlin.

On 4 January 1941, in the presence of von Ribbentrop at the Berghof, Foreign Minister Filoff announced Bulgaria's readiness to enter the Axis. Ten days later the new Romanian President, Antonescu, arrived to discuss his country's internal political problems, asking whether the German-Italian guarantees then in force were valid in the event of an attack by the Soviet Union. Mussolini and Count Ciano stayed as guests at the Obersalzberg from 18 to 20 January, their talks with Hitler and von Ribbentrop covering the implications of Italy's failed assault on Greece. At the same time Hitler summoned senior *Wehrmacht* commanders, provided them with a picture of the increasingly aggressive politics of the Soviet Union in the light of Molotov's visit to Berlin in November and alerted them to the coming confrontation with Stalin.

On 14 February, at Hitler's request, President Cvetkovich and Foreign Minister Cincar-Markovich of Yugoslavia arrived at the Berghof for talks about their country's attitude to developments in the Balkans, and on 4 March the Yugoslav Prince Regent discussed with Hitler the dangerous situation being, as they saw it, engineered in the region by both the Soviet Union and Great Britain. On 27 March Hitler decided that he had no choice but to occupy Yugoslavia, and on the 31st OKH began preparations to transfer its headquarters to Wiener Neustadt, south of Vienna, for the attack.

On 1 April Hitler announced his decision to launch a land campaign to lend support to Mussolini in Greece. There was no time to erect a fixed FHQ establishment, and, in contrast to the OKH field detachment, Hitler was unwilling to consider the use of an alternative military installation in Austria such as a barracks: its modest facilities notwithstanding, he was in favour of using the *Führerzug's* command carriage as workplace for himself, Keitel and Jodl. Accordingly, a party consisting of *FHQu-Kommandant* Thomas, *SS-Standartenführer* Rattenhuber (the head of Hitler's *SS-Begleitkommando*), one officer and a senior *Reichsbahn* official travelled from Berlin to Wiener Neustadt the same day to search for a secure location to accommodate the *Führerzug*. They chose a tunnel two kilometres north of Mönichkirchen that was of sufficient length to house not only the *Amerika* at the north end but also the WFSt's *Atlas* at the other. Two other stretches of tunnel north of Friedberg (south of Mönichkirchen) were considered suitable for Göring's two trains, the short *Minenräumer* and *Asien*. It was also decided on 1 April that the task of expanding the telephone network at the chosen localities would be handled by the FHQ signals unit, the control exchange being sited at Kirchberg, ten kilometres north of Mönichkirchen. The new FHQ was ready a few days into April, the telephone exchange having been set up first and lines run down to the tunnel. The security battalion built the exchange housing.

On 3 April the Soviet Union signed a Friendship and Non-Aggression Pact with Yugoslavia, and on the 6th German aircraft opened the campaign against the latter by subjecting Belgrade to a heavy air raid.

FHQu-Kommandant Thomas arrived in Mönichkirchen on 9 April, and two days later the *Führer-Begleitbataillon*, which by now had a fighting strength of 1,157 men, occupied its assigned quarters.

The *Wehrmachtführungsstab's Sonderzug, Atlas*, left Berlin during the evening of 10 April and arrived twenty-four hours later at Taucher-Schaueregg. *Führersonderzug Amerika* arrived at Mönichkirchen at 0720 on 12 April, delayed two hours by heavy snow, and ground to a halt outside the tunnel near the station. This stopping place for Hitler's train was codenamed FHQ 'Frühlingssturm' (Spring Storm), a remote halt on the single-line stretch of track between Mönichkirchen and Markt

Aspang. Because of the train's great length, a temporary wooden platform had been erected to facilitate alighting and boarding.

Himmler's *Sonderzug, Heinrich,* followed Hitler's train from Berlin through Munich to Wiener Neustadt but was then diverted to Brück-an-der-Mur, about 60 kilometres from Mönichkirchen. Göring's two trains probably stayed in their allocated tunnels north of Friedberg, although this is unconfirmed. The various sections of track were then all blocked off. Von Ribbentrop's train, *Westfalen,* remained at the Süd-bahnhof in Vienna. OKH were allocated the Wiener Neustadt Military Academy for their field headquarters. Once the installation of tele-communications equipment had been completed, the various dispersed command posts were all operating on 9 April.

Hitler directed the Balkans campaign from FHQ 'Frühlingssturm' from 12 to 25 April 1941, living in *Amerika,* the locomotive for which stood permanently with steam up, ready to push the fifteen coaches into the nearby tunnel should the need arise. The *Führer-Begleitbataillon* kept watch over the surrounding area. The only occasions when Hitler left the train were for walks to the nearby small Mönichkirchen Hof hotel to watch the latest wartime newsreels.

On 19 April Hitler received King Boris III of Bulgaria and the German ambassador to Turkey, Franz von Papen, and the following day he inspected a *Führer-Begleitbataillon* honour guard and on the station platform accepted congratulations on his 52nd birthday from FHQ personnel and the Italian Foreign Minister, Ciano. Afterwards there was a concert. On 24 April the Hungarian regent, Count Horthy, arrived to discuss what share Hungary could expect when Yugoslavia was divided up.

Once victory over Yugoslavia had been assured, Hitler left Mönich-kirchen in the early hours of 26 April for Graz, where he visited the Nationalpolitische Erziehungsanstalt (NAPOLA, or National Political Education Institute), and Marburg, capital of annexed southern Styria. He spent that night at Maria Saal, north of Klagenfurt, where, next day, he paid homage to Austrian servicemen of the Great War by visiting the Infantry Memorial. In the Weapons Room he met his old history teacher, Dr Leopold Potsch of Linz, to whom he had dedicated some lines in

Mein Kampf. The *Sonderzug* left for Berlin at 1800 that evening, and the various other trains returned directly to the Reich capital after the Yugoslav defeat. The *Führer-Begleitbataillon* evacuated its quarters in Mönichkirchen and Aspang on 26 April and proceeded to the Doberitz barracks, where it remained until 21 June 1941. At the end of May the battalion received a Panzer company formed at Wunsdorf and for the first time had a definite battlefield component. The strength of the battalion now stood at 1,250.

On 11, 16 and 28 May *FHQu-Kommandant* Thomas carried out inspection of FHQ 'Askania Nord'. Hitler returned to the Berghof on 9 May 1941 for a stay of 33 days, during which he was preparing Operation 'Barbarossa', the invasion of the Soviet Union. He entrusted the invasion of Crete, Operation 'Merkur', which began on 21 May, to the *Luftwaffe*. On the 10th he received news that his deputy of long standing, Rudolf Hess, had made an unauthorised flight to Scotland with a view to negotiating peace between Great Britain and the Reich. To determine how this could best be glossed over, on the 13th Hitler summoned all *Reichsleiter* and *NSDAP-Gauleiter* to the Obersalzberg for a conference. Hess had rarely been present at FHQ and had little influence there. His immediate subordinate, Martin Bormann, now became *Chef der Parteikanzlei* (Head of the Party Office). Bormann had been a constant member of Hitler's travelling circus since 1935, and of the innermost circle since at least the Polish campaign. His talent for organisation had enabled him to bring order to Hitler's often chaotic environment, where clear boundaries and sharp divisions of competence were frequently lacking.

On 11 May Hitler received Admiral Darlan and approved the release of all French prisoners of war currently in German captivity who had served in the Great War, and in return he obtained Darlan's promise of support for German measures fomenting insurrection in Iraq in order to oust the British. On 6 June Hitler met the Croat leader Pavelich for talks held 'in the spirit of hearty friendship which binds together the German and Croat peoples'. A plea was made by his guest for economic aid for Croatia.

National Socialist Germany attacked the Soviet Union on 22 June 1941. At noon the following day Hitler boarded his *Sonderzug*, bound for

'Askania Nord', his new FHQ in East Prussia, which was henceforth to be known as Wolfschanze. Goebbels had seen Wolfschanze and thought 'it looked more like a summer holiday retreat than the headquarters of the German High Command'. Gorlitz railway station was at the centre of the 250-hectare Wolfschanze estate, and in due course Hitler made a number of excursions by train around the Reich for various purposes, starting and finishing at Gorlitz. It was as more southerly railway out-posts of FHQ Wolfschanze that 'Askania Mitte' and 'Askania Süd' had been created, but, having regard to the expected rapidity of the German thrust eastwards, it is not clear why those particular locations were selected.

FHQ 'Askania Mitte' lay about 40 kilometres east of Lodz, in a large forest near the small town of Tomasov on the River Pilica. In October 1940 OT set up a site management office and two months later received the expected contract to erect structures of 'an improvised character' for a secure FHQ and small OKH unit. The plans were completed in January 1941, although a labour force of 4,500, all employees of German construction firms on account of the need for secrecy, was at work the previous month. The *Führersonderzug* was to rest within a tunnel or a tubular train shed, either of which would have reinforced concrete walls two and a half metres thick. OKH would also have a siding, an air-raid bunker and several barracks huts. 'Askania Mitte' was exclusively for Hitler and the OKH: no quarters were envisaged for the *Luftwaffe*, for Himmler or for von Ribbentrop. The project was to be tackled with the 'greatest haste', and April 1941 had been designated as the completion date.

The FHQ was in three parts. 'Askania Mitte I' was a railway tunnel excavated into a mountainside. On the floor of the tunnel was a sleeper-based track 300 metres in length. The total floor space of the tunnel was 1,900 square metres, while 120 square metres of galleries connected the tunnel to a 500-square-metre generator house and a pump house of 26 square metres which supplied fresh water and ventilation. A total of 40,500 cubic metres of concrete was used to build this tunnel. Three barracks huts, a converted forestry house of 200 square metres' floor space and a *Teehaus* the same size were erected for Hitler's entourage, namely the WFSt *Feldstaffel*, NSDAP representatives, adjutants, doctors, stenographers and the security force.

'Askania Mitte II' was in the open. Thirty thousand cubic metres of concrete went into building a tubular train shed of reinforced concrete. The exterior machinery, the pump houses and their connecting gallery, all similar in floor area to that of the tunnel rooms, required 5,600 cubic metres of concrete, and 1,100 metres of new track were laid along the existing platform, which was roofed over.

'Askania Mitte III' consisted of a Type 102 V 'double group' bunker of only 42 square metres' useful floor space, fabricated with 800 cubic metres of concrete. Other accommodation was supplied in the form of six large barracks huts totalling 3,000 square metres and two block-houses each 65 square metres in area and made up of 800 cubic metres of concrete. The dwellings were for the OKH workforce and security force. Altogether 2.3 kilometres of permanent way were laid. Whereas the water for personnel and the locomotives was pumped from the mountain, there was no provision for sewage disposal in the tunnel and waste water had to be brought out in buckets. Details of how the two shelters were sited in relation to each other are unavailable, but, in view of the need for separate machinery housing, one assumes that they were not close.

The work was completed in September 1941 after 812,500 working days had been expended on it. The *Wehrmacht* installed the communications equipment. The total volume of concrete consumed by 'Askania Mitte' was 75,100 cubic metres, producing 6,849 square metres of floor space of which 4,520 square metres were allocated to the trains and auxiliary rooms.

Hitler's Army ADC Engel, *FHQu-Kommandant* Thomas and *Reichsminister für Bewaffnung und Munition* Todt all visited 'Askania Mitte' from time to time to update themselves as to progress. The position of 'Askania Mitte' was never likely to be of any military significance, and it is thus hardly surprising that, despite all the effort that went into building it, Hitler never stayed there.

OT began work began on the two 'Askania Süd' sites in October 1940, although the plans were not finalised until February 1941. The project to build two bomb-proof concrete train sheds for *Amerika* and *Atlas* at separate locations 20 kilometres north and north-west of Krosno took up to 7,000 labourers almost a year, involving 1.2 million days' work. At Strzyzow an existing tunnel was expanded using 15,000 cubic metres of steel-reinforced concrete to make the walls, which were two and a half metres thick. The tunnel had been engineered before the Great War by the Viennese firm Universale during works to link the railheads of Reichshof and Jaslo. In the immediate vicinity OT put up barracks for the security force and a *Teehaus* for Hitler.

At Frysztak, a few kilometres away in a valley north of the station, 35,000 cubic metres of concrete went into the manufacture of numerous segments for a tubular, 200-metre-long concrete train shelter over seven

An artist's impression of the protected train siding at Frysztak (after Kuhn). The tubular shelter remains intact. 1. Tubular concrete train shelter; 2. Machinery and pump houses; 3. Concrete bunker; 4. Concrete defensive cupolas. D. Frysztak village.

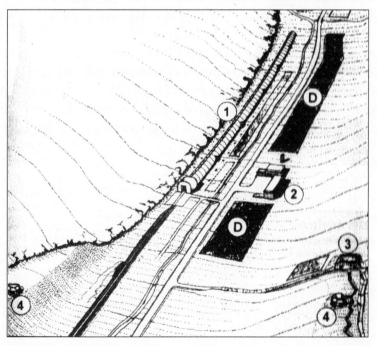

metres high to the top of the dome and practically identical to the model at 'Askania Mitte II'; in addition, 2.9 kilometres of new permanent way were laid at Frysztak.

The generator houses at each location occupied a similar floor space, but the tunnel construction consumed eight times the amount of concrete—34,000 cubic metres—needed at the Frysztak location. In all, 61,500 cubic metres of concrete produced a useful floor area of 16,430 square metres, equivalent to two football pitches. The *Wehrmacht* installed the communications equipment.

The consumption of materials and the personnel deployed for this project, which was completed within a year, is difficult to comprehend. It is easy enough to see that a lot of concrete is needed to make two 600-foot-long cathedrals with walls eight feet thick and some machinery housing, but to produce, mix and pound 61,500 cubic metres of concrete with simple tools and equipment in such a short time demands not only a timetabled supply of water, cement and the binding ingredients but also a massive and dedicated labour force. The average working day at 'Askania Süd' was ten hours. As a guide, 61,500 cubic metres of concrete would fill a pit the size of a soccer pitch and twenty-five feet deep.

All this tremendous expense and effort guaranteed the safety of Hitler and Mussolini for one night. The two leaders stopped over in their respective trains in the protected environments at Strzyzow and Frysztak on 27 August 1941 before visiting troops on the Eastern Front.

Chapter 4

Wolfschanze:
The Russian Front, 1940–1

T HE first symbolic spadeful of earth was dug at Gorlitz by some
unknown OT labourer in the winter of 1940. From then until 25
January 1945, when General Jacob's sappers destroyed the establishment by explosives, less a thirteen-month break between 1 September
1941 and 1 October 1942, FHQ Wolfschanze was always in the process
of being excavated and renovated, of having drains and sanitation pipes
laid, and of being fortified and camouflaged. Even on the day when Hitler
left it for good in November 1944, *Dipl. Ing.* Welker's 2,000-strong force
of OT labourers was still hard at work on the establishment, improving
it for the future.

The straight building costs for Wolfschanze ran to 36 million *Reichsmark* and the conversion work is nowhere recorded. It was originally
designated 'Askania Nord', but Hitler renamed it 'Wolfschanze' when
he moved in. One of his female secretaries recalled: 'When I asked him
why practically all his headquarters were prefixed "Wolf", he told me it
was because that had been his cover-name in the early years of the
National Socialist movement.' The reply avoided answering the implicit
question as to why 'Wolf' had been chosen as his cover-name.

Wolfschanze consisted of:

1. Hitler's headquarters as *Oberbefehlshaber der Wehrmacht* (*C-in-C Wehrmacht*), situated in the Görlitz Forest east of Rastenburg, where he
and a small entourage including the WFSt *Feldstaffel* occupied a
complex of bunkers for accommodation and work, plus a barracks
equipped with a concrete anti-shrapnel mantle. The OKH and *Luftwaffe* command centres, the *Feldkommandostelle* (Field Command

93

Post) of the *Reichsführer-SS* and the seat of the *Reichsaussenminister* (German Foreign Minister) all lay between twenty and sixty kilo-metres away.

2. The OKH headquarters complex, about eighteen kilometres north-east of Wolfschanze near the Mauersee in the dense Steinorter Forest. The headquarters bore the cover name 'Mauerwald', after the forestry house there. The Rastenburg–Angerburg highway bisected the terrain into areas dubbed 'Fritz' and 'Quelle'. In 'Fritz' were the offices of the *Generalstab des Heeres* and in 'Quelle' were located the *Generalquartiermeister* (Quartermaster-General) with his administrative and logistical staffs. The total number of personnel was 1,500. The OKH *Feldstaffel* was analogous to the WFSt *Feldstaffel* and had only recently been formed. The location was an extensive camp of barracks huts and small air-raid bunkers. OKH also occu-pied existing barracks at Angerburg and Lotzen. A *Wachbataillon* (guard battalion) of older soldiers unfit to serve in the field handled the exterior security, while two (and later three) companies of *Geheime Feldpolizei* (Secret Field Police) guarded the installations inside. The *Chef des Generalstabs* (Chief of the General Staff) and his entourage travelled daily to Görlitz Forest to attend Hitler's situ-ation conferences by means of a local train run exclusively for that purpose. Hitler's only visit to 'Mauerwald' was on 5 October 1941, when he went there to consult *Generalfeldmarschall* von Brauchitsch, who at the time was still *Oberbefehlshaber des Heeres* (C-in-C of the Army).

3. The *Luftwaffe* Command Staff barracks and bunkers at Niedersee and Goldap, together with sidings for Göring's trains. Whenever he was in East Prussia, Göring preferred to stay near Rominten in his luxurious *Sonderzug Robinson*, which consisted of eight coaches with 34 axles—two anti-aircraft and maintenance wagons, three first- and second-class coaches, two saloons cars equipped with library and desks and a bath/hairdressing coach. On frequent occasions the *Minenräumer* would precede it, the locomotive for which hauled a variety of wagons, including one with a turntable loading ramp and capacity for up to ten road vehicles, and a light

maintenance wagon for supplying current to work the onboard refrigerating units.

4. The 'Hochwald' SS headquarters of barracks and bunkers, located in an area of woodland at Grossgarten about 20 kilometres north-east of Wolfschanze and with a siding for the SS train. For two weeks in November 1942 the HQ was moved temporarily to Kruglanken, about seven kilometres to the south.

5. The castle-like main edifice of the Steinort am Mauersee estate, owned by the Lehndorf family, where von Ribbentrop used to reside whenever he came to East Prussia. The greater part of his several-hundred-strong party was accommodated at the distant Sporthotel Jagerhohe on the Schwenzaitsee. Von Ribbentrop's *Bevollmächtigter* (representative) to Hitler, Ambassador Hewel, had to closet himself at Steinort with von Ribbentrop for conversations regarding affairs of state.

6. The residence of the head of the *Reichskanlei*, Dr Lammers, which was at Rosengarten.

The OKM remained in Berlin until air raids in the summer of 1943 dictated a move to Bernau in the north-eastern outskirts of the capital. *Kapitän zur See* von Puttkamer was the *Marineadjutant* to Hitler, and an admiral was the *Oberbefehlshaber der Marine*'s permanent representative at FHQ.

At Wolfschanze, FHQ adopted for the first time an organisational complexion which espoused the idea expressed in the OKW *Kriegstagebuch* entry of 5 September 1940 regarding the proposed invasion of Great Britain, namely that all *Wehrmacht* arms of service should consolidate in proximity to FHQ. Because they all remained completely subordinate to the leader of the regime, however, it was immaterial where they were located geographically. This was recognised by Himmler when he had his *Feldkommandostelle* stationed close to FHQ yet was himself in attendance only very rarely. The same went for von Ribbentrop, for whom a field headquarters had been reserved in close proximity to FHQ even though since the beginning of the war he had been as good as eliminated from the policy- and decision-making processes.

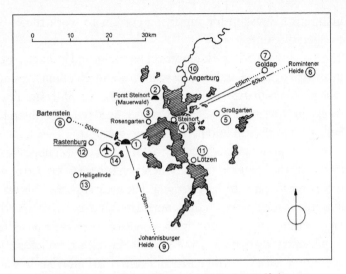

FHQ Wolfschanze and its satellite centres (1941–4): 1. Wolfschanze; 2. Hauptquartier OKH; 3. Reichskanzlei (1941–4) and Luftwaffe operations unit (1944); 4. Reichsaussenminister; 5. Reichsführer-SS; 6. Göring's headquarters; 7. Luftwaffe operations unit (1942–4); 8, 9. Luftwaffe operations unit (1944); 10, 11. Sections of OKH; 12. Sections of Führer-Begleitbataillon; 113. FHQ telegraphy centre; 14. Airfield.

Significant was Bormann's admission into the innermost circle around Hitler at FHQ as head of the *Parteikanzlei* after Hess's defection. His presence there served no political or military necessity, but it was decisive in that, according to Longerich, Bormann 'through his constant presence in Hitler's entourage and by virtue of his position of trust was able to channel access to Hitler.'

Whilst the site was under construction, and even when occupied, Allied intelligence never identified it as an FHQ; Hitler's emphasis on secrecy paid off. Although the Soviet airline Aeroflot continued to make its scheduled flights between Moscow and Berlin until 22 June 1941, the day of the German attack, and Rastenburg was directly under the flight path, the Soviets never divined the purpose of the building work either. The Stuttgart landscaping firm Seidenspinner put down artificial trees, camouflage netting and mosses to disguise gaps in the woodland, and from altitude the impression offered was one of thick, continuous forest. German aircraft regularly took photographs as a means of checking its integrity, and the entire complex was included in the early-warning system of *Luftflotte 'Reich'*. The possibility of enemy paratroop operations against his headquarters was of special concern to Hitler. The choice of location, its secrecy and the adequacy of camouflage measures were considered highly important, to the extent that at the end of 1940 Hitler stated specifically that at Wolfschanze, 'as regards camouflage, paratroop drops are to be taken into account.' This apprehension continued to pre-occupy him throughout the war, as is evident from his discussion with Himmler on 14 July 1944 and from the situation conference of 17 September that year.

The 250-hectare FHQ compound for Hitler and the WFSt lay in 800 hectares of woodland stretching two kilometres either side of the asphalt highway bisecting Görlitz Forest east to west towards Rastenburg. Parallel to this road was a single-track railway with a station, Forst Görlitz. In summertime before the war this had been a favourite destination for many excursionists, who used to stay at the nearby inn. The line was closed to civilian traffic in the spring of 1941, and in August that year two platforms were added at the station and the existing platform greatly lengthened for the benefit of the numerous *Sonderzüge* which would use it. This was the first time that an FHQ had had a railway station inside its perimeter fencing, and here Hitler would wait to greet high-ranking visitors. Occasionally Göring's luxurious train would pull in. At Gorlitz station one locomotive was always kept ready with steam up beneath camouflage netting. Two *Führer-Kurierzüge* (Courier Trains) passed each other once daily on their respective journeys between Berlin and Rastenburg. An asphalt road connected Rastenburg to FHQ Wolf-schanze.

Wolfschanze was the third largest of all nineteen FHQs either completed or still under construction at the end of the war. The two larger complexes were 'Wolfsschlucht 2', in France, and Riese, which was just over half complete when the Soviet Army overran Silesia in 1945. The total ground area developed at Wolfschanze was 154,501 square metres, about the size of 21 soccer pitches. Of this area, less than 4 per cent—5,394 square metres—comprised bunkers. OKH, at Mauerwald, Angerburg and Lotzen, had the lion's share of the total, with 81,328 square metres, Hitler's headquarters comprised 41,720 square metres (27 per cent) and the *Führungsstab der Luftwaffe* (Command Staff) 29,316 square metres (19). Von Ribbentrop and Himmler had about 2 per cent each, 2,654 and 2,983 square metres, respectively.

The figures for the bunkers present a different picture. Of the total of 5,394 square metres of bunkered accommodation, Hitler had 78 per cent, OKH 15, RFSS 3½ and the *Führungsstab der Luftwaffe* and *Reichsaussenminister* (Foreign Minister) about 1½ each. Of the 173,260 cubic metres of concrete prepared, 69 per cent went into Hitler's security area, 16 into OKH, 4.6 each to the bunkered structures of the *Luftwaffe* and *Feldquartier des Reichsführer-SS* (*Reichführer-SS* Field headquarters) and the rest to the *Reichsaussenminister*. With 173,260 cubic metres of concrete one could build a column over 900 feet in height and 80 feet in diameter.

From 1941, *Sperrkreise* were set up within the FHQ. They tended to separate the establishment into a nucleus, a support group and a number of subsidiary groups, as had been the practice at FHQ Felsennest. A pass was needed to facilitate entry through a perimeter gate at FHQ, and a further special pass had to be produced for *Sperrkreis I*. In 1943 another prohibited compound area, *Sperrkreis A* was set up within *Sperrkreis I* and, after the failed attempt on Hitler's life in 1944, a concentric *Führer-Sperrkreis* was added.

The output of labour for the East Prussian headquarters and its 'dependencies' was 1.7 million days. On average, 4,600 German OT employees—foreign workers were excluded to preserve secrecy, and all workers were thoroughly vetted by the RSD—worked on the project initially. The peak periods of activity were between September 1940 and June 1941, and from July 1943 to November 1944.

The grass airfield near Wilhelmsdorf, for use by the entire FHQ, was sited five kilometres away. Hitler's *Führersonderstaffel* (Special Flight) and *-kurierstaffel* for the Berlin flight were parked here. A paved road led from the airfield to Wolfschanze.

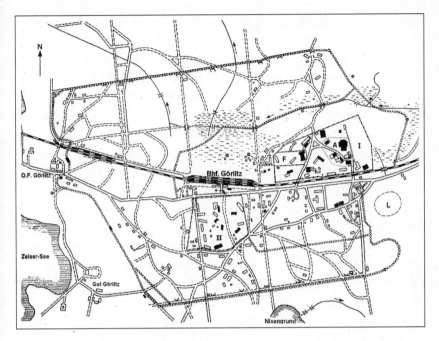

Layout of FHQ Wolfschanze (after Hoffmann): I, II, A and F = fenced security areas; L = short field for Storch aircraft.

The responsibility for telecommunications installations and their maintenance, together with the erection of housing for the various pieces of equipment, fell to the 314-strong *Stabssignalskompanie OKW*. Calls were connected through small telephone/telex exchanges in *Sperrkreise I* and II. Schulz states that three exchanges were set up by the *Führer-Nachrichtenabteilung* in *Sperrkreis I*; Hoffmann mentions one bunker in *Sperrkreis I* and two in *Sperrkreis II*, all 'state of the art'. An independent telegraphy unit existed at Heligenlinde, about twenty kilometres to the west of Wolfschanze. Whilst soldiers were employed at FHQ as telephone operators under the supervision of a senior official of the Signals Service, technical *Reichspost* specialists were responsible for the installation, development and maintenance of the communications network.

Building work by the OT at FHQ Wolfschanze continued after its occupation. New barracks huts with a mantle of brickwork and concrete ceilings for protection against bomb splinters were erected, increasing the available work area and consequently the working conditions, and new concrete bunkers were put up and the existing structures, including the blockhouses, reinforced with steel window shields.

There were originally ten bunkers, each with a wall thickness of two metres. The floor in the rear part was two metres below ground level and used for sleeping; the front part was used as a workroom. Inside the work bunkers a narrow corridor led to the workroom door. Generally there was room inside each for two desks. The windows, over which steel plates could be bolted from the outside, were so high that only the tree-tops could be seen from inside. The windowless dormitory bunkers had two entrances over an airlock. The cabins, panelled with bright wood, were each about the size of a railway sleeping berth compartment and furnished with a bed, wash basin, fitted wardrobe and telephone. A tiled lavatory/bathroom with running water was situated near the bunker entrance.

All rooms had ventilation machinery which drew fresh air through the ceiling, a slight excess of pressure offering protection against gas attack. The air-conditioning system in the situations room in the *Führer-bunker* was of especially advanced design: a ventilator sucked out the air, passing it through a carbon filter, a cooling unit, a chemical bath and a second carbon filter before forcing it back into the room under pressure. Detectors were fitted for the immediate identification of battlefield gases.

All rooms also had electrical heating, and warm air could be circulated through the ventilators, but the humidity in the rooms and the ventilator noise proved intolerable and because of this a number of WFSt officers had to move into the *Sonderzug Atlas* at Schwarzstein-am-Moysee station. When the *Franken I* and *II* trains arrived, the officers preferred to remain in *Atlas*, despite the fact that most of its office facilities were located in former third-class compartments. Others rented a room at the inn inside *Sperrkreis II*, sharing it with officers of the *Führer-Begleitbataillon*. Until a proper dining hall was built for them, WFSt officers also ate at the inn.

The barracks-building programme of 1942 was greeted with relief by everybody. Gerda Daranowski and Christa Schroeder, Hitler's secretaries, preferred not to sleep in their bunker, cursing the ventilator which brought fresh air into the cabin but made a terrible racket as it did so. If they turned it off, they had the feeling that they were going to suffocate. Christa Schroeder wrote to a friend: 'The ventilator runs all night. The noise goes right through your head until every hair hurts.'

After the *FHQu-Kommandant* had satisfied himself at the end of May 1941 as to the progress of the building work, *1. Bataillon Flak Regt 604* moved in on 6 June as the long-term solution to the anti-aircraft protection of Hitler's headquarters. This unit, as noted, had been formed at the outbreak of war as *Reserve-Festungs Flakabteilung 321*, when it consisted of five batteries, three equipped with 10.5cm guns and one each with 3.7cm and 2cm guns. Its total strength was barely 600. The first mention of the unit occurs in the FHQ KTB of 6 June 1940 as *Reserve-Festungs-Flakabteilung 604*, which took up duties at the Felsennest and 'Wolfsschlucht 1' FHQs, and then at Adlerhorst on 18 July 1940, by which time its title had been shortened to *Reserve-Flakabteilung 604*. For effective anti-aircraft defence, a permanent observation of the air space over a large area had to be maintained, and regional organisations needed to be set up and integrated into the communications network. The 'Goldap' group, subordinated to the 'Masuren' regional anti-aircraft establishment, had responsibility for warning the FHQ's AA defences at Wolfschanze and their satellite command posts. According to unconfirmed information supplied by *FHQu-Kommandant* Thomas, a similar AA unit of four to six batteries was available to FHQ in East Prussia. In combination, the two units formed an impressive air defence system for the Mauersee region.

The full *Führer-Begleitbataillon* did not occupy 'Askania Nord'/Wolfschanze until 22 June 1941, whereupon it at once assumed the strictly regimented security routine. Small guard houses were positioned at the three entrances, Nord, Süd and Ost. The entire estate was surrounded by a barbed-wire fence. Sentry tracks ran the length of the wire between blockhouses for the guard personnel, one of whose three companies would always be on duty. Machine-gun positions and flak emplacements kept careful watch on woodland and skies from behind a 50-metre-deep minefield.

The uniformed police officials of the *Reichsicherheitsdienst* had performed gate and guard duty inside the *Reichskanzlei* since 1935, and their employment continued at the FHQs. Apart from the usual watch for fire and flood, their duties inside a *Sperrkreis* included the monitoring of movements, the prevention of sabotage and unauthorised entry into the *Sperrkreis*, and the prevention of unauthorised contact with the stenographic service. Whilst Hitler's bunker was protected by the *SS-Begleitkommando*, an RSD official was always patrolling the exterior of the building, a second kept permanent guard at the door to the stenographers' barracks hut and a third carried out a general foot patrol in the inner *Sperrkreis*. RSD officials shared *Sperrkreis* gate duty with the *Führer-Begleitbataillon*.

Beyond the perimeter, reserve units attached to the *Wehrkreis I Generalkommando*, based at Königsberg, were responsible for security. Like the *Führer-Begleitbataillon*, they were equipped with the best and most modern weapons available. At Wolfschanze, security personnel were billeted in wooden barracks huts in which each group was allocated its own room equipped with camp beds. Catering was arranged in the surrounding villages.

The *Führer-Begleitbataillon* was probably the best equipped and most modern unit in the German Army, and by 1942 it comprised five companies. During 1941 parts of it were deployed on the Russian Front in specially assembled battle groups with Army Groups North and Centre—even the *Flakbataillon* was occasionally used away from FHQ—although an adequate component remained at Wolfschanze. In an emergency, a *Luftwaffe* paratroop battalion linked up to the costly early-warning system was always on standby, initially at Goldap and later near Insterburg.

In summer, Wolfschanze suffered from a mosquito plague against which chemical measures proved ineffective. The best personal protection was a veil, which security personnel wore regularly, although in the rooms poisoned fly-papers seemed to work satisfactorily. Hitler was heard to make the acid remark that the swampiest, most mosquito-ridden and climatically unfavourable place in the entire Reich had been deliberately singled out for his headquarters.

On 24 June 1941, two days after Operation 'Barbarossa' had begun, *Sonderzug Amerika*, consisting of two locomotives, an AA wagon, a luggage car, the *Führerwagen*, the command coach, the *SS-Begleitkommando* coach, the first *Speisewagen* (dining car), two guests' coaches, the bathroom coach, the second *Speisewagen*, two sleeping cars, the Press carriage, a second luggage coach and another AA wagon at the rear—that is, fifteen coaches in all—ground to a halt beside the long platform at Forst Görlitz station and Hitler and his entourage alighted.

Besides Hitler, the bunker occupants of *Sperrkreis I* were Keitel, Bormann and *Reichspressechef* Dr Dietrich. The remaining bunkers were assigned to the telephone/telex exchange, the situation room, guests' accommodation, the officers' mess, and accommodation for female secretaries and stenographers. Jodl and all the ADCs. together with the *SS-Begleit-* and *RSD-Kommandos*, inhabited roofed blockhouses in *Sperrkreis I*. Picker put the figure of those constantly present at thirty, but this seems far too low: including the female secretaries and auxiliaries, it must have been at least sixty.

Other personnel in *Sperrkreis I* from time to time were various *Führer-Begleitbataillon* sentries and patrols, the *Stabssignalskompanie* , personnel running the social amenities (officers' mess, the *Teehaus* and barbers' and hairdressing salons), house servants, drivers and chauffeurs. A figure of 200 constantly admitted to, or present in, *Sperrkreis I* might not be too high.

The WFSt field staff's *Sonderzug* had left Berlin-Grunewald during the afternoon of 23 June for an undisclosed destination, and had arrived at Görlitz just before 0400 the next morning. A few hundred metres south of the platform General Warlimont and his staff found the quarters which had been prepared for them. It is significant that, although Jodl was billeted there, the 120 or so members of the WFSt *Feldstaffel* were not integrated into *Sperrkreis I*. When asked how the figure of 120 was arrived at, Warlimont is alleged to have remarked that that was the greatest possible number that could be packed into the WFSt's 'special work train'. Their headquarters were located south of the railway line in *Sperrkreis II* together with the staffs of the *FHQu-Kommandant* and the

Führer-Begleitbataillon. If the remoteness of the locality interfered with the performance of their duties, it appears that neither Keitel nor Jodl made any attempt to remedy the situation.

Warlimont commanded the WFSt field staff, whose officer corps in 1941 numbered 40 or so and was supported by up to 170 *Unteroffiziere* (NCOs) and men, the excess being drafted in when Hitler relieved OKH of competence in OKW-designated theatres of war. The maximum WFSt figure at this time never exceeded 220 in all. According to Warlimont, 'the WFSt remained Hitler's military office, his speech tube; or, to put it another way, he used it as an organ to edit, publish and monitor the execution of his orders in the military sphere.' It had been excluded from helping to plan the invasion of the Soviet Union, and at Wolfschanze it handled questions of organisation, personnel and armaments: 'The WFSt stood on the sidelines.' The *FHQu-Kommandant* Staff numbered about twenty, but an accurate figure cannot be put on the strength of the *Führer-Begleitbataillon* staff, liaison officers of the various *Wehrmacht* arms of service and resident technicians of the *Führer-Nachrichtenabteilung*, although an overall estimate of about 200 would seem justified.

These figures for *Sperrkreise I* and *II* take no account of the main body of the *Führer-Begleitbataillon*, whose rosters changed daily, the duties taking them outside the perimeter fence and anywhere inside it. Their strength in 1941 was 1,277 men.

Foreign visitors to Wolfschanze were exclusively representatives of states allied to Germany or from satellite governments. On 6 August Hitler made the first of his four visits to the front in 1941 when, in company with interpreter Dr Paul Schmidt, he travelled to Berditshev to award the Knight's Cross to the head of Romanian forces 'in recognition of the liberation of Bessarabia'. After attending the Army Group South situation conference with von Rundstedt, he returned to FHQ the same day. Following the '*Treffen der Achsenpartner*' (Meeting of the Axis Partners) at FHQ on 25 August, when two extra heavy anti-aircraft batteries were brought in from Königsberg, 'just in case', Hitler flew with Mussolini to Brest-Litovsk the next day to show him the huge 60cm 'Karl' mortar which had played a role in the taking of the fortress. After lunching with the troops at a field kitchen, Hitler returned to Wolf-schanze, while Mussolini went on to Gorsk in his personal train. The next morning Hitler's *Sonderzug* conveyed him to Strzyzov. The two leaders spent the night aboard their respective trains in the protected sidings at FHQ 'Askania Süd'. On the 28th they flew in Hitler's FW Condor D-2600 from Strzyzov to Uman in the Ukraine to visit an Italian division. *Generalfeldmarschall* von Rundstedt and *Generaloberst* Löhr received the guests. At 2000 that evening Hitler boarded the *Sonderzug* at Strzyzov for Rastenburg.

On 24 September Hitler flew with Himmler, Heydrich and Hans Frank to Borissov, where at Army Group Centre headquarters he gave *Generalfeldmarschall* von Bock orders for the offensive against Moscow—'the last powerful shove against the Soviet Union'.

FHQu-Kommandant Oberst Thomas and the military *Adjutanten* Schmundt and von Below flew to Tallinn in the eastern Baltic to scout for a suitable location for a forward FHQ south of Leningrad. In October and November, two new FHQs were ordered to be built on captured Soviet territory much further to the south. In October, OT engineer Reinhold Valjavec took charge of the work on Bärenhöhle, a 19-hectare plot of desolate woodland requiring forestry work, draining and replanting. The complex was an abandoned former Red Army headquarters near Gnyesdovo, about nine kilometres west of Smolensk. Bärenhöhle was planned exclusively for Hitler and his inner circle of staff and consisted of 42 block-houses and specialised conversions of existing structures.

Work on the second FHQ began in November 1941. So that he should be 'nearer the spearhead of the attack', a wooded area of terrain eight kilometres north of Vinnitsa and lying just east of the highway to Shitomir was selected as a permanent headquarters for Hitler and his *Arbeitsstab* (work staff), with other locations around Shitomir itself for the OKH, the *Führungsstab der Luftwaffe*, the *Reichsführer-SS*, *Reichsminister* Lammers and the *Reichsaussenminister*. The structures for Hitler and the WFSt *Feldstaffel* were codenamed 'Wehrwolf' and 'Wald', respectively.* Schmundt

---

* Hitler personally specified the spelling of the word 'Wehrwolf': it is a play on the words 'Wehr' (meaning armed forces) and 'Werwolf' (werewolf).

chose the nucleus for the site, a wooded tract close to an electrical sub-station which would make possible the rapid installation of a telephone network with FHQ as its centre. 'Oberbauleitung Ukraine' of Organisation Todt set up its own operation, codenamed 'Eichenhain' (Oak Grove), a settlement of rustic blockhouses, barracks huts and bunkers. One of the conditions laid down by Hitler, bearing in mind his sufferings at FHQ Wolfsschlucht, was that the timber used in the construction should be untreated.

On 2 December Hitler flew in bitter winter weather with Schmundt, valet Linge and medical consultant Dr Morell to Maripol on the Sea of Azov in the rearward operational area of Army Group South, stopping *en route* at Kiev and Poltava. From Maripol the *Kommandeur der Leib-standarte*, Sepp Dietrich, drove him to Taganrog to meet *Generalfeld-marschall* von Reichenau, whom Hitler considered a prospective successor to von Brauchitsch. When the weather closed in the next day, Hitler had to break off his return flight at Poltava and, cut off from any telephone contact with the outside world, spend the night in the bug-ridden castle.

As a rule, only a limited circle attended the midday situation conference at Wolfschanze in 1941. Keitel and Jodl were always present, usually with Schmundt and one or other of the military ADCs and, during the year, on a gradually diminishing basis, the *Oberbefehlshaber des Heeres* with the *Generalstabschef* (Chief of the General Staff) and the *Chef der Operations-abteilung* (Chief of Army Operations). If not too many others had been specially summoned, *Gruppenführer* Wolf, Himmler's *Verbindungsoffizier* (liaison officer), and *Generalmajor* Bodenschatz, Göring's permanent representative, would attend. Göring himself had licence from Hitler merely to appear. if he felt so inclined. and listen, even if he had nothing material to contribute. Raeder called in very rarely. Jodl's reports tended to dominate proceedings. Although Warlimont was responsible for the preparation of these reports, he seldom accompanied Jodl to the situation conference. This was disadvantageous for the flow of information which would be filtered by Jodl, who seems to have distanced himself deliberately from his staff, and so caused more work. Percy Schramm, the *Kriegstagebuch* chronicler who lived in *Sperrkreis II*, considered that this attitude might have been provoked by Hitler's known reluctance to see new faces in his 'inner circle', although he thought it more likely that Jodl sought for himself the role of Hitler's sole counsel on all operational questions. Of the non-military personalities, Himmler and Speer came to the situation conference occasionally and Goebbels infrequently: if Goebbels had anything to convey, the Foreign Minister's representative consulted Hitler, usually outside the situation room, after the conference.

As *C-in-C Wehrmacht* but with the expertise of a First World War lance-corporal, Hitler nevertheless considered himself competent to intervene in Army operations and planning. During the huge encirclement battles at the beginning of the 'Barbarossa' campaign he criticised the insufficient flank protection of the Panzer formations driving into the Russian interior. His first great error, with which he persevered against the expert advice of the military, was 'the switching of the fast troops to the north' in order to capture Leningrad and Kronstadt instead of using the consolidated strength of the *Wehrmacht* to take Moscow as the Army planners had wanted.*

When von Brauchitsch resigned after the German advance had ground to a halt with the onset of winter, Hitler did not name a successor but took on the role of *Oberbefehlshaber des Heeres* himself. There now developed a strategic constant of holding every foot of ground won—a dogma which even Jodl was unable to shake.

The assumption of command over the German Army required a change to Hitler's daily routine. In the early hours of the morning, the *Generalstab des Heeres* on the Eastern Front presented to Warlimont at WFSt their situation reports for the previous day. After these had been consolidated with reports from other theatres and other *Wehrmacht* branches of service, an internal discussion followed at 1100. Jodl presented the report to Hitler at the midday conference, after which Halder, the *Chef der Generalstab des*

---

* Von Below stated in his memoirs that Hitler's plan from the very outset was to seize Leningrad in the north and Rostov in the south before winter, leaving the less important objective of Moscow until 1942. Having captured Rostov, the German Army did not set off in hot pursuit of the retreating Russians in accordance with their orders, but rested for 72 hours and thus missed the opportunity to begin the great encircling movement behind Moscow. OKH did not commit a sufficient force to take Leningrad in time. Von Below, Hitler's *Luftwaffenadjutant*, emphasised that the chance of victory in the first year was lost because OKH did not follow Hitler's plan wholeheartedly.—Tr.

Heeres, would make a special situation report with reference to large, 1:300,000-scale maps. The midday conference would often last several hours, whereas the evening conference was by comparison usually short and attended by only a handful of officers.

Chapter 5

Wolfschanze and Wehrwolf: The Russian Front, 1942

HITLER had scant regard for the advice of his generals. His was the strategy which had brought swift victory over the French in 1940, and, following the crisis outside Moscow in the late autumn of 1941 he began to involve himself in command decisions as far down as divisional level, to the extent of ordering movements on the field of battle. His *Luftwaffenadjutant*, Nicolaus von Below, who never denied his sympathetic feelings towards Hitler and played an ambiguous role as regards the Army at FHQ, wrote that

> Hitler forbade retreats from the front, even operational necessities to regain freedom of manoeuvre or to spare the men in the field. His distrust of the generals had increased inordinately and would never quite be overcome . . . he reserved to himself every decision, even the most minor, tactical ones . . .

The visible consequence of this attitude was the dismissal of a number of field commanders from the beginning of 1942, including the C-in-C of the three Army Groups in the East. After General List asked to be relieved, Hitler took Army Group A under his direct command for a period. Political followers, career opportunists and many who did not understand his real intentions may have supported him in all this, but, for those who did not, few chances presented themselves for debating, let alone openly opposing, any course of action Hitler had decided upon. *Luftwaffe* General *Freiherr* von Richthofen, always a welcome face at Hitler's FHQ, recalled that

> The *Führer* hears you out and then decides against you. I stick by my alternative opinion. Orders are orders, however, and I do everything in the way it is ordered to be done. But, seen from an operational point of view, I am just a highly paid NCO.

A further measure in 1942 to 'tighten the screw' was Hitler's decision to appoint his *Chefadjutant der Wehrmacht*, General Schmundt, to run the *Heerespersonalamt* (Army Personnel Office). There would have been nothing of significance regarding the Army officer corps that Schmundt did not discuss with Hitler. The head of the OKH *Generalstab* was relieved of any say in the officer appointment process, and, with two *de facto* Army *Generalstäbe*, Hitler now controlled the Army through Schmundt and Jodl. The former Army and *Luftwaffeadjutanten* Engel and von Below both described in their memoirs how it was at Schmundt's urging that Hitler took over command of the Army in late 1941.

On 8 February 1942 Dr Todt was killed when his personal He 111 aircraft crashed on take-off at Wilhelmsdorf. This led to one of the most significant appointments to be made by Hitler at Wolfschanze as, the same day, he sent for Speer as Todt's successor. With Hitler's support, Speer co-ordinated the armaments effort and achieved a staggering level of efficiency using the self-adminstration system of committees, commissions and cartels set up by Todt with the assistance of the leaders of industry. It was Speer's success that enabled the course of the war to run for several months longer than would otherwise have been the case. His *Reichsministerium für Rüstung und Kriegsproduktion* (Ministry for Armaments and War Production) was the only state institution to have substantial influence at FHQ, and, as he remarks in his memoirs, his success brought him into rivalry with Himmler, prompting the latter to attempt to seize the important areas of production for himself by the unscrupulous use of the concentration-camp workforce.

On days at Wolfschanze that were not filled with official engagements, as a rule Hitler would invite a small circle to take afternoon tea with him in his study. The party would include one each of the military and personal *Adjutanten*, one or two of his female secretaries and Martin Bormann. However, one could not 'unwind' at these rituals. In a letter to a friend dated 27 February 1942, Christa Schroeder wrote: 'As the tea circle is always made up of the same people, and there is no stimulus from outside and nobody has any new personal occurrence to relate, the conversation is often lame and really drags, tiresome and heavy.'

At some point in 1942 the *FHQu-Kommandant* was relieved of the function of commanding the *Führer-Begleitbatallion*. He was left with a small military/civilian staff accountable to Keitel although receiving instructions from Schmundt. His role was to ensure that operational efficiency was maintained and that the best use of buildings and resources was made, the FHQ telephone/telex system being his major concern. The *FHQu-Kommandant* exercised control over the communications unit by the issuing of directives, although its day-to-day running was the responsibility of an official of the *Leiter des Nachrichtenbetriebs* (LdN, or Head of the Signals Branch).

In May 1942 the 'thousand-bomber raid' on Cologne exposed the weakness of the German air defence system and foreshadowed the horror of the air bombardment to come. On 4 June 1942 Hitler made an excursion taking him beyond his domain or sphere of influence for the only time when he ordered his pilot Baur to fly him, Keitel, *Reichspressechef* Dr Dietrich, Schmundt and ambassador Hewel to Micheli near Viborg in Finland, to congratulate Marshal Carl Mannerheim on his seventy-fifth birthday and to urge the Finns to become more involved in the struggle against the Soviets. The visit lasted six hours. Hitler spent the period 11–20 June at the Berghof. Baur brought Mannerheim from Helsinki to FHQ on 27 June for a grand celebration, but whether Hitler succeeded in making an impression by his words and the large party he threw remains uncertain. On 12 July General Grandes, the commander of the Spanish Blue Division on the Eastern Front, was received by the *Führer* at FHQ.

In mid-June the two FHQs under construction on Soviet soil, Bärenhöhle and 'Eichenhain' (Wehrwolf), were nearing completion. The third, FHQ Wasserburg, would be started on 17 November 1942: it was actually located in Estonia, 300 kilometres south-west of Leningrad and about four kilometres north-west of Pleskau, dominating a sharp bend in the River Welikaya. At the centre of the village was an old baronial type mansion, parts of which dated back to the eighth century, originally erected to protect the local fishery. *FHQu-Kommandant* Thomas and two military ADCs had visited the Baltic states in September 1941 to look for a suitable location, and the suggestion to build an FHQ in this locality came from *General der Artillerie* von Küchler's Army Group North. OT had already built a 1,500-bed hospital, a delousing centre and accommodation for a field training battalion nearby, and possibly Küchler got the idea for an FHQ from them. Architect *Dip. Ing.* Valjavec prepared the plans.

On the Russian Front, between 20 June and 16 July 1942, FHQ were relocated in successive stages to 'Eichenhain' between Vinnitsa and Shitomir in the Ukraine in order that Hitler might prosecute the summer offensive in the Caucasus and against Stalingrad from a position close to the front lines. Thus, on 20 June, *1. Schützenkompanie* (1st Rifle Company) of the *Führer-Begleitbataillon* arrived, followed on 25th by *4. (schwere) Kompanie* (4th Heavy Company) and on 11 July by *5. (Panzer) Kompanie* (5th Panzer Company). *1. Abteilung FlakRgt* 604 now comprising eight batteries, was operational there on 25 June.

After Wolfschanze and the Berghof, Hitler spent the third longest period of residence during the war at 'Eichenhain': in the year 1942 he spent 100 days there—from 16 July until 1 November, less a visit to Berlin lasting from 27 September to 4 October.

A courier and military/passenger train left Berlin-Charlottenburg every evening at 1951 and, after a 34-hour journey via Warsaw, Brest-Litovsk, Kovel, Povno and Berditshev, arrived at 'Eichenhain' at 0645 on the second morning. The corresponding train in the other direction left Vinnitsa at 2238 and pulled into Berlin-Schlesisch station at 0957 on the second morning. A Heinkel He 111 aircraft took off from Berlin-Staaken daily at 1400 and landed at 'Eichenhain' four hours later, having made an intermediate stop at Shitomir. There was a corresponding flight in the other direction. When Hitler received the Turkish ambassador and a Bulgarian emissary on 15 August 1942, the two diplomats and their entourages had spent nearly three days getting from Berlin to Vinnitsa by train for the one-hour audience. Von Ribbentrop would often summon his officials to Vinnitsa for some footling discussion and have them wait all day at his pleasure.

Hitler was at once dissatisfied with his accommodation, in the first few days complaining of 'severe headaches.' The cloudless skies and baking heat oppressed him and he broke into a rage at the least provocation. The fortified blockhouses looked nice but had not dried out inside. Christa Schroeder wrote:

> It is always the same: everywhere, in every headquarters, you start off with damp bedding, you feel the cold right through to your bones and are quite convinced that eventually this will bring on rheumatism. The daytime temperatures are extreme (it is quite often that we have 45 to 50 degrees Centigrade); at night it is relatively cold. The weather often changes as quickly as lightning.

The mosquito infestation was worse than at Wolfschanze, and everybody had to take Atibrin as a prophylactic against malaria.

The OKH occupied converted buildings on the Vinnitsa University campus. *Chef des Generalstabs* Halder could not speak highly enough of the work conditions. The *Generalquartiermeister* was billeted at an extensive castle codenamed 'Waldheim', which, situated a few kilometres from Vinnitsa, had once been used as a mental asylum.

At Wehrwolf, the nineteen-hectare patch of woodland eight kilometres north of Vinnitsa, Hitler's entourage had an allocation of nineteen blockhouses with a total floor area of 4,928 square metres, together with 12,705 square metres of *Luftwaffe* and RAD barrack huts for the FHQ staff and security force. The three small air-raid bunkers had required 9,900 cubic metres of concrete, to provide a total area of 81.5 square metres— no less than 121 cubic metres of concrete for every square metre of floor.

Overhead cables from the Vinnitsa sub-station supplied the power, individual buildings being wired into a four-kilometre-long ground cable. Three diesel generators in a special machinery house stood ready to supply light and power to drive the water pumps in case of electrical failure. This back-up system needed 2,580 metres of overhead wiring and 1,330 metres of ground cables.

Water was graded into drinking, general and fire-hydrant quality. Two 120-metre-deep wells had been bored for drinking and general water. The hydrant water was drawn from the River Bug and pumped into a ring circuit, a large water tank being kept topped up should a serious emergency arise. Sewage from the complex drained into a biological purification plant inside the main compound and went from there into the Bug. The system had eight kilometres of drainage channels with control shafts.

As the establishment lay in an abandoned pine forest, after necessary felling the gaps were camouflaged using 12,000 square metres of turf, 800 trees and several thousand bushes. OT also laid six kilometres of all-weather roads and two kilometres of footpaths.

Up to 8,000 OT labourers and 1,000 Russians were engaged in the first building phase, from November 1941 to September 1942. The total work output amounted to 179,500 work days. A second phase became necessary when a reassessment required the building of a further eight blockhouses of 2,452 square metres and seven barracks of 1,565 square metres, while all completed blockhouses needed to be checked over and proofed against the harsh winter climate. The increase in the developed area led to the need for 2.4 more kilometres of all-weather roads and another 1.7 kilometres of footpaths. The existing six kilometres of perimeter wire-mesh fencing and twelve kilometres of 'Flanders hedge' barbed wire entanglements had to be extended by another 1.6 kilometres. This work kept 1,250 OT labourers occupied from January to July 1943; by then, mainly for reasons of secrecy, Russians were no longer employed. Finally, a network of underground guard posts was installed for use by the *Führer-Begleitbataillon*, field gendarmes and the *SS-Begleitkommando* in order to increase the effectiveness of the security.

Following its completion, Wehrwolf had the outward look of a pleasant summer camp rather than a command centre. Even Dr Schmidt, Hitler's chief interpreter, held the opinion that the headquarters were 'by several degrees nicer' than Wolfschanze, although 'for normal people it was still grim enough'. Felix Hartlaub, a member of the WFSt field staff, noted in his diary of Wehrwolf:

> Pine woodland to the forestry management handbook. Nobody knows from whence it came. Looks like it was specially grown for just this purpose by a forward-looking German forester, perhaps at the end of the last century. Of narrow, tongue-like outline, regimented in numbered paths (each blocked by a barrier) in all directions, easy to see anything between them. Regularly spaced at the edge of the wood, tall oaks with built-in look-out nests. *Sperrkreis I* is in the eastern part away from the highway and cordoned off by fencing taller than a

man. Across the meadow runs an extensive barbed wire entanglement, a spirally bulge. The pines are 20–30 centimetres thick and many have been cut down, the tops of their stumps a greyish-green. Vegetation from the woods is carefully arranged on the roof of the uninhabited cube-shaped bunker; on the numerous barracks, camouflage netting is dappled with sea grass. Black ash on the footpaths, fat hydrants, boxes of hose reels on the barrack walls. At the *Führer-Begleitbataillon* barracks somebody is working on antlers with a saw. Only September but already fires burn in the grates: each of the long work barracks sends up dozens of vertical, thin columns of smoke. Where the trees are thicker, parking places. At the edge of the wood armoured scout cars keep watch from beneath sun-dried camouflage netting. Outlined under a wrap of tarpaulin—an anti-tank gun.'

The barracks and schools at Vinnitsa, with 120,000 square metres floor space—equal to sixteen soccer pitches—converted for OKH in the first building phase required only cosmetic repairs during the second phase.

Steinbruch, erected for the *Führungsstab der Luftwaffe* in the first building phase, lay thirty kilometres north of Vinnitsa on the highway to Shitomir and was close to Kalinovka aerodrome and an electricity sub-station. A good highway connected it to Wehrwolf. Security personnel were accommodated in the airfield buildings. The complex had twelve 300-metre standard barracks huts and a *Westwall*-like Type 102 V double-group bunker of 42.5 square metres and made up of 800 cubic metres of concrete, for the safety of Göring's immediate support staff. The transformer stations supplying current were equipped with 60 and 90kW sets. Emergency power was available from two 175kVA diesels, with a 40kVA reserve, in splinter-proof housing. A newly bored, 120-metre-deep well supplied Steinbruch with water, the drinking water being fed to four storage tanks each fabricated from 100 cubic metres of concrete. Almost two kilometres of plumbing supplied the individual houses. A similar biological sewage farm to that at Wehrwolf had been installed, nine kilometres of tubing and pipes having been laid for this purpose.

Steinbruch was surrounded by five kilometres of wire-net fencing and twelve kilometres of 'Flanders hedge'. The camouflage work was more extensive than at Wehrwolf—12,000 square metres of newly sown grass, 2,100 square metres of ground disguised and several thousand trees and bushes transplanted. In all, 1,760 metres of highway was repaired and 2,800 metres of rails and sleepers laid on a new embankment for the

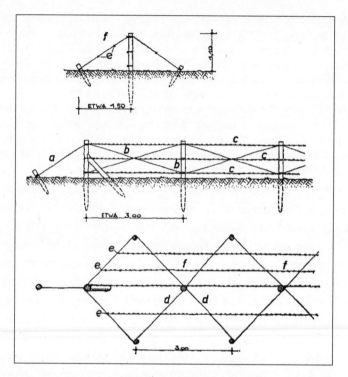

'Construction Method of the "Flanders Hedge" as a Field Obstruction' (from *Behelfmassiges Bauen im Kriege, Teil II, 1942*). *a. end anchor; b. central stakes anchored by taut cross of smooth wire; c. horizontal lengths of barbed wire, the lowest close to the ground to impede anyone crawling underneath; d. lateral anchorage to small stakes with fine wire; e. lateral lengths of slack barbed wire; f. enemy side.*

Sonderzüge required by Göring and von Ribbentrop. The 400-metre long station platform was plumbed into the drinking water supply and the fire-hydrant water ring. Not including that demanded by the installation of the telephone system, the expenditure of labour amounted to 104,500 working days.

Hegewald, on the outskirts of the town of Shitomir, was allocated to the *Reichsführer-SS, Reichsminister* Dr Lammers and the *Reichsaussenminister*. Four hundred and ten workers devoted 27,000 working days to the project between 10 October 1941 and 1 July 1942; 1,200 cubic metres of concrete went into making the two fifteen-square-metre air-raid bunkers and 21,500 square metres of existing buildings, mostly barracks, was upgraded. The local grid supplied the electricity, and diesel generators stood by in reserve for emergencies. The existing water piping, drainage facilities and footpaths were adequate, and only 500 metres of extra all-weather road needed to be laid. Hegewald was fenced in by three kilometres of wire mesh and five kilometres of 'Flanders hedge', while 1,200 square metres of terrain was camouflaged by substitute trees, grass and netting. The unit had been provisionally designated 'Waldhof', but on his arrival on 15 July 1942 Himmler changed the name to 'Hegewald'.

The total output of labour for 'Eichenhain' expressed in working days was 332,000. This effort produced 183 square metres of bunkers, 21,500 square metres of fortified housing and 140,505 square metres of barracks and other lightly built structures—a useful area of 161,688 square metres, equivalent to 22 soccer pitches. Occupancy at the site totalled 3,532 persons. The 11,400 cubic metres of concrete was a relatively small quantity in comparison to that required by other FHQs, although the ratio of about 60 cubic metres of concrete to every square metre of floor space indicates that the 'Eichenhain' bunkers were the sturdiest of all those at FHQ strongholds.

Hitler came to Vinnitsa to direct the German offensive aimed at destroying the Soviet political system. One of the most fateful of Hitler's decisions, taken against OKH advice, was to divide Army Group South into two groups—Group A to seize the Caucasus oilfields and Group B to capture Stalingrad and block off the Volga to barge traffic. Hitler signed an instruction to that effect on 23 July 1942 in the belief that the Red Army had been decisively weakened in the vast encirclements of 1941 and needed only to be pursued to its destruction. The *Generalstab des Heeres* considered that a head-on clash between the two armies was inevitable. When the various foreign armies fighting alongside the *Wehrmacht* in the central Don region proved to be of mediocre quality, *Generalfeldmarschall* von Kluge, C-in-C Army Group Centre, requested at Wehrwolf on 8 August 1942 that the 9th and 11th Panzer Divisions be brought up to repulse the Soviet breakthrough at Rzhev. When Hitler refused, von Kluge said, 'Then you take upon yourself the responsibility, *mein Führer*.'

On 22 August *Generalfeldmarschall* List, C-in-C Army Group A, attended the situation conference at Wehrwolf, dispelling Hitler's doubts regarding the apparently poor progress on the Caucasus front. After lunch with the intimate circle in Hitler's blockhouse, Hitler meriting List's observation that he was 'an unusually attentive host', List left FHQ for Stalino with a bagful of new tasks but no extra troops.

On 23 August Hitler invited von Küchler to Vinnitsa to discuss with him the capture of Leningrad and, with Finnish help, the cutting off of the Murmansk highway. The next day von Kluge returned with a request to pull back the Ninth Army at Rzhev in order to straighten the front. Hitler refused, and it was during this conference that there occurred the decisive clash between Hitler and *Generalstabschef* Halder that led to the latter's dismissal. Hitler had accused the military commanders of not being hard enough:

HITLER: I expect from the commanders the same hardness as from the troops at the front.

HALDER: I take your point, *mein Führer*, but out there brave musketeers and lieutenants are falling in their thousands simply because the *Führung* [High Command, i.e. Hitler himself] cannot order the only possible solution and their hands are tied.

HITLER: *Generaloberst* Halder, what sort of tone is that to use to me? You are telling me what it is like for the man at the front? What is your experience of being at the front? Where were you in the First World War? And you reproach me by saying I don't know what it is like at the front! I absolutely forbid it! I never heard of such a thing!'

A month later Halder was gone.*

There now began a period of severe setbacks for Hitler. In North Africa, on 1 September Rommel broke off his offensive against El Alamein. The occupation of Malta had proved impossible. The intentions of the

---

* According to Laternser, of the seventeen Army field marshals to serve during the war, ten were relieved of command by Hitler, three were executed for complicity in the assassination attempt, two fell in action and one was taken prisoner. Only one, Keitel, served to the end. Of the 36 Army generals of the highest rank (*Generaloberst*), 24 were relieved of command, two were dishonourably discharged, seven fell in action and only three served to the end.

Western Allies regarding landings in France were inscrutable. The Finns had not been able to sever the Murmansk highway. At Leningrad, the Red Army had seized the initiative. Partisans were using terror tactics to create serious difficulties for Army Group Centre. The most awkward situation of all was in the southern sector of the Eastern Front, where the objectives were Stalingrad and the Caucasus oilfields.

Hitler had sent Jodl on a fact-finding mission to Army Group A headquarters. On his return, on 7 September 1942, there occurred an altercation at Wehrwolf in which Jodl strenuously rejected Hitler's reproach that he had taken the side of List and was attempting to promulgate the latter's view as to how operations in the Caucasus should be conducted. Voices were raised in what seems to have been a highly emotional and heated exchange once each had accused the other of lying. Hitler denied having ordered List to carry out any operations in the Caucasus area that had gone seriously awry. Jodl argued to the contrary. To prevent such bitter disagreements in the future, a dozen stenographers were brought from the *Reichstag*, sworn in and put to work in pairs, taking down verbatim what was said at situation conferences.

Life at FHQ changed on account of the discord that this incident engendered, and Hitler now avoided his staff, leaving his sunless blockhouse only after dark and using only the rear entrance. Situation conferences were held in this blockhouse and no longer in the appointed situation room. Only the most indispensable report-makers were admitted. The atmosphere was icy and talk was limited to the bare essentials. The custom introduced by Schmundt that at least one officer of the military *Arbeitsstab* should dine with Hitler was terminated. Whereas initially the younger officers had fought for the opportunity, those at table now had been more or less commandeered. Hitler no longer dined there, Bormann deputising for him. From then on, Bormann was also at Hitler's elbow during the situation conferences—a fact which did not pass unnoticed by the military. On 9 September, List advised Hitler that he wished to be relieved of command. The tension which existed between them is indicated by the dismissal of List next day. For a time, Hitler took over command of Army Group A himself.

In addition to the many NSDAP and military men and members of the Nazi judiciary who visited Wehrwolf between July and September 1942, the Romanian dictator Marshal Antonescu and the Croat leader Pavelich were also in attendance, on 23 and 24 September, respectively. On 27 September Hitler flew to Berlin for a week, addressing 10,000 officers the next day at the Sportpalast. He expressed his 'unconditional certainty of victory and his rock-firm confidence in the superior fighting skill of the German soldier'. The tirades against the Allies were met with hesitant applause. He returned to Wehrwolf on 4 October, spending the next month there (until 1 November) following the fortunes of his armies on the Eastern Front. The special radio bulletins spoke of victories everywhere.

The proposed FHQ Bärenhöhle, nine kilometres west of Smolensk and a former Red Army headquarters, had been the subject of conversion work and improvements since October 1941. The nineteen-hectare site lay in woodland revitalised by OT with 400 trees and several thousand bushes within 1,750 metres of wire-net fencing. Hitler's immense bunker had only 43 square metres of floor space, but the structure contained 900 cubic metres of concrete. Thirty-one standard barracks huts totalling 9,416 square metres had been erected for Hitler's staff, 870 square metres of RAD barracks huts having been allocated for the security personnel. All accommodation was furnished with confiscated Red Army furniture, curtains and carpets.

Two 120-metre wells were sunk for drinking water, which was pumped into a storage tank after purification. Supply piping totalled 1,750 metres for drinking water, 1,040 metres for fire hydrants and 910 metres for other non-potable water. Waste water passed through frost-free drainage channels to a sewage farm for purification before flowing back into the Dnieper.

Bärenhöhle was supplied with power over the Smolensk high-tension grid, individual structures being fed by cable or overhead wire. Diesel generators of 80 and 150kVA located in a machinery house provided emergency back-up, and bunker lighting was further guaranteed by batteries. The renamed *Stabs-Nachrichtenkompanie FHQu* (Staff Signals

Company FHQ) equipped the telecommunications network. Roads and footpaths were laid inside the establishment, together with the access roads to the Smolensk–Rollbahn highway, totalling 1.8 kilometres, and an extra 800 metres of track extended to Gniesdovo station, where the platform was lengthened to 450 metres.

At the high point of the effort, in April and May 1942, the workforce consisted of 2,400 German OT employees and 950 Russian civilians. For the ten months from October 1941, OT labourers toiled for 237,000 working days and the Russians for 200,000, from which figures it would appear that, at Bärenhöhle, the Russian's working day with twice as long as his German counterpart's.

During the Second World War, 12.9 million working days, each lasting between eight and sixteen hours, would be expended on building FHQs. As the war progressed, the OT workforce expanded to 1.5 million. Eighty per cent of these people were non-German workers, the majority sub-contracted to OT with their firms and equipment. Added to this figure were the prisoners of war (the only workers who, under international law, contributed their labour for no wage), forced labourers and concentration-camp inmates. Remuneration was set down precisely in the *Tarifordnung für die Frontarbeiter der Organisation Todt* (Tariff Regulations for Organisation Todt Front Workers) issued in October 1942—65 *pfennig* an hour for basic grades, 72 for skilled grades, 80 for expert grades, 85 for specialised expert grades, 92 for foremen and 96 for borers and shaft-workers. Food and lodgings were provided free. This tariff put OT workers on a par with the fighting services, in accordance with the wishes of the *Wehrmacht*.

Subject to the exceptions mentioned below, non-German labourers were subject to the same conditions of work as German nationals, but their wages were scaled up or down to correspond to the worth of their labour in their home country. A Frenchman, for example, earned from 38 to 50 *pfennig*, a Belgian from 40 to 53 . Russians, Poles and workers from the Baltic states qualified for remuneration under their own special tariff schemes. Labour costs were financed from the *Reichshaushaltskasse* (Reich Household Budget). Firms contracted to OT or the SS applied directly to the *Reichshaushaltskasse* for the reimbursement of forced labourers or concentration-camp prisoners in their employ who earned from between 4 and 6 *Reichsmark* per day, depending on grade. No Organisation Todt worker received payment for overtime.*

Food in Germany was scarce, and the allowance was equivalent to the civilian scale. In 1943 OT non-prisoner labour was entitled to a daily ration of 700 grams of black bread, 30 grams of sugar and 40 grams of fat; in 1944 the ration was cut to 500, 20 and 30 grams, respectively. The official allowance for all prisoners of war, penal prisoners, concentration-camp inmates and Jews at labour was 500 grams of black bread, 150 grams of fresh sausage, 30 grams of fat, 6 grams of coffee substitute and 10 grams of sugar, and differed very little from the others.†

By mid-August 1942, when building work on it was more or less complete, Bärenhöhle was no longer required as an FHQ and it was abandoned to Army Group Centre as a reserve HQ. A maintenance team composed of an OT senior builder and twelve men stayed on once the labour force had withdrawn with their machinery.

By November 1942 Hitler had spent so much time in bunkers since arriving at Wolfschanze in June the previous year that Schmundt recommended he have a change of scenery for the sake of his health. On 8 November he attended the annual commemoration of the National Socialist movement's 'witnesses in blood during the march to the *Feldherrnhalle*'; on the 11th he went to the Berghof. He was forced to break off his stay at Obersalzberg on 22 November when *General der Infanterie* Kurt Zeitzler, *Chef des Generalstabs des Heeres*, brought him the ominous news regarding the impending disasters on the Caucasus front and at Stalingrad. The return to Wolfschanze by *Führersonderzug* took 24 hours. After leaving Berchtesgaden at 2155 it had to halt once an hour, on average, because of air raid warnings.

---

* The author is not, of course, suggesting that concentration-camp prisoners and Jews actually received wages due under the Tariff.—Tr.
† This last group, however, was forced to perform heavy manual labour for sixteen hours every day of the week. The daily ration of a one-pound loaf of bread plus a tablespoonful of margarine and a piece of sausage, all washed down with a cup of *ersatz* coffee, was enough to keep a prisoner in this group alive, drawing on his bodily energies, for perhaps a couple of months.—Tr.

On 10 December the leader of the Dutch fascists, Anton Mussert, had a 'long, confidential discussion' with Hitler, as reported in the 13 December issue of the *Volkischer Beobachter*. General Munoz Grandes, the commander of the Spanish Blue Division on the Eastern Front, made his second visit to Wolfschanze on 13 December to receive the Oak Leaves to his Knight's Cross. Hitler explained to him the reasons why he could not supply weapons to Spain.

On 18 December the Italian Foreign Minister, Ciano, visited Wolfschanze at Hitler's invitation. In view of the military situation in North Africa and the Italian débâcle at Stalingrad, Ciano made the suggestion for the first time that a peace accord should be sought with the Soviets. The next day Göring and von Ribbentrop joined Ciano to hear the French President, Laval, being dressed down by Hitler over the inadequate contribution by France to the fight against Bolshevism. On 20 December Ciano and Hitler discussed the role of Spain and the vexed question of getting supplies to North Africa.

For the *Führer*, the year 1942 did not end on a high note.

Chapter 6

France: Preparing for the Allied Invasion, 1942–3

I T will be recalled that, when the second phase of the French campaign, Operation 'Rot', opened on 5 June 1940, it was decided to provide Hitler with a field headquarters close to the front, and a 650-metre long railway tunnel near Margival had seemed suitable. Accordingly, Dr Todt and *FHQu-Kommandant* Thomas had issued OT with the necessary instructions. On 17 June, however, two days after the workforce had begun to arrive, the French forces capitulated and the idea became redundant.

Two years later, the work at Margival was recommenced under the cover-name 'W 2'. At the Channel coast, Organisation Todt was working feverishly on the Atlantic Wall obstructions aimed at preventing Allied landings that, it was assumed, might take place anywhere between the Scheldt and Brittany. Hitler was anxious to lead the *Wehrmacht* defence personally if the Western Allies attempted to invade, and for this purpose he needed a choice of two headquarters in France ready for occupation. These were codenamed 'W 2' and 'W 3'.

It is doubtful whether Hitler chose the 'W 2' site himself: more probably, he agreed with Schmundt's recommended locality because he had seen action between Laon and Soissons as a private soldier in the Great War. OT director Xaver Dorsch awarded the new project to chief FHQ architect Siegfried Schmelcher, and in due course, over the twenty-four months from September 1942, several bomb-proof accommodation and work bunkers, together with a series of barracks huts with concrete, anti-shrapnel casings, were erected ten kilometres north of Soissons, near the railway line to Laon. For Himmler and von Ribbentrop, two *châteaux*, at Vregny and Mailly, were developed to include an air-raid

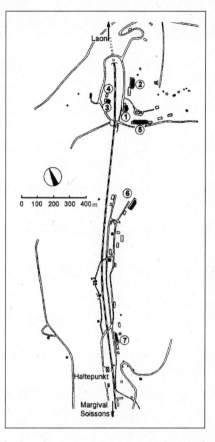

bunker. On 25 October 1942, Hitler's *Heeresadjutant, Hauptmann* Engel, arrived to discuss the expansion of 'W 2' with Classen, Schmelcher and architect Müller, and on 17 December Engel met Müller at 'W 2' with fresh instructions. The total useful ground area of 'W 2' was fixed at 43,050 square metres.

At the heart of the complex was the railway tunnel. It was fitted with armoured sliding doors retracting into the rockwall, one door 120 metres from the southern end and the other 80 metres from the northern. Smoke extractors and ventilation shafts guaranteed the fresh air supply, even when the locomotive of the *Führersonderzug* was present within and had raised steam.

The defended site occupied some 90 square kilometres, roughly six kilometres in all directions from the centre, where were located six 'large' and eight 'flat' bunkers and twenty protected barracks huts, plus an assortment of large, unprotected wooden huts.

The large bunkers were built into the slope of the hillside. Walls and ceilings were up to 3.5 metres thick, whereas those of the flat bunkers did not exceed 80 centimetres in thickness and are unlikely to have been built as air-raid shelters. The latter were long (110 metres) and narrow and were intended to house command positions, as work places and for

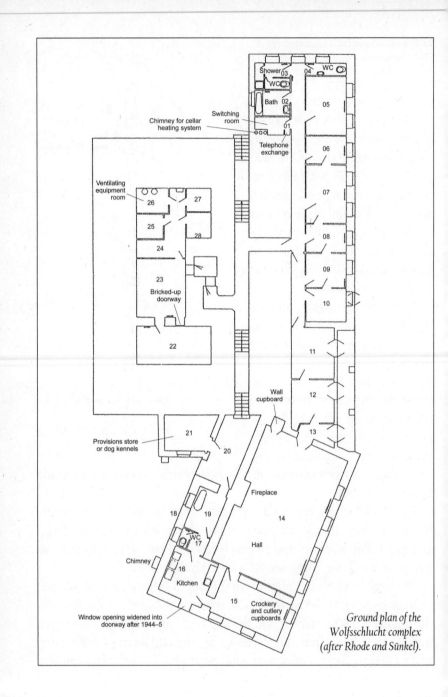

Shower
WC
Bath
Chimney for cellar
heating system
Switching
room
Telephone
exchange
03
04
WC
02
01
05
06
07
08
09
10
Ventilating
equipment
room
26
27
25
28
24
23
Bricked-up
doorway
22
11
12
13
Wall
cupboard
Provisions store
or dog kennels
21
20
Fireplace
18
19
14
WC
17
Hall
Chimney
16
Kitchen
15
Crockery
and cutlery
cupboards
Window opening widened into
doorway after 1944–5

*Ground plan of the
Wolfsschlucht complex
(after Rhode and Sünkel).*

communications installations. Ventilation shafts with gas filters supplied the air. Sheets of armour plating could be bolted over the windows, and at each narrow end the entrances were protected by gas-proof armoured doors. The work rooms were situated either side of the central corridor. The *Führerbunker* was undoubtedly the edifice with a 90 square metre hall and dog kennels; certainly the portico resembled the entrance to the *Neue Reichskanzlei* (New Reich Chancellery) in Berlin. A flight of seven steps led down to the air-raid bunker, the walls and ceiling of which were 3.5 metres thick. No fewer than 450 structures of one kind or another—mostly barracks huts and defensive emplacements—were dotted about within the general perimeter, Air defence was taken very seriously, as evidenced by the large number of anti-aircraft positions.

Water was pumped in from three springs in the surrounding hills. The catchment basin was walled in for security, and water was piped from there into the 500-cubic-metre main reservoir for distribution to the consumer. The bunker in the railway tunnel had its separate, 80-cubic-metre water tank. There were three sewage farms. Solid matter was treated in a lower foul pond while waste water, after purification, flowed into the La Jocienne and Vauxaillon streams.

Electricity came from the civilian grid, a power station supplying current by means of underground cables. Ten emergency diesel generators housed in four on-site, steel-doored sub-stations were available in the event of a power cut.

As 'W 2' lay between Soissons and Laon, in a rural area without French network telephone trunk lines, the Paris ring was extended using 115 kilometres of cabling and seven switching centres. From the French capital there were two trunk lines into Germany, one connecting to the German network at Aachen through Brussels, the other at Saarbrücken via Rheims and Metz. In 1941 the French post and telephone company PTT had contracted to trunk in the Laon–Soissons–Villers–Cotterêts and Breny–Château Thierry sections, each with 56 paired circuits and switching centres at Laon and Château Thierry, plus an amplifier office at Verberie. In 1942 the 20-paired overhead wires between Charleville and the Belgian amplifier at Jemelle were replaced by underground cables and extended to Prum in the Eifel mountains to connect to the German network there. This gave 'W 2' its third underground point of access into the Reich network. During the period of German occupation, the 6,000 kilometres of telephone lines in France were extended to 11,000 kilometres. *Feldschaltabteilung z.b.V. 2* (Field Switching Detachment 2) supervised the main network. After the French defeat in 1940, this detachment worked alongside the PTT to repair damaged trunk lines and so restore both military and civilian telephone traffic. Overhead wires were repaired by PTT gangs and French prisoners of war working under the instructions of *Feldnachtrichtenkommandanturen* (Field Signals Commanders). Female signals auxiliaries were used as telephone operators in military command centres.

At 'W 2', some telephone and telex circuits were at constant readiness, and calls from within the establishment could be direct-dialled. Each operator served a switchboard able to handle between 30 and 100 connections. For the Morse transmitters, however, nothing more than the aerial shafts had been installed.

The protection of FHQs against airborne attackers or partisans was, as noted, the responsibility of the *Führer-Begleitbataillon*. Control posts, field patrols and fixed sentry points safeguarded the inner area against unauthorised entry, and bomb-proof machine-gun positions protected the outer defenders. A ring of seven heavy anti-aircraft batteries, each equipped with six to twelve 10.5cm or 8.8cm guns and rangefinding equipment, were supported by 21 light and medium AA emplacements and eighteen searchlight batteries. Vregny had four AA and searchlight positions, but whether they were ever manned is not known. Presumably, when German troops withdrew in August 1944 some of the ordnance would have been put to good use in covering the retreat.

On 20 March 1943, in Berlin, Engel and *FHQu-Kommandant Oberstleutnant* Streve met Müller, Classen and two others to consider progress, and on 4 April 1943 Müller and Engel discussed 'W 2' and 'W 3' at Obersalzberg, where Hitler was in residence. On 22 April Müller and Classen talked about electrification and camouflage, and to check the latter from the air Müller overflew the 'W 2' site in a Storch on 27 May.

Above: Hitler's *Sonderzug* (Special Train) waits at an improvised halt.
Below: Motorcycle combinations of the *Führer-Begleit-bataillon* and the SS bodyguard wait for Hitler to alight from his *Führersonderzug.*

Left: FHQ Commandant *Oberstleutnant* Kurt Thomas offers Hitler congratulations on the latter's birthday, 20 April 1941, at Mönichkirchen, Austria, during the Balkans campaign.
Below: FHQ Frühlingssturm: the *Führersonderzug* at Mönichkirchen.
Right, upper: Hitler acknowledges the salute of a *Luftwaffe* guard detachment at Frühlingssturm on the occasion of his 52nd birthday. To his right are Göring, Raeder, von Brauchitsch and Keitel.
Right, lower: One of the blockhouse-style bunker buildings at FHQ Adlerhorst near Bad Nauheim. Occupying a ground area of nearly 600 square metres, such fortified houses had two levels of subterranean bunkers.

Above: A partial view of the bunker (left of photograph) at FHQ Adlerhorst, as seen on 6 or 7 March 1945.

Left: The village of Rodert, south of Münstereifel (Sperrkreis II), seen from Felsennest, Hitler's FHQ during the Western offensive, 10 May–6 June 1940.

Above: The work hut (left) and Hitler's bunker (right) at FHQ Felsennest.
Left: Hitler at the entrance to his bunker at FHQ Felsennest, in company with his *Luftwaffenadjutant*, *Oberstleutnant* Nicolaus von Below.

Left: The terrace and entrance to Hitler's work barracks at FHQ Felsennest, screened by a camouflage awning.

Left: Hitler's living room at FHQ Felsennest.

Above: The Map Room in the barracks hut at FHQ Felsennest.
Right: Hitler strolling in the grounds of FHQ Felsennest, in company with von Below, his valet Schaub and an SS bodyguard.

Left: An OT labourer salutes Hitler during the latter's tour of the abandoned Belgian village of Brûly-de-Pesche, FHQ Wolfsschlucht 1, 6 June 1940. A fortnight later, the terms of the armistice offered to France were worked on in the church.

Below: A *Luftwaffe* reconnaissance photograph of FHQ Wolfsschlucht 1, Brûly-de-Pesche. Hitler's bunker and barracks hut, General Jodl's barracks and the *Teehaus* all lie well hidden in the woods behind the village.

Right: Outdoor furniture amongst the trees at FHQ Wolfsschlucht 1.

Far right: Hitler leading two SS and two *Führer-Begleitbataillon* aides on a fast stroll at FHQ Tannenberg in the Black Forest, sometime between 27 June and 5 July 1940. By this time, the campaign in the West was over.

Right, lower: Hitler, on an outing from FHQ Tannenberg, crosses a Rhine bridge into the re-annexed Alsace. On its left mudguard, his vehicle wears the tactical insignia of a wolf—an animal with which Hitler often identified himself during the war.

Above: Hitler about to board the *Führersonderzug* at Oppenau station for Freiburg and a motor tour of the Alsace battlefields. FHQ Tannenberg, 30 June 1940.
Below: Returning to FHQ Tannenberg following a visit to the former front lines in France, Hitler's motorcade drives through the ruins of a French customs post and across a pontoon bridge straddling the Rhine between Alsace and Baden-Württemberg, June 1940.

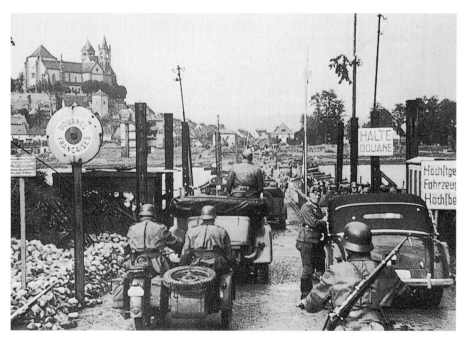

Above: France, late 1942: the improvised wooden platform for the *Sonderzug* at the approach to the Laon tunnel, FHQ Wolfsschlucht 2. The building on the right is the *Teehaus*, but the bunker complex on the slope below it has not yet been started.

Below: The *Führerbunker* at FHQ Wolfschanze after reinforcement work in late 1944. Camouflage netting is evident in the trees. In the background is *Teehaus II*.

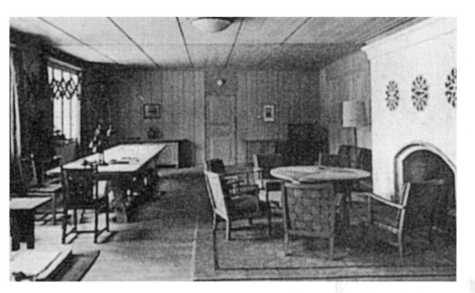

Left, upper: The reinforced concrete shed for Hitler's *Sonderzug* at Askania Mitte, east of Lodz. This FHQ was never used by Hitler, because the speed of the German advance into Russia left it far behind the front lines.
Left, lower: The '*Reichssiedlung Rudolf Hess*' (Sonnenwald settlement) at Pullach near Munich before the war. The buildings and bunkers for FHQ Siegfried, or Hagen, were erected on the terrain in the foreground.

Many structures in the compounds either side of the Heilmannstrasse, which is the lower thoroughfare, are used today by the Federal German Intelligence Service.
Above: Hitler's study at FHQ 'Eichenhain' (Wehrwolf).
Below: An aerial photograph of the estate on the River Welikaya at Pleskau in Estonia selected for FHQ Wasserburg in October 1942. It was never visited by Hitler and eventually became Army Group North's headquarters.

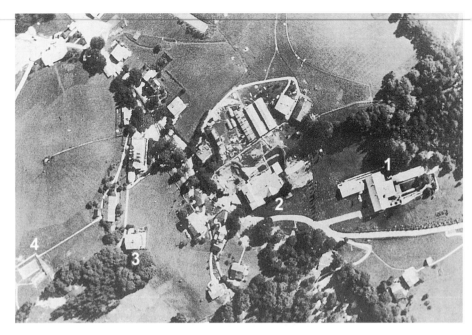

Above: An aerial photograph of FHQ Obersalzberg showing (1) the Berghof, (2) the RSD complex, (3) the *Bormann-Haus* and (4) Göring's residence.

Left: FHQ Obersalzberg: the converted Berghof at the northern foot of the Hoher Goll mountain.

Right, upper: Schloss Fürstenstein, about 20km north of the FHQ Riese site in Lower Silesia, was rebuilt by OT with a view to its becoming one of Hitler's postwar residences and a government guest house. FHQ Riese itself is one of the war's greatest mysteries.

Right, lower: A bunker blockhouse at FHQ Maybach II near Berlin-Zossen, to the design of a family dwelling house. Eleven such houses were built on a residential estate to a 'banjo' ground plan, and seven of these were allocated to Hitler. In 1945 Bormann considered Maybach II safer than the *Reichskanzlei*.

Above and below: *Führerhauptquartier* 'S-III': the building site, with work in progress at the western (above) and eastern en[

More concrete—almost a quarter of a million cubic metres—went into the building of 'W 2' than at any other completed FHQ. Hitler's awesome bunker alone consumed 231,000 cubic metres, enough to erect a pyramid 300 feet high with a base the size of a professional soccer pitch. This, and the remaining 17,450 cubic metres of concrete, provided 26,495 square metres of useful area made up of bunkers, reinforced housing, concrete-encased barracks, blockhouses and simple wooden huts for adjutants, the entourage and the OKW and the WFSt *Feldstaffel*.

The OKH, concentrating its attentions primarily on the Eastern Front, was allotted 865 square metres; 225 square metres of this was bunkered, for which 8,100 cubic metres of concrete had been used. At Vregny, Himmler had 8,395 square metres, and even the *Reichsaussenminister* at Mailly had nearly eight times as much space as the Army with his 6,775 square metres. The latter two *châteaux* had an air-raid bunker each, the concrete required being 4,400 and 4,950 cubic metres, respectively. The Vregny bunker was arranged into two pairs of rooms either side of a central corridor, with toilets at the far end. Below the *château* were two subterranean floors, used as magazines. The installation was provided with four defensive bunkers with twenty gun turntables and four AA positions. The Château Mailly bunker was similar in ground plan to that at Vregny, but it had no porch and was reached by descending a stairway from the château. Security troops were based in bunkers nearby.

'W 2' was a masterpiece of logistics. The plans had been drawn up by *Einsatzgruppe West der OT* (OT Operational Group West), and supervision was the responsibility of the management team at Soissons under *Bau-assessor* Classen. Altogether 2.79 million working days—24.6 million hours—went into creating this FHQ. The workforce was about 13,000, most of it provided by French building firms co-opted to OT and then duty-bound to provide equipment and personnel. The number of forced labourers and prisoners of war were employed is not known.

The transport of sand, cement and shingle required as great an effort as the lodging and feeding of the workforce. A 60cm-gauge light field railway was laid to ship in the materials. Iron and wood came to Crouy station near Soissons, the cement in barges to Missy-sur-Aisne. As the

145

grit and shingle in the Margival area was unsuitable for the manufacture of concrete, this also had to be brought in. Cement, sand and gravel came principally from Belgium. Materials were stored in local caves. Petrol for the many lorries involved in making deliveries was kept in a 600,000-litre tank at Couvailles. The workforce lived in camps of barracks-type huts or at the Charpentier Barracks in Soissons, from where they commuted to the site by train.

In November 1943 Müller called on the site overseers and urged them to step up the pace before the visit of Hitler's *Luftwaffenadjutant, Oberstleutnant* von Below, who was responsible for all FHQ internal matters. On his return journey from Paris to Munich, Müller discussed the outstanding matters with the head of *Einsatzgruppe West der OT, Oberbaudirektor* Weiss. He made a final visit to Soissons on 10 January 1944 to inspect the air conditioning system, at which point the construction work for 'W 2' seems to have been complete.

The second FHQ in France had to be at a location that would enable Hitler to direct operations from a central point near the coast. Hitler or somebody else may have recalled the railway tunnel used to shelter the *Führersonderzug* in preparation for the talks with Marshal Pétain on 16 October 1940. The location was on the Loire, south-west of Paris, 50 kilometres north of Tours and 15 kilometres west of Vendôme on the single-line stretch of track to Montoire. The 509-metre long tunnel had been cut through hilly terrain around 350 feet high. An impending Allied invasion was thought to be a 'high probability', and on 9 July Hitler drafted extra troops into France and ordered a series of other measures to counter the threat. OT resumed building 'W 2' in September 1942: this would become the largest of the completed FHQs, but 'W 3' was also deemed suitable for accommodating the *Führersonderzug*.

On 27 June 1942, a delegation headed by *FHQu-Kommandant Oberst* Thomas arrived at St-Rimay to carry out a detailed survey. *Baurat* Simon of *Einsatzgruppe West der OT* was appointed to head the project, assisted by architect Luis Gerland of Schmelcher's FHQ building group, but who signed the instructions, and when, is not known. Simon commissioned an expert geological opinion of the hillside through which the railway tunnel ran. The survey reported that the chalk structure of the *massif* had its good and bad points. Drilling work could proceed rapidly, and under bombardment chalk absorbed blast more effectively than hard rock. However, the stability of the chalk was a doubtful factor, since the material did not split but crumbled. Accordingly, Simon decided that the ceiling and walls of the tunnel would have to be strengthened. This was done by creating an outer, 30-centimetre-thick wall of limestone. A 20-centimetre wide space between the surfaces was filled with stones.

The geological report also stated that the material above the tunnel had to be at least 30 metres thick to guarantee that the *Führerzug* would survive unscathed in the event of direct hits on the hillside. Only the central section of the tunnel had this much overhead cover. To avoid having to strengthen the entire tunnel ceiling with steel-reinforced concrete over 81 and 36 metres at the respective ends, Simon had two hinged doors of 4cm steel plate, each five by five metres in size, erected at the 40- and 35-metre points. These opened in one direction only and would be hooked back against the tunnel wall. The locomotive driver was required to position his train between the two doors, thus ensuring that it was favourably located for safety. The doors would be shut upon receipt of an air raid alarm for the area.

In the immediate vicinity of the north-eastern mouth of the tunnel, a large bunker with walls of four-metre-thick concrete was built for Hitler. The rooms followed the standard plan for FHQ *Führerbunker* of similar size. A general bunker with walls of similar thickness was erected for Hitler's entourage. Between the bunker entrances and interior was a gas sluice. The two bunkers had an aggregate floor space of 190 square metres and required 9,000 cubic metres of concrete in their manufacture.

It was planned to put up 7,000 square metres of barracks huts outside the tunnels as accommodation for the security force. Four anti-aircraft emplacements, protected by two-metre-high walls, were installed in open country. Brick-built, ready-use ammunition lockers were situated on either side of the access ramps.

On average, 1,200 OT workers were engaged in the construction of 'W 3'. In the main, French firms supplied the workforce and equipment.

After Müller inspected the foundation work on 13 October 1942, the labour force was increased to 2,500 for the three months from November 1942. in total, 400,000 working days were expended on the project between June 1942 and August 1943, representing a working day of 9½ hours (assuming Sunday to have been a free day).

The trunk lines from 'W 3' to the coast and to Paris were installed by *Feldschaltabteilung z.b.V. 2*, which had responsibility for France. Two multi-purpose underground cables were laid from Le Mans to Orléans and another from 'W 3' to Tours. By the end of 1942, the 70-kilometre-long stretch between 'W 3' and Le Mans and the 55-kilometre length between 'W 3' and Tours had been laid, and work on the stretch between 'W 3' and Orléans was proceeding apace in 1943. When building work was suspended at 'W 3' in August 1943, however, the site was linked alongside the French network at three points. The Paris–Orléans and Paris–Le Mans trunk circuits both continued into Germany, and connections from 'W 3' into the Reich network were guaranteed by cable along the same stretch.

Although it was reportedly Hitler's wish, having regard to the enormous quantities of concrete which were going into the building of the Atlantic Wall, that only one *Führerhauptquartier* should be established on French soil, the work on 'W 3' ran for almost a year in parallel with that for 'W 2'. That the origin of the orders to build FHQs was sometimes a mystery, and that what was 'in the pot' at any one time was not known for sure (even to Hitler), is amply demonstrated here. Hitler had said that there was to be only one FHQ on French territory. Before September 1942, OT head Xaver Dorsch had appointed Siegfried Schmelcher to design 'W 2' near Soissons, but who ordered Dorsch to proceed is not known. On 27 June 1942 *FHQu-Kommandant* Thomas had come to St-Rimay, the site of 'W 3', to carry out a survey. *Baurat* Simon of OT Operations Group West was appointed to head the project, and so one assumes that Thomas told him to go ahead. In September 1942, Speer wrote to Dorsch ordering him 'not to begin building a second FHQ establishment [in France] without my express permission . . .' From this, it is not clear if the first establishment was 'W2' or 'W 3', although it

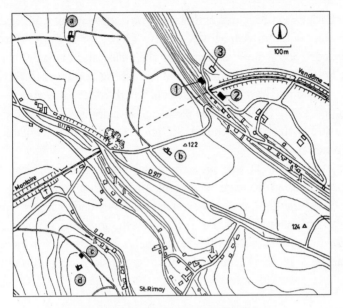

Sketchmap of 'W 3' (after Rhode and Sünkel):
1. Presumed Führerbunker; *2. General bunker for entourage;*
3. Bunker with removable roof; a–d. AA emplacements.

stands to reason that Speer was ignorant of work having actually already started on both.

On 25 October 1942, *Hauptmann* Engel, Hitler's *Heeresadjutant*, inspected 'W 2' and 'W 3' with Schmelcher and Müller, and so, presumably, Hitler either knew that there were two establishments under construction in France before that date or was not particularly interested in how many there were. In 1944, a third FHQ was being worked on in France, at Diedenhofen in Lorraine, and, although he knew about this one, he seems not to have briefed himself on its layout and structure. The answer to all this seems to be that at some time he must have more or less devolved responsibility for FHQ construction to a committee consisting of the *FHQu-Kommandant* and the four military *Adjutanten*. If Speer, not being a military man, was left out of the consultations, this would account for his bringing pressure on Dorsch through written instructions which betrayed his ignorance of the true situation.

On Hitler's express instructions, the interior walls of bunkers were to be clad with untreated wood only, 'since, for reasons of health, varnished wood is not conducive for the *Führer* and his staff.' It is not clear, however, whether the internal furnishing had reached the stage where 'W 3' could have been operational when work on it was suspended in August 1943. The telephone exchange had apparently not yet been completed at this time, although sufficient circuits were available into the French network.

Since the local OT management team, 'Atlas' , took over at 'W 3' immediately upon receiving news of the Allied landings on the Normandy coast on 6 June 1944, it can be inferred that they had orders to prepare the installation for Hitler's arrival. In the event, however, 'W 3' was never occupied as an FHQ: the Allies made such substantial territorial gains during the first month that Hitler would not risk placing himself so far west.

Chapter 7

Wasserburg and Olga: The New FHQs on the Russian Front, 1943

O N 18 November 1942, *Einsatzgruppe Nord der OT*, under the direction of architect Valjavec, began work at Pleskau in Estonia. FHQ Wasserburg was the command centre from which Hitler was proposing to direct Army Group North's offensive against Leningrad when the thaw came in 1943. The estate was situated on a south-facing bend of the River Welikaya, the principal building being a baronial mansion whose foundations went back to the eighth century. The mansion was enlarged and refurbished for Hitler's occupation. Adjacent to it was built the *Führerbunker*, a standard Type 102V (the so-called 'double-room

Double-room bunker Type 102V, Version B (after Gross).

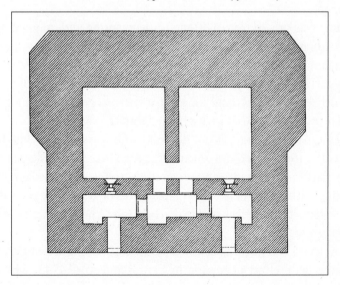

design' from the pre-war *Westwall* programme) fabricated from 900 cubic metres of concrete. Its ground base was 13.6 by 10.6 metres, providing an internal floor space of 42 square metres.

The mansion had a central tower which was converted into the officers' mess. Field staff not accommodated in the mansion or the farm buildings were allocated space in one of two *Luftwaffe* barracks huts, while the security force shared seven RAD huts. Living space at the mansion totalled 4,300 square metres, with 2,540 square metres in the huts, all of which was stove-heated: 135 such stoves were shipped in from the Eska ceramics firm in Munich, Hitler's stoves being distinguished by having a superior glaze. OT management saw to all furnishings, most of which came from Estonian suppliers. Coconut matting and curtains completed the decor.

On the foundations of an old building, OT erected a large garage, heated so that automobile engines would start in even the most severe winter temperatures. Pleskau power station supplied electricity over a high-tension grid to a newly built transformer station. Overhead wires from a ring cable delivered current to the various FHQ buildings. In all, 350 metres of cable, 5,000 metres of overhead wiring and 3,500 metres of domestic wiring was rigged. The *Wehrmacht* built the telephone/telex exchange.

Water was drawn from a 40-metre-deep spring and pumped into a tank feeding individual standpipes. The fire-hydrant system operated from a tank with a capacity of 300 cubic metres located below the main courtyard. There were two farms for the biological purification of sewage, for which 400 metres of domestic and 680 metres of external piping were laid. The purified water was discharged into the river.

At FHQ Wasserburg, OT put down 1.4 kilometres of gravel highway with a dust-free surface and repaired the road between Pleskau and the estate. Extensive clearance and restoration work was carried out in the adjoining parkland, where 800 square metres of grass were seeded and 1,800 metres of 'Flanders hedge' barbed-wire entanglements laid to strengthen security.

A total of 53,700 working days went into the building of FHQ Wasserburg, the main effort occurring in March and April 1943, when the workforce comprised 570 labourers. Ferdinand, *Prinz* von der Leyen, an officer on the OKH *Stab des Generalquartiermeisters*, described it thus:

> At Pleskau—Pskov in Russian—I saw one of the many absurdities of the age. On a piece of terrain enclosed by daunting wire fences, some old buildings had been converted into a fortress comparable to an Imperial stronghold of the Middle Ages. I was told it was for Hitler, so that he could stay there while touring his newly conquered provinces following 'final victory'. This was in 1943. I did not succeed in gaining entry to the huge, SS-guarded installation.

After the disaster at Stalingrad on 1 February 1943 and the retreat of the front to the Taganrog–Bielograd line, Hitler accepted the invitation of *Generalfeldmarschall* von Manstein to observe the German counter-offensive towards Donetz and Kharkov, as a result of which the *Wehrmacht* was hoping to regain the initiative on the Eastern Front. With a small entourage that included the new *Chef der Generalstabs des Heeres*, *General der Infanterie* Kurt Zeitzler, and Jodl, he flew from Wilhelmsdorf on 17 February to Saporoshie, where he was met at the airfield by von Manstein and von Richthofen. Hitler and his party were given lodgings in von Manstein's headquarters, an office building in the town.

At the situation conferences, Hitler could be persuaded only with difficulty that the recapture of the Donetz basin and the city of Kharkov, which he favoured, would be less decisive than securing the Dnieper crossings in the south. On 19 February 1943, he proclaimed to the troops of Army Group South and von Richthofen's *Luftflotte 4* that he was entrusting to their hands 'the fate of Germany's present and future'. With new weapons and new divisions, the advance of the Red Army would be stopped: 'I have therefore flown to you so as to explore all possibilities to lighten your defensive struggle and turn it at the end into victory.'

On the advice of von Manstein and von Richthofen, Hitler decided to shuttle back and forth from FHQ Wehrwolf because of the danger that Saporoshie airfield might be captured by a Soviet battle group. Even as his aircraft was taking off on 19 February, Hitler heard Russian artillery and the rattle of machine-gun fire from nearby Silsinikov.

On 22 February, Hitler flew from Wehrwolf to Wolfschanze, probably with the intention of attending the celebrations in Munich on the 24th to mark the founding of the NSDAP, but in the event he sent a message instead and returned to Wehrwolf on the 25th. Because of the worsening situation in North Africa, Rommel and Kesselring came under attack in the situation conferences. On 7 March, Speer discussed with Hitler his proposals to get 800,000 men of conscriptable age off the shop floor and into military service.

Generalfeldmarschall von Manstein had lived up to expectations and was honoured by a visit from Hitler at Saporoshie on 10 March, when he received the Oak Leaves to his Knight's Cross. That same day Rommel came to Wehrwolf to discuss the serious plight of the Axis in North Africa. Hitler awarded him the Diamonds to his Knight's Cross and sent him on sick leave. Göring also arrived on 10 March, from Rome, and spoke so optimistically of the situation in the Mediterranean and Tunisia that Hitler preferred Göring's version of affairs.

On 13 March, Hitler decided to return to Rastenburg. On the way he stopped at Army Group Centre at Krasnibor near Smolensk to deliver to von Kluge the orders for Operation 'Zitadelle', the Kursk offensive. After he had lunched in the *Kasino*, Baur flew him to Wilhelmsdorf in the Condor. A bomb had been placed in the fuselage of the aircraft by *Oberst* von Tresckow, *Erst Generalstabsoffizier* (Ia) of Army Group Centre, but since it was (apparently) ordained that no assassination attempt could ever succeed against Hitler, the chemical detonator failed to work.

At the insistence of his doctors, Hitler decided to take a three-month working holiday on the Obersalzberg, where he arrived on 22 March. He conferred with the leaders of Romania, Hungary, Slovakia and Croatia at Schloss Klessheim, Salzburg: the only visitor to the Berghof was the French President, Laval, on 29 April. In the presence of von Ribbentrop and the Italian Under-Secretary Bastianini, he demanded of France her support for the federated nations in the 'life and death battle' against the Allies. Until now, said Hitler, France had been handled 'with kid gloves'. To enable him to ask further sacrifices of his people, Laval required a joint German-Italian declaration as to the future of France, but both Hitler and Bastianini declined this. The German communiqué stated:

With full objectivity, the question was examined of what share France was expected to contribute to the effort and sacrifice which the Axis powers have taken upon themselves for the reconstruction of the new Europe in the struggle against Bolshevism and the Anglo-American plutocracy allied with it, and what benefits would materialise for France from her involvement.

Hitler spent his 54th birthday quietly at the Berghof. The Army presented him with a very expensive case decorated with infantry battle scenes in oil. Hitler was in Berlin for nineteen days from 2 May, returning to Obersalzberg on 21 May. Except for a conference with leading industrialists at the Platterhof, arranged by Speer on 2 June, he had few official engagements. In view of the worsening situation on the northern flank, on 30 June Schmundt ordered that work be halted at FHQ Wasserburg, Pleskau. The installation was by then almost finished, and so Army Group North occupied the site as its headquarters. Hitler never visited Wasserburg.

On 20 June 1943—a date when Hitler was not in residence at Wolfschanze, and from which one may again infer that Schmundt had powers of decision with regard to FHQ construction—OT *Oberbauleiter* Müller had preliminary conversations at Rastenburg with respect to a new site for an FHQ in Russia. On 27 June, Müller travelled to the location to examine the possibilities, and within a few days OT started work on a small headquarters codenamed 'Olga'. The plans envisaged a *Führerbunker*, some blockhouses and several barracks huts just off the main highway near Orsha in the Vitebsk area, about 200 kilometres north-east of Minsk.

The military logic of building an FHQ in the summer of 1943 in such a forward position is only comprehensible if one assumes, as one must, that Hitler believed he could hold the existing front line, which ran from east of Smolensk to Orel and Kharkov, and that his presence would be influential. He had placed great faith in the plan for 'Zitadelle', which opened on 5 July, and this probably explains it.

Following the unexpected US landings in Sicily on 10 July 1943, Hitler flew from Wolfschanze to Salzburg on the 18th, and after an overnight stay at the Berghof he continued to Treviso for a three-hour conference with Mussolini and his generals at San Fermo. All were of the opinion that Italy had shot her bolt and, at least knowing where he stood with them, Hitler returned to Wolfschanze on 20 July.

On 27 August Hitler made his last visit to Vinnitsa in the Ukraine. He was driven to FHQ Wehrwolf and there met von Manstein, who informed him of the pressing need to abandon the Donetz basin if Army Group South could not count on at least an additional twelve divisions. Hitler promised him 'all forces not otherwise engaged', the sum total of which was nil. By nightfall Hitler was back at Rastenburg.

After the recapture of Kharkov by the Soviet Army, on 8 September Hitler flew to Army Group South at Saporoshie for a conference with the commanders of Army Group South and Army Group A—von Manstein and von Kleist, respectively—and *Generaloberst* Ruoff of the Seventeenth Army. Hitler consented to a withdrawal of the right flank to the Melitopol–Dnieper line and promised to supply von Manstein with units equipped with the new self-propelled gun and with another four divisions to protect the Dnieper bridges. Upon his return to Rastenburg the same afternoon, he received news of the Italian capitulation.

In October, Hitler gave up FHQ Wehrwolf, leaving von Manstein to take it over as Army Group South headquarters. On 28 December 1943, Hitler ordered Wehrwolf to be dynamited. Another casualty of the Russian advance was FHQ Olga. By October 1943, German forces had been forced back to the Vitebsk–Lenino–Gomel–Kiev line. Hitler's bunker at Olga was incomplete when the programme was abandoned because of the military situation. By that time 400 cubic metres of concrete had been prepared and 3,599 square metres of blockhouses and wooden barracks had been erected.

Chapter 8

Improving Obersalzberg
and Wolfschanze, 1943

MARTIN Bormann, who before the war, in his capacity as *Stabsleiter der NSDAP* (head of the NSDAP Staff), had become indispensable to Hitler as his *Privatschatulle* (private treasurer) and administered the royalties from Hitler's book *Mein Kampf*, directed the building work on the Obersalzberg. Hitler's devoted and reliable servant, and executor of the *Führer*'s wishes, Bormann inveigled himself into a yet closer position after Hess flew to Britain. Appointed to succeed Hess as the '*Sekretär der Führers*' (*Führer*'s Secretary) in 1943, Bormann became ubiquitous. As Hitler's confidant, he interpreted his master's wishes and instructions at his own discretion, dabbled in inner-political affairs and attempted to subjugate the *Wehrmacht* to the dictats of the NSDAP. He exercised considerable influence on the mobilisation of the *Heimatfront* (Home Front), in which the *Volkssturm* was to be the Party's army in the 'final struggle'.

Bormann had the *Reichskasse* (Exchequer) reimburse the cost of his own stays and those of his Party co-workers at the various FHQs. On 22 November 1939 he indented for 118,505 *Reichsmark* for the Polish campaign. *Reichsminister* Lammers rejected the demand because it was not accompanied by receipts as required by the Reich budget ordinances, but Bormann refused to account for how the sum was arrived at: it had to do with payments for flights, the vehicles attached to the *Kraftwagenkolonne* (motorcade), expanding the car parking facilities, motor repairs and hotels—things like that. Lammers gave in and referred the demand to the *Parteikanzlei* (Party Chancellery) central account at the Commerz-Bank A. G., Munich, for payment. Much encouraged by this success, throughout the war Bormann continued to make demands upon the

Reichskasse: on 6 December 1940, for example, for 356,359 *Reichsmark*, and on 31 October 1941 for 261,465. By 20 August 1942 he had obtained 1,800,000 *Reichsmark* from the *Reichskasse* by this means. When the last account rendered was settled on 19 February 1945, Bormann had acquired 5.4 million *Reichsmark* on his personal assurance and never once did he supply a receipt. He had become bolder as time went on: on 21 November 1944, for example, he was paid 582,939 *Reichsmark* for 'new cars' and 103,420 *Reichsmark* in respect of 'transport costs for paintings etc.' It is not suggested that these funds went into his own pocket, but rather that he viewed his work as a labour of love and invested most of the money in expanding the NSDAP properties on the Obersalzberg. Himmler, by comparison, limited his demands for reimbursement solely to personnel aboard the SS *Sonderzüge Heinrich* and *Steiermark*, and he also supplied receipts or proper invoices. There must have been a strict regime in force aboard these trains, for the *Reichskasse* paid out huge sums for juices and fruits from the warmer south, especially citrus. By 10 February 1945 the accounts settled totalled 1,900,000 *Reichsmark*.

Some of the major projects realised on the Obersalzberg during the war under Bormann's direction included:

1. The completion of the Platterhof. The interior furbishment of the hotel was to the design of Professor Michaelis. The decoration in every room was technically perfect. Despite the shortage of metals in the armaments industry, no effort was spared with regard to brass and chrome fittings. In a separate building nearby were flats for about 160 hotel employees. On the completion of the enterprise, the building workers acknowledged that this was no '*Volksgasthaus*' (Peoples' Guest House) but a full-blown luxury hotel for the Party bosses. Guests would be expected to pay five *Reichsmark* a night and more, which in those days was expensive. The reception hall at the Platterhof, to give it its official title—Hitler would not permit the term '*Hotel*' to be used—was refitted on several occasions because its appearance did not conform to the image in Bormann's mind.

2. The *Bechsteinhaus* on the Obersalzbergstrasse was converted and modernised.

3. The great eyesore of the huge *Koksbunker* (coke bunker) was erected on an exposed site just outside the main complex on the road between the Platterhof and Klaushohe settlement. It occupied a ground area of 1,064 square metres and was fourteen metres high. Several hundred Italian experts had been called in and had built it over a six-month period in 1940. The structure was concrete with a cladding of stonework: its capacity was 1,500 tonnes of coke, loaded through eight chutes. Once it had been officially declared open, a flow of hundreds of lorries each made the journey to deliver a load of several tonnes. When Bormann came to inspect it he noticed that the masonry joints appeared a little irregular, and he had the entire façade removed. The replacement work took a year. The cost of this coke bunker was 770,000 *Reichsmark*.

4. The construction of dwellings for Obersalzberg personnel. After the completion of the giant parking place on the street between Oberau and the Platterhof, for which thousands of cubic metres of earth had had to be removed, the Klaushohe settlement was begun in 1941 to plans by Professor Fick. It consisted of four rows of six houses each, for two or three families. On completion, the buildings were occupied by administration employees. The large Buchenhohe settlement was begun in 1942 to plans by Professor Hermann Giesler. Both these estates were designated 'important for the war effort', and the 1941 blueprints were accordingly stamped '*Geheim*' (Secret).

5. The construction of air-raid bunkers from August 1943. The project leader was *SS-Obersturmbannführer* Dr Hoehne of the *SS-Wehrgeologen-Bataillon* (Military Geology Battalion). The first gallery system, of 745 square metres, was below the Berghof and included a bunker labyrinth of about 275 square metres for the Bormann household. Other subterranean galleries were built for the Göring household, the guests at the Platterhof, the troops of the SS barracks, the families on the Klaushohe and Buchenhohe settlements and the farm. There was another air-raid cellar, 'Antenberg', for the occupants of the barracks camp. The galleries extended for 2.7 kilometres and, with the exception of those between Göring's and Bormann's

bunkers, were linked together. Steps led about 40 metres down from individual buildings into the underground caverns.

When it became known that Hitler might be spending Christmas 1943 on the Obersalzberg, Bormann pressurised the builders into completing the 130-metre long Berghof gallery within only eight weeks. Hitler never found the time even to look it over. To support the building firms in their endeavours, a 110-strong *Waffen-SS Stollenbaukompanie* (gallery construction company) and an additional 100 Italian civilian labourers were drafted in. Five tipper trucks were made available by the *SS-Führungshauptamt* from the lorry depot at Oranienburg to remove the spoil. Even Himmler became personally involved in the progress of the work when, in his *Tagesbefehl* (Order of the Day) of 18 July 1943 he wrote:

> I expect that each one of you, wholeheartedly setting aside his personal pleasures, will devote his free time to the common task at the Obersalzberg together with the building experts and our *Stollenbaukompanie*. It is for us SS men a joyful duty to be able to build the air-raid cellars on the Obersalzberg.

Himmler had the *Baukommando* 'Obersalzberg' inform him daily by telex as to how the work was coming along. Immediately after the completion of the *Führerbunker*—during his last stay on the Obersalzberg in the summer of 1944, when Hitler had begun to experience some difficulty negotiating steps, work was started on a lift from the Berghof down to the bunker, but never finished—the great underground expansion began.

Most of the galleries were round-arched, 1.75 metres across and 2.5 metres high. The approaches were strongly fortified with rounded steel, the entrances concealed by a thin layer of earth and masonry. Fifty metres down the passageway was a steel-reinforced concrete block covering the gallery beyond. This had a dual purpose: it contained a machine-gun nest to protect the entrance against commando attack and was designed to absorb and reflect bomb blasts. The footway skirted the block and, after passing through a gas-sluice, descended a flight of stairs to arrive at caverns to the right and left of the corridor. Here the minimum overhead cover was at least 40 metres. The caverns, dynamited from the rock at right angles to the passage, were 3.5 metres wide, 2.8 metres at the highest point and generally up to 15 metres long. Each gallery system had tunnels leading to emergency exits with steel doors. Below the main gallery ran a conduit containing wires, piping and cables for the water supply, lighting, heating, air-conditioning and sewage disposal.

Since the Obersalzberg is permeated by many water-bearing veins, the subterranean galleries required damp-proofing. A dressing of *papier-mâché* and rubber strips isolated the rock-wall, coated with a 30–60cm layer of concrete, from the 25cm thick wall tiling. Filters in the concrete underlayer led the water off into channels below.

By the war's end, 5,000 metres of galleries had been bored into the rock, of which 2,000 metres involving 75 caverns and another 4,000 square metres of floor were habitable. Below the Berghof and Platterhof hotel alone there were 745 square metres of caverns, for which almost 60,000 cubic metres of rock had been excavated in haste and under the most difficult conditions.

The caverns were partitioned off into living and storage spaces and the ablutions. To prevent water dripping in, the partition walls were of special filtering bricks plugged with rubber. The gallery walls were painted white. With the exception of those prepared for Hitler and Eva Braun, the bunker rooms were unfurnished. The kitchens and toilets had floor tiles, the bedrooms and living rooms were parquet-floored or carpeted, the walls were panelled in wood and the doors and frames were painted and varnished. All rooms had built-in cupboards, wall-lighting and wireless, 'to supply visitors with music and the latest news bulletins'. The *SS-Rohstoffamt* (Raw Materials Office) supplied the cabling. Endless special requests for air-conditioning, more storage space, dressing rooms and extra sanitary installations prolonged the work. The Bormanns had so much food hoarded in their 275-square-metre bunker in 1944 that a nutrition expert calculated they could have survived into the 1950s without ever seeing the light of day. If anybody rang, a family member could have taken the call on any one of Bormann's 800 separate telephone extensions.

During the war there was an average workforce of 3,000 on the Obersalzberg, lodged near the construction sites in camps of wooden barracks huts, eighteen to a room. German workers and members of the foreign contractual labour force received wages according to a set tariff plus an 'Obersalzbergzulage' (Obersalzberg Supplement) of 50 *pfennig* a day and one Reichsmark a day '*Trennungszulage*' (Separation Allowance) for married men whose families lived outside the area. German workers were allowed one weekend's home leave each month. All workers were fed in the camp canteens, where, irrespective of whether they were contracted to civilian firms or working for the SS, they were provided with the *Verpflegungssatz III* (Grade III) ration of 650 grams of bread daily (reduced to 600 grams from 1 October) and 640 grams of fish weekly. Two SS doctors ran the medical practice.

In July 1943 the anti-aircraft defences on Obersalzberg were augmented by further guns and a smoke-making installation. In a *Tagesbefehl* dated 18 July 1943, Himmler had exhorted *Flak* and smoke crews to be 'tirelessly alert by night and day.' There were now sixty guns sited on various favourable heights—twelve 10.5cm, sixteen 8.8cm, twenty-four 3.7cm, six 2cm and a pair of 2cm *Flakvierlinge*, one on the Rossfeld and the other on Ahornkaser. The Kehlstein was left clear on Bormann's orders, 'since the *Führer* likes very much to walk there and the *Flak* would spoil it all'. Even so, it was used to store the barrels of acid for the smoke installations.

The *Führerflugmeldezentrale* (Air Raid Centre) was 30 metres below the Goringhugel rock. It was linked to the national system and had a wall map equipped with numerous electrical circuits which lit up to show 'real-time' enemy air movements over the Reich. If aircraft approached to within 100 kilometres, the air-raid alarm went off. Since a paratroop drop was also considered a possibility, on the roof of the produce warehouse an observation bunker had been erected, from where aerials and a scissors-type artillery binoculars could be deployed.

Hitler spent only four days at the Berghof in the last six months of 1943. In September that year, he decided to tighten up security at FHQ Wolfschanze and ordered the creation of a new restricted area, concentric within *Sperrkreis I*. Partitioned off by high wire fencing, *Sperrkreis A* would embrace the *Führerbunker*, Keitel's bunker and wooden hut, the personal *Adjutantur*, *Kasino I* (Officers' Mess I), the *Teehaus*, Bormann's buildings, small sections of Schmundt's *Heerespersonalamt* (which also served as a storehouse) and the *Wehrmachtadjutantur*. A new kind of identity card would be required for visitors, and only the cars of the *Reichsminister*, *NSDAP-Reichsleiter* and field marshals would be allowed entry. The three gates to *Sperrkreis A* were each manned by an *Unteroffizier* of the *Führer-Begleitbataillon* and an RSD official. On a normal day, Hitler would now only leave *Sperrkreis A* for the daily situation conferences. Every morning before breakfast he received a short situation report in the *Kartenraum* (Map Room). The communal breakfast in *Kasino A* frequently lasted over an hour because Hitler, who always sat at table facing a large wall map of the Soviet Union, would hold forth about Russia and Bolshevism.

The main situation conference took place at about 1300. Jodl and the Chief of the Army General Staff would make their reports, after which the discussion would begin. Once the conference had finished—and this was frequently well into the afternoon—lunch would be taken in the *Kasino I* bunker at a table for twenty. At 1700 Hitler would take tea or coffee with his female secretaries. At 1900 his inner circle would meet for dinner with a handful of invited guests, retiring afterwards to the *Führer*'s study, where there was a round table before the open grate. This group would often be composed of the two female secretaries, one personal and one military *Adjutant*, a doctor, and Bormann with his adjutant Dr Henry Picker, a stenographer appointed to take down Hitler's monologues for Bormann's information. After the war these notes were published in several volumes.

The full text of the new security order is given below:*

Führer HQ, 20 September 1943

1. *Sperrkreis A* is newly created within *Sperrkreis I*. The new regulation comes into effect at 1700 on 22 September 1943.

2. The following houses belong within *Sperrkreis A*: *Generalfeldmarschall* Keitel; the *Führer*'s personal adjutants; *Kasino I* and *Teehaus*; the *Führer*; *Reichsleiter* Bormann; *Heerespersonalamt* etc.

* Institut fur Zeitgeschichte, Munich, MA 163-43.

3. *Sperrkreis A* has been set up on the basis of an instruction by the *Führer*. The *Führer* has ordered: All steps are to be taken to ensure that events, intentions, conversations etc. held in his presence or that of his immediate circle at FHQ are kept secret. The *Führer* has ordered that any person who speaks to another person of a matter which is secret and must not be divulged is to be reported to him for disciplinary action. Secrecy and the safety of the *Führer*'s person are the factors behind the creation of *Sperrkreis A*.

4. The *Führer*'s orders may bring about stringent measures which mean hardship to this or that party. However, personal wishes must be subordinated to the need for increased security and secrecy.

5. The circle of persons rightfully in *Sperrkreis A* are those having duty with the *Führer* but not their aides. This rule does not apply to those persons resident in *Sperrkreis A*.

6. It is most vital that visitor traffic in the *Sperrkreise* is restricted. However, some visits to *Sperrkreis I* command centres for conferences as well as courier traffic are unavoidable and the creation of *Sperrkreis A* will serve the purpose of limiting visitor movement.

7. Persons resident in *Sperrkreis A*, or resident outside it but whose duties will bring them continually into *Sperrkreis A*, will be issued with a long-term pass bearing the holder's photographic likeness. Other long-term passes for *Sperrkreis A* will be issued by the *FHQu-Kommandant* only with the approval of the *Chefadjutant der Wehrmacht* to the *Führer* or his deputy and in agreement with *SS-Obergruppenführer* Schaub and his deputy. The passes valid hitherto will be withdrawn.

8. A day pass for *Sperrkreis A* may only be issued by the guardroom if previously authorised by a personal or military *Adjutant* to the *Führer*. Corresponding requests must be made in good time to permanent *Adjutanten*. No person may enter *Sperrkreis A* without a pass, not even in company with another person who holds a valid pass. Only those RSD officials on gate duty are authorised in exceptional cases to admit a person to *Sperrkreis A* without a pass; however ,they must always accompany that person. The official must bring the visitor to his destination to confirm the right of entry. The duplicate pass must then be issued and worn, or the visitor escorted by the RSD official back to the gate. No person must be alone in *Sperrkreis A* without a pass. Officials and sentries have instructions that in the event of such an occurrence, the person concerned is to be directed out of the *Sperrkreis* or arrested. The requirements for *Sperrkreis I* remain in force as per instructions issued on 9 September 1943.

9. Motor traffic in *Sperrkreis A* is to be discouraged as much as possible. Parking in *Sperrkreis A* is forbidden. Only the cars of the *Reichsaussenminister*, *Reichsleiter*

IMPROVING WOLFSCHANZE AND OBERSALZBERG, 1943

and field marshals may enter. These persons and anybody accompanying them must be in possession of a valid pass and produce it for inspection whenever requested to do so. All other persons must leave their vehicles at the gate, excepting officers resident in *Sperrkreis A* and those driving delivery vehicles.

10. Foot traffic to command centres: *Chef OKW, Adj. der Wehrm. B. Führer*, HPA, Admiral Voss, General Scherff and WNO must enter by Gate IIIA, vehicles by Gate IIA. Foot traffic to the *Parteikanzlei*, to the personal *Adjutantur* and the kitchens enter by Gate IA.

11. Couriers must not enter *Sperrkreis A*. Couriered material is to be delivered to an agreed place for immediate collection by the command centre in *Sperrkreis A*.

12. The entry gates to *Sperrkreis A* (Gate IA at Bunker 12, Gate IIA at the *Reichsmarschall's* house, Gate IIIA between Houses 7 and 77) are each manned by an *Unteroffizier* of the *Führer-Grenadierbataillon* and an RSD official. The duty of the *Unteroffizier* is to check the pass of all persons requiring entry. He may not allow any person to enter without a pass, except where the RSD sentry accompanies the visitor personally into *Sperrkreis A*. The passes of persons leaving the *Sperrkreis* are to be examined with the same attention to detail as those entering. In the event of any irregularity being detected, the visitor is to be brought to the guardhouse by the RSD sentry or the guard sent for.

13. *Sperrkreis A* will be constantly patrolled by one RSD official, who has the duty to monitor all persons and to escort unauthorised persons out of the *Sperrkreis*.

14. The same soldiers are always to be appointed as messengers for Press and telex and issued with the appropriate pass.

15. By order of the *Führer*, the circle of persons dining in *Kasino I Speiseraum I* (Dining Hall I of Officers' Mess I) is his closest entourage. (See attached list.)* Guests additional to this list and for meals at the *Teehaus* will receive invitations from *Obergruppenführer* Schaub or *Generalleutnant* Schmundt, or their respective deputies, only at the request of the *Führer*. Applications are to be submitted in good time.

16. All persons from outside who have been ordered into the presence of the *Führer* or to a command centre within *Sperrkreis A* must await their summons in *Sperrkreis I* and *Kasino II*, where they will be treated as guests of the *Führer*.

[Signed] Albert Bormann, *NSKK-Gruppenführer*
[Signed] Schmundt, *Generalleutnant*

---

* This list bears 38 names and is not included here.

It may be pure coincidence that this strange order was issued on 20 September 1943, just five days after a meeting between *Rüstungsminister* Speer, *Leiter der OT* Xaver Dorsch and *Oberbauleiter* Müller in the OT offices at Moysee, not far from FHQ Wolfschanze, on 15 September. What was discussed was the plan for the greatest FHQ of all—'Riese' (Giant), in Lower Silesia. What exactly its true purpose was, and what went on there, remains a secret to this day.

Chapter 9

Allied Invasion
and Bomb Plot, 1944

ITLER'S last stay on the Obersalzberg lasted almost five months. After addressing the Party *Alte Kämpfer* (old warriors) in Munich on 23 February 1944, he braved the snow to arrive at the Berghof next day. During the ensuing period he received six State guests at Schloss Klessheim near Salzburg, but he entertained General Oshima, the Japanese ambassador, at the Berghof for just over an hour on the afternoon of 27 May with talk of his preparations for the expected Allied landings in France, speaking confidently also of the prospects in the East. Oshima confessed that Japan had underestimated the industrial power of the United States and knew 'that they would have to beat the Americans on their own'. Apart from the official excursions to Schloss Klessheim, Hitler left the Berghof only for walks, weapons exhibitions and funerals.

In addition to 'W 2' and 'W 3' in France to counter the expected Allied landings, a third installation came into existence early in 1944. It lay north-west of Diederhofen in Lorraine, near Angevillers/Arzweiler. and was possibly planned after German intelligence had been misled by the Allies into believing in the possibility of landings in the Pas de Calais. In collaboration with Hitler's *Wehrmacht* ADCs, on 18 March 1944 *Oberbauleiter* Müller selected a number of Maginot Line tunnels for restoration. After discussing his ideas with Hitler's *Luftwaffenadjutant*, *Oberstleutnant* von Below, and *Generalmajor* Niemeyer on 28 March and 7 April, and with Niemeyer separately on 24 March, he ordered OT to reopen three sections of the underground fortress.

It would appear that 1,300 square metres of wooden huts were erected in the open, together with two surface bunkers, one manifesting striking similarities to the *Führerbunker* at 'W 2' but with an air-raid cellar in place of the front annexe. Below ground, 15,300 square metres of galleries were to be reopened, 6,200 being allocated to FHQ, 5,500 to the OKH and 3,600 to the *Reichsführer-SS*. There was no space here for von Ribbentrop. The concept of the partially mobile FHQ had evidently been resurrected, since arrangements were being made to shelter nine *Sonderzüge* in the Metz area, mostly in the St Hubert tunnel, with another eight across the Saar-Pfalz. Connecting only some of these tunnels into the *Wehrmacht* command telephone system would have necessitated extensive work involving junction boxes and lines by the *Reichspost* and signals troops at a time when their normal duties stretched resources to the limit.

On 12 April Hanna Reitsch piloted Müller, Niemeyer and von Below from Salzburg to Diedenhofen in a Dornier 217 bomber. By this time the decaying Maginot Line galleries had been cleaned, freshly painted and wired for light so that the magazine rooms were ready for dividing up. Müller recalled that they were 30 metres below ground and were reached by a passageway which led down at an oblique angle. A narrow-gauge freight railway penetrated about a kilometre into the interior of the installation. The forward casemate had already been sectioned off into rooms, the largest of which was converted into a store. The floors were painted red because no other colour was available.

On 17 April 1944, Hitler attended the State funeral in Munich of Adolf Wagner, *Gauleiter* of Munich and Lower Bavaria. He celebrated his last birthday in daylight on 20 April at the Berghof, where Keitel, Dönitz, Milch and Himmler conveyed the congratulations of the four *Wehrmacht* arms of service. That afternoon he decorated *Generaloberst* Hans Hube, who had led the First Panzer Army out of the Kamenez-Podolsk cauldron, as the twelfth recipient of the Swords and Diamonds to the Knight's Cross with Oak Leaves. The next day Hube was killed when his aircraft crashed on take-off near Salzburg; his funeral was held at the *Reichskanzlei* on 26 April. On 3 June, the marriage of *SS-Gruppenführer* Fegelein, *Verbin-dungsoffizier der SS* (SS Liaison Officer) to Hitler, to the sister of Eva Braun was celebrated at the Berghof.

The most important event to confront Hitler during his stay at the Berghof was the Allied landings in Normandy on 6 June 1944. The first reports came in at 0300. Towards 0600, *Generalfeldmarschall* von Rundstedt, *Oberbefehlshaber West* (*OB West*, or C-in-C West), requested the mobilisation of the OKW Reserve, consisting of four motorised/armoured divisions. No decision had been taken by midday when Hitler set off for Schloss Klessheim at Salzburg for the State visit of the Hungarian Prime Minister. To demonstrate that no immediate threat existed, Jodl, with Hitler's approval, went next day on a five-day inspection tour of German installations in the Apennines. Thus Hitler underestimated for a full week the danger which these landings represented.

Work on FHQ Zigeuner, also known as Brunhilde, resumed as soon as news was received of the Allied invasion. The same day, Schmundt, Niemeyer and von Below went with Sander, *Leitend Fernmeldeoffizier des FHQu* (Senior FHQ Telephone Communications Officer) and *Generalmajor* Josef Wolf, Commander of the *Führer-Nachtrichtenabteilung*, to inspect the installation. Up to 2,300 OT workers were engaged on the site. *Oberbauleiter* Müller remained at Diedenhofen from 18 June to 21 August to make sure that the work progressed expeditiously. and the headquarters was declared 'in general, ready for occupation' by the end of August. The telephone and telex system, which was about the same size and to the same technically advanced standard as that at FHQ Wolfschanze, was also operational by then.

Eleven days after the Allies' invasion of Normandy, Hitler used 'W 2' at Margival as his base for a visit to the front. On 16 June his pilot, Hans Baur, flew him from Salzburg to Metz in an Focke-Wulf Condor with an escort of three fighters. For the duration of the flight, all German anti-aircraft guns fell silent and all *Luftwaffe* aerial activity fell away. From Metz. Hitler was driven the following day to Margival, escorted by the *Führer-Begleitbataillon* below an umbrella of fighter aircraft. His entourage included Jodl and Schmundt. In the *Teehaus* at 'W 2', Hitler met von Rundstedt and Rommel, C-in-C Army Group B, and their respective *Generalstabschefs*, *General der Infanterie* Blumentritt and *Generalmajor* Speidel. The situation conference lasted from 0900 until 1600 in the annexe to the *Führerbunker* and was interrupted repeatedly by warnings of enemy aircraft, so that the party spent a good deal of time in the bunker itself.

Here Hitler sat on a footstool, toying nervously with his spectacles and pencils while the officers stood before him.

Because of the Allies' air superiority in 1944, considerable efforts had been devoted to upgrading the anti-aircraft defences at 'W 2'. The number of guns had been increased, emplacements and command posts had been reinforced and splinter shielding had been introduced for the gunners and fire-direction personnel and around ready-ammunition lockers. These measures were not generally in force elsewhere, not even at Wolfschanze where the inadequate 2cm *Flak* atop the main bunkers had no protection at all. The initial reaction at Wolfschanze had been to encase the bunkers with more concrete, but the ultimate solution, as carried out at FHQ Riese, was to situate everything at least 30 metres below ground and leave the AA batteries in the open.

The problem facing the *Wehrmacht* in Normandy on 17 June 1944 was that the Allies were threatening to break through the German front at Caen, either side of the Bayeux highway and at St-Lô. Hitler expressed his displeasure at the continual retreating and ordered his generals to hold Cherbourg at all costs. Rommel reacted by saying that operations ordered from a desk were based on considerations which differed from those prevailing at the front. He gave voice to his fears that the German fronts in Italy and Normandy could not be held and that the Allies might soon set foot on German soil. For that reason, he considered it advisable to end the war before Germany was totally isolated. Hitler ordered him 'not to interfere in politics' and 'to worry himself about the Normandy front and nothing else'. Lunch in the *Teehaus* was 'a stew with his very closest circle', from which one infers that Hitler dined with Schmundt. Two SS men employed as tasters stood guarding his back throughout the meal.

The *Kommandierender General* (Commanding General) of LXV Army Corps, *Generalleutnant* Erich Heinemann, then responsible for the V-weapons campaign, reported to 'W 2' with *Oberst* Wachtel, *Kommandeur des Flakregiments 155(W)*, for the midday situation conference. and afterwards both received Hitler's best wishes for the V-1 flying-bomb offensive against Britain, which had begun on 12 June with mixed results.

Hitler was due to visit Rommel's Army Group B at La Roche-Guyon on the Lower Seine on 19 June, but he returned to the Berghof the day previously on an excuse. On 29 June at Obersalzberg, at a conference with Göring, Guderian, von Rundstedt, Rommel and Sperrle, *Oberbefehls-haber Luftflotte 3* (C-in-C Air Fleet 3), the last three made their opinions known that further resistance to the Allied armies was useless. This resulted in the eventual replacement of von Rundstedt and Sperrle, while Rommel dug his own grave. On 14 July, Hitler left the Berghof for the last time. At Wolfschanze he intended to direct the Eastern campaign following the collapse of Army Group Centre. Six days later would come the attempt on his life there.

On 16 August 1944, the battle headquarters of *Generalfeldmarschall* Model was the *château* at La Roche-Guyon. On 19 August when forced to evacuate by the US First Army, Model withdrew to 'W 2' for nine days. Under pressure from the US 3rd Armored Division on 28 August, he summoned *V. Panzerkorps* to demolish the installation after his depart-ure. This unit had been cut off, and *II. SS-Panzerkorps*, which had orders to recapture Margival, considered the chances of doing so to be hopeless. Accordingly, 'W 2' was in immaculate condition when occupied by the Americans the following day.

Work at Diedenhofen was abandoned on 21 September 1944 at the request of *General der Panzertruppe* Balck, commander of Army Group G. As a result, 322,500 working days and 2,300 cubic metres of concrete had gone to waste.

The extent to which Hitler had been informed about FHQ Dieden-hofen, or indeed whether he had even approved it, is unknown. Since, at the situation conference of 31 July 1944, he had requested the immediate construction of a new FHQ in the West that would be 'not too far away, preferably in the Vosges', it can be construed from his response to von Below's mention of Diedenhofen that he knew of it, if nothing much about it. The actual conversation was reported by Heiber thus:

HITLER: It is essential to secure immediately a headquarters that is not too far away, preferably in the Vosges; if that is not possible, in the Black Forest. But best of all would be in the Vosges.

171

BELOW: The one near Diedenhofen [FHQ Brunhilde] is ready.

HITLER: Is that more or less safe against modern bombs?

BELOW: I don't think it would be safe against the six-tonners.

HITLER: Neither do I. Is it camouflaged so that nobody can see it?

BELOW: It's not visible from above; it is completely below ground. They are the old Maginot Line fortresses which can't be seen from above.

HITLER: Can't you just show me some photos?

JODL: One would have to take whatever was available. There is no time to build anything else.

HITLER: I would just like to have a look at the file then.

It is interesting to note that, at the time of this conversation, aside from Diedenhofen, there were two other FHQ establishments considered immediately ready for occupation near the western border. Adlerhorst was ready, except that it was not wired into the *Wehrmacht* telephone network, and Felsennest, at Rodert near Munstereiffel, was in all respects ready. After Hitler left FHQ Felsennest during the French campaign in 1940, it had been taken over by *VI. Armeekorps* on 11 June, and following negotiations later that year it passed to the NSDAP on 31 January 1941 in deference to Hitler's wish that the historic site be converted into a national memorial park so that future generations might see it as a place symbolic of the *Wehrmacht*'s invincibility.

In the spring of 1944, Jodl and Schmundt addressed Hitler on the subject of their deliberations regarding how an attack on FHQ Wolf-schanze might be repulsed. They were working on the hypothesis that two or three divisions of Allied paratroopers would land in the Rasten-burg area. After explaining it all to Hitler, they received his permission to bring Wolfschanze to a state of maximum readiness and set up three concentric defensive rings—the outer perimeter, the perimeter of *Sperr-kreis I* and *II*, and at the centre *Sperrkreis A*. The primary objective was to draw in the outer perimeter. However, no steps appear to have been taken in this direction during July 1944, although on the 14th Hitler discussed with Himmler the possibility of paratroop attacks against Wolfschanze.

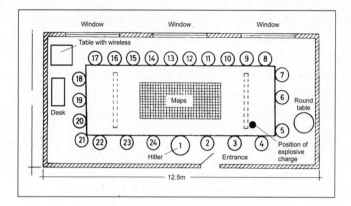

*Occupation of the barracks hut at the time of
the assassination attempt on Hitler, 20 July 1944.*

Once the possibility of bombing raids on FHQs could no longer be ruled out, Hitler became so concerned for the safety of his own person and the protection of the telephone system that on 20 June he ordered the construction of a telecommunications bunker, Annabu, and a general air-raid shelter to be built for the OKH at Mauerwald. For the desired improvements to his own bunker, he made a sketch.

His living space was 2.8 by 3.5 metres. The exterior walls and ceiling were of concrete three metres thick. He wanted a second, outer concrete 'jacket' 3.5 metres thick, and between the two concrete walls a 50cm layer of sand to absorb blast and prevent the penetration of armour-piercing bombs. No bomb of the time could have seriously damaged such an extraordinary structure. Conversion work began at once.

July 20 was a hot summer's day at FHQ Wolfschanze, and the midday conference was held in the *Lagebaracke* (Situation Hut) at 1230, half an hour earlier than usual because Mussolini was expected during the afternoon. The building was wooden, 25 by 5 metres in area, but, despite its name, it was not used regularly for situation conferences. However, as explained, Hitler's bunker was undergoing modification, and the guests' barracks hut was too small to accommodate an assembly of 24 officers.

The explosive charge planted by *Oberst Graf* von Stauffenberg detonated at 1244, killing four persons, including Schmundt, and seriously injuring seven others. The hut was wrecked. It had a protective outer wall of concrete-reinforced brick, but the blast smashed down the end walls and dissipated. Hitler received relatively light injuries—ruptured ear drums and nerve damage to his left arm—but was well enough to receive Mussolini at 1530. Interpreter Schmidt's note of the encounter opens:

> At the beginning of the talk the *Duce* congratulated the *Führer* with heartfelt words on his survival of the bomb attempt. The *Duce* was deeply moved upon hearing the details related to him by the *Führer* concerning the train of events surrounding the assassination attempt. He interpreted the *Führer*'s escape as a clear indication of the intervention of the Almighty. It was certain that anybody who always miraculously survived the assassination attempts of his enemies must also be led to a victorious finale in the current conflict.

Hitler showered his guest with reams of armaments statistics in order to impress upon him that the current military crisis was merely a temporary setback. He hinted at fantastic new weapons to hearten Mussolini. When the former Italian dictator bade farewell at Wolfschanze that day, however, it would be for the last time.

In a radio broadcast on 20 July, Hitler asserted that the attempt on his life had been plotted 'by a quite small clique of ambitious, unscrupulous and at the same time stupid officers'. This 'quite small clique', however, included at least 4,000 persons subsequently judged and executed for complicity of one kind or another in the plot.

In deference to the anti-paratroop plan drawn up by Jodl and the now deceased Schmundt, by 1 August 1944 the *Luftwaffe* had evacuated its most easterly command posts at Niedersee and Goldap for Bartenstein, 40 kilometres north-west of Rastenburg, although between 20 August and 15 November, when they abandoned Wolfschanze for Potsdam, they lodged at Rosengarten, north-east of FHQ. Göring's *Sonderzug*, *Robinson*, was also gradually withdrawn westwards. Göring himself placed little faith in defensive plans of this kind, although in the autumn of 1944 he did form a *Volkssturmbataillon*, 'Lubsin', to protect the Rominter Heide, where one of his many residences, the Reichsjägerhof, was located. According to a *Generalstab* report of 26 October 1944, the estate master was left as the sole custodian of the property, and he put it to the torch on the 20th of the month to deny it to the advancing Soviets.

The assassination attempt of 20 July was a shattering blow to the *Führer-Begleitbataillon* and cast in doubt its ability to protect FHQs effectively. Whether it was responsible for checking officers' attaché cases and car boots at the *Sperrkreis* gates is not known. The immediate transfer of elements of the *SS-Leibstandarte* into Wolfschanze, apparently initiated by Himmler with the object of ridding FHQ of the Army element altogether, was only a short-lived measure: not until the Ardennes offensive did he manage to introduce a permanent company of the *Leib-standarte—Sonderkommando A*—to protect FHQ Adlerhorst, ordering at the same time that non-SS men seconded to the protection of Hitler were to be vetted for political reliability by the RSHA first.

The general deterioration of the prospects in the East and the collapse of Army Group Centre made it appear advisable to set up an active defence force at Rastenburg. The first measure was to split the Army command structure at FHQ into two. Accordingly, on 1 September 1944, *Oberst* Otto-Ernst Remer, who, as *Kommandeur des Berliner Wachbataillons*, had played a significant role in helping to put down the attempted *putsch* of 20 July, was made '*Kampfkommandant des Führerhauptquartiers*' (*Führer* HQ Battle Commandant). He thus assumed responsibility for internal and external security at Wolfschanze. *Oberst* Streve, the successor to *Oberst* Thomas, was relegated to '*Lagerkommandant*', an administrative and logistical role.*

In the middle of 1943, the *Führer-Begleitbataillon* was still exclusively a security unit, but a change of title to *Führer-Grenadierbataillon* in about September that year hints that it was beginning to be seen more as a fighting organisation. Only *7. Kompanie*, with its motorcycle combinations and scout cars, continued the tradition of the escort role the earlier group had enjoyed. After the July Bomb Plot, the *Bataillon* grew to the size of a regiment, and, unless it was being considered for the anti-paratroop defences, it is not easy to understand why it was the subject of such a dramatic reformation.

* Aside from technical troops, the only security units remaining under the control of the *Lagerkommandant* were the special forces at eight FHQ installations. Two of these, 'Anlage Robert' and 'Anlage Bruno', are thought to have been telephone centres; 'Robert' was probably at Berchtesgaden, but the location of 'Bruno' has never been established.

Towards the end of 1944, the *Führer-Begleitbrigade* was composed of the following:

> I. *Führer-Begleitbataillon* (armoured)
> 4 *Panzergrenadier* companies
> 1 *Panzer* company
> 1 *Flak* battery
> II. *Führer-Begleitbataillon* (motorised)
> 2 Grenadier companies (motorised)
> 1 assault engineer company
> 1 'heavy' company
> *Panzerabteilung* (Armoured Section)
> 3 companies
> *Flakabteilung* (Anti-Aircraft Section)
> 7 batteries
> *Aufklärungskompanie* (Reconnaissance Company)

It appears that at least three companies of the *Luftnachrichtenabteilung* were subordinated to *Oberst* Remer. This unit had installed a costly reporting network for incoming aircraft. On 23 July 1944 it had observed: 'Surprise air attack against FHQ must be reckoned with. Despite the most scrupulous observation of targets, misidentification and confusion of enemy aircraft with our own will occur and false alarms are not, therefore, out of the question.'

Towards the end of 1944, the *Flak* forces at Wolfschanze numbered in the region of 3,500; for the next planned stage, FHQ Riese they would number 6,600.

The living and working conditions at the FHQs, with their narrow and austerely furnished rooms, were in marked contrast to the pompous architectural fantasies and expensive lifestyles enjoyed by the NSDAP bosses before the war. That FHQs looked like concentration camps and were furnished accordingly was due to the influence of the hermit Hitler. The historian Fest remarked that, as the war progressed, Hitler became 'noticeably even less pretentious'. A *Wehrmacht* signals soldier stated he

ALLIED INVASION AND BOMB PLOT, 1944

had noticed that Hitler only required for himself 'a relatively modest lifestyle', while one of Hitler's female secretaries described the appointments of his bunker as 'really quite primitive'. Speer spoke of 'the prestige of having no pretensions', and Martin Bormann, emperor of the Obersalzberg underworld, described the outward differences between his own manner of living and that of the *Führer* in the following terms in a letter to his wife dated 1 October 1944:

> At least I am now sitting in a large room, six by seven metres in size, have four large windows and a lot of daylight, and can sleep at night by an open window. The *Führer*, on the other hand, lives down there in his bunker, and has only electric light and a rarefied atmosphere—the air pressure is always too high in his room because fresh air has to be pumped in continuously. It is just as if he enjoys living in an unlit basement. At the end of the day, to dwell in a fortified cell is unhealthy, and in the long run quite insufferable for every living thing. Every normal plant would die for lack of air and light ... he sniffs around our huts with their brick protective walls which, so he says, will be knocked flat in the first heavy air raid, and then everybody will have to make do with a great deal less space!

Hitler inspected the progress of work on his bunker on 11 October 1944 and moved back into the mammoth concrete edifice with its eleven-foot-thick walls and ceiling at midday on 8 November. The gas-protection and air-conditioning units installed by the Draeger company were set to a pressure of seven atmospheres. There was uncertainty regarding the life expectancy of the poison-gas filter. The instructions for its use stated that it was supposed to be changed 'when the canary kept in the room died', but it had not been established whether the *Führer* would put up with a canary in his bunker. The personal *Adjutanten* were reluctant to make a firm enquiry on the point, and so they insisted that a gas detector be fitted to the tubing carrying the air supply. There were no poison-gas attacks on Wolfschanze in the ensuing week, at the end of which, on 20 November 1944, Hitler left his great bunker, and FHQ Wolfschanze, for ever.

It is noteworthy that, despite the scarcity of raw materials, the network of military trunk-lines was extended by 15,000 kilometres over the five years from 1940. The system made it possible, for example, to remain in touch, along 4,500 kilometres of routing through Denmark, Norway and

177

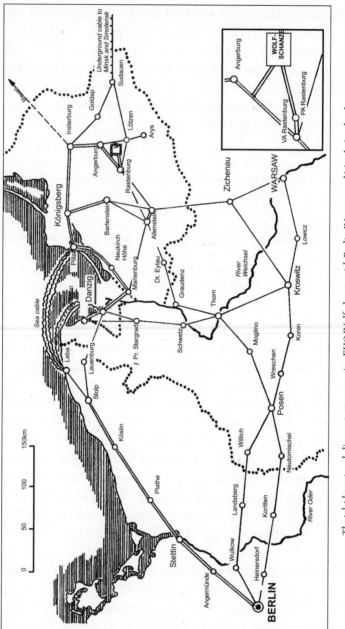

The telephone trunk-line system connecting FHQ Wolfschanze with Berlin, Warsaw and Minsk-Smolensk.

Finland, with the isolated Army Group Kurland. In January 1945, Jodl noted that the total number of telephone calls and telex messages daily between Berlin and German land units was 120,000 and 33,000, respectively. According to Maser, 'It made almost no difference whether I was calling Berlin, Rome, Oslo or Belgrade. If the connection was poor, I sent a telex instead.'

The efficiency of the German telephone network not only was of inestimable value for military commanders; it also enabled Hitler to continue to impose his influence on operations. No matter what the situation looked like at the front, the man poring over the FHQ situation map with his spyglass always knew best. As Speer remarked, 'The more difficult the situation, all the more did modern technology widen the gap between reality and the fantasy being operated from that table.'

In late 1944, the telephone-exchange bunker in *Sperrkreis I*, which had replaced the pleasant barracks hut, was windowless, its air pumped in under pressure. The staff worked a shift system, each shift comprising six telephone operators and three telex and telegraphy operators. Contrary to practice elsewhere, no female auxiliaries were employed. According to Schulz, 'The telephone exchange consisted of six double cabinets. On the left side were approximately 200 direct subscriber or trunk circuits. On the right side there was a telephone dial like you see on older telephones. The operators used it to direct-dial local numbers or VIPs over the trunk network.'

From *Sperrkreis I*, a total of 40, and from the FHQ as a whole 74, trunk lines led into the centre of Berlin—to the OKW, to the four arms of service, to ministerial trains, to the various operational centres of the *Luftwaffenführungsstab*, and to other exchanges. From this one infers that carrier frequency equipment was in use. There were twenty telex direct lines from Forst Görlitz used in the same manner. Schulz again: 'Through the various exchanges and offices in Berlin one could connect to all fronts as well as any place in the Reich, and to friendly or neutral countries too.

On 22 November 1944, two days after Hitler had abandoned FHQ Wolfschanze for good, preparations were taken in hand to destroy the bunker complex upon receipt of the codeword 'Inselsprung', until when the installations were to be maintained in good order. On 23 January 1945 *General der Pionere* Jacob ordered the demolition to commence. The work lasted two days. Despite the use of the most effective industrial explosives available, the demolition of the large bunkers was only part- ially successful, at best causing them to collapse inwards. On 27 January, the Red Army arrived at Wolfschanze. In their occupation of Rastenburg they behaved 'with unspeakable bestiality and cruelty' towards the civil- ian population, and on 31 January they incinerated the whole of the old town.

Chapter 10

Munich and Berchtesgaden: The 'Standby' FHQs

H AGEN, or Siegfried, was a completed FHQ about which un-
certainties remain. The village of Pullach lies about 15 kilometres
south of Munich. Before the war, an estate known as '*Reichssiedlung Rudolf Hess*' (Rudolf Hess Reich Settlement) and officially designated Siedlung Sonnenwald, consisting of 26 one- and two-family houses,
had been developed on a parcel of land between the Heilmannstrasse
and the Munich–Wolfratshausen railway line. The houses were occupied
mainly by Party functionaries who worked in the NSDAP staff building
at the centre of the settlement. The housing complex was arranged in a
rectangle around a nursery school. Hess ran the NSDAP from Pullach
before the completion in Munich of the new Party building in the
Arcisstrasse. Following the change, Bormann took over the former
NSDAP staff building at Pullach, which ever after was known as the
'*Bormann-Haus*'. At the end of July 1939, Hitler visited the Bormann family
there, but this was the only occasion when he came to Pullach.

All conversions during the war seem to have been carried out without
the knowledge and consent of Hitler's personal and military adjutants.
Possibly Bormann wanted to keep the estate as a reserve FHQ for Hitler
in the event that Obersalzberg was destroyed. On the other side of the
Heilmannstrasse was a 40-hectare tract of woodland in which most of
the construction work was carried out. This area was bounded by Burg
Weg, beyond which was woodland skirting the river.

Work on Hagen/Siegfried began in March 1943 and was completed
by November 1944. The appropriation was 13 million *Reichsmark*. A total
of 25,000 cubic metres of concrete went into the making of 1,642 square
metres of bunkers and 5,625 square metres of barracks foundations. There

were four bunkers and probably twenty barracks huts. The workforce of OT labourers, which varied between 200 and 800 in number, put 173,750 working days into the project. The FHQ was codenamed 'Siegfried': according to Wichert, the *Bormann-Haus* and bunker were 'Hagen'. However, a report by the Joint Intelligence Objectives Agency prepared in May 1945 states that Hagen comprised the central bunker in the wooded terrain, apparently intended for Hitler's use, was Hagen. The JIOA report must be preferred, because in autumn 1944 the *FHQu-Kommandant* stationed a '*Sonderkommando Hagen*' here, and FHQ security forces were never deployed on NSDAP property.

Immediately adjacent to the *Bormann-Haus*, OT built an underground bunker, accessed by a flight of twenty steps leading down from the main building. The bunker walls were two metres thick, and the structure was divided in two large rooms each of 20 square metres, four bedrooms each of eight square metres, a telephone exchange of nine square metres and several smaller rooms. All the rooms had wood ceilings and panelled walls. Two other bunkers, one built below the nursery school and the other near the drivers' and security accommodation, served as air-raid shelters.

Entry to the wooded terrain was afforded by means of a broad footpath at its north-east corner. Behind the main gate was a drivers' lodge in front of a vehicle parking hall. On the plot itself were seven 43-by-12-square-metre RAD accommodation huts. Four other barracks, from 12 to 15 metres broad and 45 to 70 metres long, were designed for air-raid protection and for this purpose stood within a one-metre thick brick wall surround, had an 80cm concrete roof and steel window guards. Two branch lines from the Isartal railway ended in sidings for two *Sonderzüge* within the compound.

The 70 by 20 metre underground bunker, large enough for Hitler, his entourage and military staff, was to the design of Professor Hermann Giesler. That only 3,200 cubic metres of space were available in a bunker made of 13,400 cubic metres of concrete speaks for the enormous thickness of the shell structure—a two-metre-thick ground layer, three-metre-thick ceiling and three-and-a-half-metre-thick outer walls,

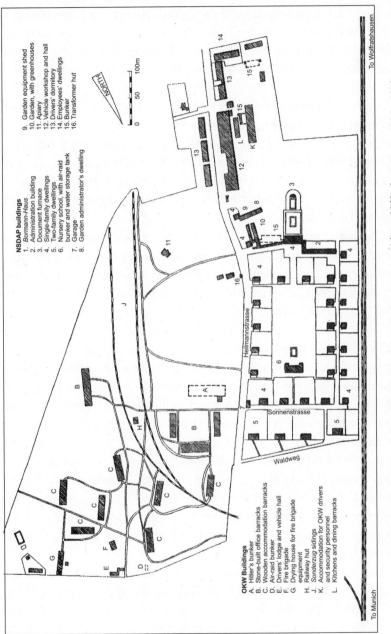

NSDAP buildings
1. *Bormann-Haus*
2. Administration building
3. Document furnace
4. Single-family dwellings
5. Two-family dwellings
6. Nursery school, with air-raid bunker and water storage tank
7. Garage
8. Garden administrator's dwelling
9. Garden equipment shed
10. Garden, with greenhouses
11. Apiary
12. Vehicle workshop and hall
13. Drivers' dormitory
14. Employees' dwellings
15. Bunker
16. Transformer hut

OKW Buildings
A. Hitler's bunker
B. Stone-built office barracks
C. Wooden accommodation barracks
D. Air-raid bunker
E. Drivers' lodge and vehicle hall
F. Fire brigade
G. Drying house for fire brigade equipment
H. Railway hut
J. *Sonderzug* sidings
K. Accommodation for OKW drivers and security personnel
L. Kitchens and dining barracks

The NSDAP Parteikanzlei (Party Office) and FHQ at Pullach, reconstructed from old files by G. Vetter, 15 May 1979.

reinforced by 80cm-thick, steel-reinforced concrete for extra strength. The bunker had thirty rooms, of which a dozen were for work purposes. All had a 65cm-high empty space below the floor for the various installations. The bunker was defended by an anti-aircraft tower with a full field of fire.

A camouflaged bunker on the barracks terrain housed the telephone exchange and was accessed directly from the operators' quarters. As befitted Bormann's nickname *'General der Fernschreiber'* (Telex-General), a huge number of circuits was available. As at Berchtesgaden, much of the cabling was simply strewn across open ground, so that by the end of 1944 the *FHQu-Kommandant* had *'Sonderkommando Hagen'* hard at work digging trenches.

The main bunker in each compound had a dual heating/ventilation system. The emergency diesel room, the transformers and ventilation machinery in Hitler's bunker occupied 400 cubic metres, an eighth of the available bunker space. Fresh air was drawn in through three 30cm thick shafts, filtered and mixed with purified, used air before being forced by high-pressure ventilators into the rooms through apertures in the ceilings. Vents behind the panelling adjusted the pressure level. Waste air was sucked out through the flooring, the diesel gases through an S-shaped exhaust pipe. The ventilation system also served for heating or cooling purposes, hot or cold water being circulated in tubing, the temperature adjustable by means of thermostats in the individual rooms. In the climatised rooms, the air pressure was a little higher than normal so as to inhibit the entry of poisonous gases in the event of attack. In such a case, the exhaled air within the bunker could be purified in chemical tanks equipped with active carbon filters before being re-circulated. By this means the bunker would be independent of an external air supply for a considerable period. The installation could be worked manually or by electrical power.

All the bunker entrances had gas-proof steel doors and a gas sluice. Gas sluices also separated the work and accommodation areas. Entry to the Hagen bunker was by means of a stairwell or lift positioned at the north-eastern corner. A long corridor of steps on the eastern side served

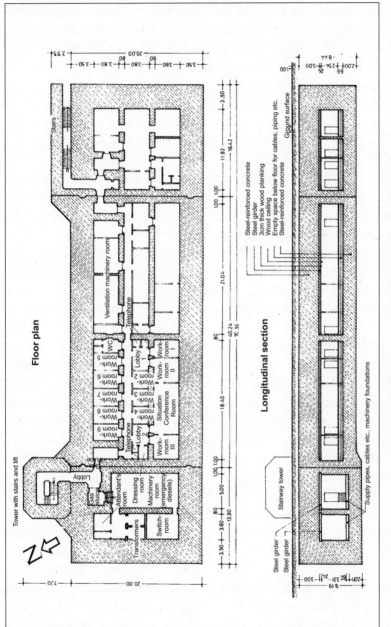

Floor plan of, and longitudinal section through, Hagen bunker (after Vetter).

as an emergency exit. All the buildings were well camouflaged. Those parts of the bunkers not fully underground were earthed up and put to grass or planted with bushes. The rail sidings were netted over. From the air it was difficult to distinguish the eastern compound as something other than an extension of the village of Pullach.

The machinery room containing the two emergency diesel generators, fuel tank and two electrically driven sewage pumps was seven metres below ground but operated from a central control panel. Water was supplied by the local utility.

The other FHQ under Bormann's control was Berchtesgaden. Because Obersalzberg was administered by the NSDAP, the *Parteikanzlei* arranged the anti-aircraft defence, and the unit concerned—a special *SS-Flak-bataillon und -Nebelabteilung* (smoke company), raised initially in 1941 from *Flak* troops performing their six months' compulsory work service with the *Reichsarbeitsdienst* (RAD)— remained operational even when Hitler was not in residence. When Hitler left the Berghof for the last time in July 1944, mostly teenage RAD conscripts had taken over the AA batteries, so as to release the original *SS-Flakbataillon* for service at the front.

SS-Kommando 'Obersalzberg' had 250 RSD officials and 2,265 SS-men under the command of SS-*Obersturmbannführer* Dr Bernhard Frank in the following divisions: *Führerfahrkolonne* 252, SS-*Wachkompanie* 364, fire brigade 23, *Nebelabteilung* 646, gallery building company 180, *Flakabteilung* 800. The release of 1,446 SS men from the *Flakabteilung* and *Nebelabteilung* left 819 at Obersalzberg for the remainder of the war.

In the winter of 1944, Frank was responsible for creating and training the Obersalzberg *Volkssturmbataillon*. Germans working at the site had to sacrifice their Sunday off for the purpose, but nobody seems to have taken this form of soldiering very seriously. In the second half of 1944, Bormann ordered a new and safer gallery system to be bored into the Obersalzberg at least 100 metres below ground. The entrances would have immensely heavy, hinged or sliding doors of steel-reinforced concrete. The new complex would be of the same dimensions as the existing system but 50 metres beneath it. It would accommodate several thousand people, a food warehouse, an arsenal and a car park for more than a hundred vehicles. Bormann issued one building order after another, even though most of the firms involved had been bombed out of their home towns. There was a lack of fuel, telephone lines in the Reich were down and the delivery of building materials was becoming ever more difficult, but Bormann was confident that Obersalzberg would ride out the storm. Only sensitive files and valuable works of art were trucked away, and settlement dates for builders' invoices were rescheduled for later. At the capitulation, the total debt for work done and not paid for was 17 million *Reichsmark*.

Telephone lines from Obersalzberg ran to the Salzburg trunk exchange. The small amplifier station at Berchtesgaden, through which all connections to and from the Berghof FHQ passed, was unprotected against shrapnel. *Reichspost*, Army and *Luftwaffe* cables lay bound together in the open: one bomb could have left Obersalzberg without telephone connections. The installation on the Obersalzberg was the concern of the NSDAP *Kanzlei*, and the *Führer-Nachrichtenabteilung* worked under their instructions. When *General der Nachrichtentruppe* Praun, *Chef des Wehrmacht-Nachrichtenverbindungswesens* (Head of *Wehrmacht* Signals Communications), saw the situation at Christmas 1944, it was too late for anything to be done. Obersalzberg was a great hub of telephone traffic, most of it emanating at some stage from Bormann. After Praun had completed his inspection, he left shaking his head: nowhere had he seen such neglect. Moreover, amidst the opulence and the great underground workings with space for thousands of people and a hundred cars, the men of the *Führer-Nachrichtenabteilung* had been given the use of a small cave.

Chapter 11

FHQ Adlerhorst:
The Ardennes Offensive

FROM an entry in the *FHQu-Kommandant*'s *Kriegstagebuch* (War Diary) recording a discussion with Jodl, it is clear that, at the latest by 25 January 1942, when an OKW shortlist was issued, Schloss Ziegenberg was already in use as a *Heeres-Genesungsheim* (Army convalescent home) for *Leichtkranke* ('walking wounded') and those who were ill but 'not in need of specialised medical care' and who could accordingly be transferred elsewhere at short notice should the need arise.

In August 1944, Jodl relinquished all interest in FHQ Adlerhorst until further notice on the grounds of its inadequate air-raid facilities and, apparently unaware of the use to which they were currently being put, agreed that Ziegenberg and Kransberg castles could be used 'as a convalescence or military hospital or similar'. Nevertheless, it seems probable that in September 1944 a *Sonderkommando 'Adlerhorst' des Kommandanten FHQu* was stationed in the grounds.

On 14 October, *Generalfeldmarschall* von Rundstedt occupied Schloss Ziegenberg and the associated bunker complex after Jodl had conveyed approval to *OB West* five days earlier for the establishment of his headquarters there. As the communications equipment installed in 1940 had been removed, new cables and switching gear were required, and *Nachrichtenregiment 603, OB West*, received orders to install in Bunker VI a 300-circuit FK-16 telephone/telex exchange and in the former power room of the castle telephone exchange a 100-circuit FK-16 staff exchange, the Ziegenberg 'farm buildings' being wired to it by means of three ground cables each of twenty paired lines. At Schloss Kransberg, twenty paired overhead cables were relocated underground. It was also found necessary to re-rig the amplifier system for the trunking network. Both systems were operational by 13 October 1944, and from that time on the *OB West* exchange announced itself as 'Plato 1' instead of 'Amt 600'. The *OB West* wireless unit was relocated to Melbach near Bad Nauheim on 15 October, and a permanent telex connection was established to the OKH's 'Zeppelin' headquarters at Berlin-Zossen.

The secret plans for the Ardennes offensive stipulated Adlerhorst as FHQ, even though it was the new headquarters of *OB West*. At the planning stage, the need to inform the *Chef der Wehrmacht-Nachrichtenverbindungen* was overlooked. The *Führer-Nachrichtenabteilung*, which was installing telecommunications equipment at the Wiesental site near Kransberg castle, received no instructions to install lines for Hitler and his entourage, with the result that *OB West* had to surrender a proportion of his own. All work being carried out at an FHQ fell within the jurisdiction of the *FHQu-Kommandant*, and he had not checked. Thus he was identified as the culprit in the wake of a complaint made by Bormann respecting the negligent preparations at FHQ Wiesental.

From 1944 the *Führer-Nachrichtenabteilung* consisted of two companies and was also designated *Nachrichtenabteilung z.b.V. 3* (*z.b.V.* meaning 'for special purposes'). Its history as an organisation is sparse and difficult to reconstruct. During the Ardennes campaign its composition was:

Stab:	Commander, three officers, two officials, six NCOs and fourteen men.
1. Kompanie:	One *Kompanietrupp* plus four *Züge* (platoons) for building construction and cable-laying, technical personnel for the military telephone network mainly employed in the WFSt amplifier house and its exchange; and a field kitchen. Total seven officers, 30 NCOs and 170 men.
2. Kompanie:	One *Kompanietrupp* plus two *Züge* of telex and wireless troops, one *Zug* comprising signals personnel deployed aboard the *Sonderzüge*; and a field kitchen. Total four officers, one official, 53 NCOs and 136 men.

The total strength of the *Wehrmacht* portion of the *Abteilung* working solely for FHQ purposes was 423. There was also an SS Signals Wireless Company, but nothing is known about the duties or strength of this unit

On 11 November 1944 *Oberbauleiter* Leo Müller was sent to Adlerhorst to prepare the headquarters for Hitler. His duties included the furnishing of Hitler's bedroom with a horse-hair mattress, carefully positioning the night table the *Führer* was accustomed to have against his bunker wall, and retrieving from *Generalfeldmarschall* von Rundstedt's quarters at Ziegenberg the *Führer*'s writing table which had mysteriously disappeared sometime previously. On 12 November Wilhelm Hirsch, who was responsible for all matters pertaining to landscaping and camouflage, appeared at Ziegenberg and issued his orders.

On 10 December 1944, in the *Sonderzug* which since 1 February 1943 had borne the name *Brandenburg*, Hitler left Berlin to oversee and direct the Ardennes offensive. His train left Sonnenwald station at 1700 and steamed through the night across the great bombsite that had once been Germany. The locomotive pulled into Kloster Arnsburg station—his secretary Christa Schroeder names Hungen as the place where he detrained, this being about 22 kilometres north-east of Ziegenberg—at 0242 next morning. From there it took over four and a half hours to reach Wiesental by car.

Göring came to Adlerhorst on 17 December and stayed for a while at Schloss Kransberg. From Triberg in the Black Forest, Himmler arrived in his *Sonderzug*, *Heinrich*, at Eppstein, between Wiesbaden and Frankfurt, from where he was driven to Kransberg. He stayed there into the New Year and attended a number of Hitler's situation conferences to familiarise himself with the activities of the *Waffen-SS* division that was spearheading the offensive. Himmler had an SS security unit and a concentration-camp work party at Kransberg from the end of 1944 until the end of March 1945. Codenamed 'Tannenwald', the castle was intended as an SS field command post in connection with a secret project, 'K', but it was never occupied because it was threatened by the Allied advance.

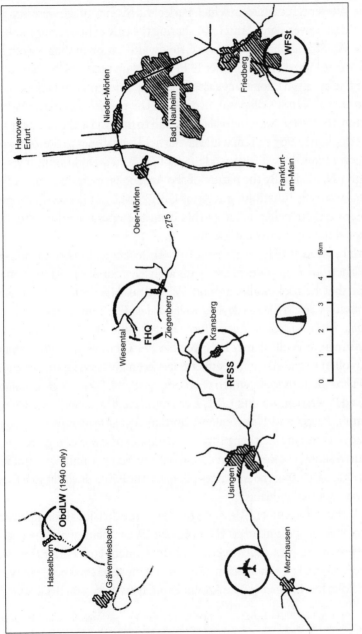

FHQ Adlerhorst during the Ardennes offensive, 1944–5.

The Wiesental complex in which Hitler and his entourage were housed received the cover-name 'Amt 600', sharing the title of his signals bunker.

The WFSt *Feldstaffel* left Berlin's Grünewald station in their *Sonderzug*, *Franken I*, at 1500 on 15 December 1944 and set up quarters in a barracks near Friedberg, ten kilometres east of FHQ. At Wiesental, only the guest-house was at WFSt's disposal. Because of the remoteness of the WFSt position, the *Führer-Nachrichtenabteilung* had to improvise the circuitry for their telephone/telex system while laying field trunk lines to the *Reichspost* junction boxes. WFSt also made use of *OB West*'s Drehkreuz lines at Usingen-Nauheim. By the nature of the Ardennes operation, the WFSt *Feldstab* was only functioning at Army Corps level, but if Jodl was happy to tolerate their being as far as this from the operational centre, the relationship was clearly a loose one.

Hitler stayed at FHQ Adlerhorst from 11 December 1944 to 15 January 1945. There are no reports of any of his activities outside working hours, except that he took walks around Wiesental. His security force was composed of *Sonderkommando A des Kommandant FHQu* and *1. SS-Grenadier-kompanie der Leibstandarte 'Adolf Hitler'*. By the time Hitler took his final departure from Wolfschanze in November 1944, the *Führer-Begleitbataillon* had swollen to the size of a regiment and been absorbed into the semi-élite *Führer-Begleitbrigade*, which was composed of *I. Führer-Begleitbataillon* (a mixed *Panzergrenadier* unit), *II. Führer-Begleitbataillon* (a motorised *Grenadier* unit), *Panzer* and *Flak* elements and an *Aufklärungskompanie* (recon-naissance company). Other proposed components, including security, armoured scout, engineers, signals and field ambulance units, were never incorporated. During the Ardennes offensive the *Führer-Begleitbrigade* took part in the actual fighting.*

On 11 and 12 December 1944, Hitler received the divisional commanders in two groups and imparted the objective of the plan, which was the recapture of the port of Antwerp, and the launch date. Hitler finished his speech with the exhortation: ;The enemy must be smashed—now or never! Long live Germany!' The Ardennes offensive began on 16 December

---

* By early 1945 it had swollen to the size of a division and had been deployed in the line against the Soviets in Silesia. Thrown into the defence of Spremberg, south of Cottbus, it was wiped out.

with a thrust towards Bastogne and the River Meuse. The Germans were at first favoured by fog, but on the eighth day conditions improved sufficiently for the Americans to counter-attack with aerial superiority.

Hitler's routine at Adlerhorst differed little from that at Wolfschanze. He had himself woken at midday, read the latest reports and received his first callers. According to the diaries of his valet Linge, during the day he would receive numerous representatives of the *Wehrmacht* and NSDAP. At about 1400 he dined with his two female secretaries, Gerda Christian and Christa Schroeder. Occasionally his vegetarian cook, Constanze Manziarly, would be present. As a rule, the daily situation conferences took place at about 1600. The most regular attenders were Göring, Keitel, von Rundstedt, Jodl, Himmler (during the last four days of 1944), the reporting officers from the front and the *Adjutanten*. Supper was taken at 2000 with the two secretaries, and the day would end with a cup of tea just after midnight. Hitler would get into bed at between three and five in the morning.

On 24 December, Guderian came to Adlerhorst to inform the *Führer* of the consequences of the Soviet breakthrough in north-west Hungary. In view of the Red Army's threatening superiority in numbers, Guderian asked for the greater weight of the German military potential to be transferred forthwith to the East, to confront the Soviet attack on the broad front which he anticipated would begin on 12 January 1945. Hitler declined, dismissing the estimates as to the size and intentions of the Red Army compiled by the *Abteilung Fremde Heere Ost* (Office for Enemy Foreign Armies East) as 'a preposterous bluff' and 'completely idiotic'. Disillusioned by this response, Guderian spent at FHQ 'a deadly grim, sad Christmas Eve in most unchristian surroundings'.

At the situation conference of 26 December (Linge noted Christmas Day in his diary), there was an altercation between Hitler and Göring. The German offensive had been brought to a standstill. Whilst Hitler had not yet abandoned hope completely, Göring suggested that it might be time to negotiate an armistice since the war was lost. Hitler raged: 'I forbid you to take any step in that direction. If in spite of what I say you do anything to defy my order, then I will have to have you shot.'

On 28 December, Hitler gathered the divisional commanders at FHQ and urged them to hold on. The following night he conferred with Thomale, *Chef der Generalinspektion der Panzertruppen* (CO General Inspectorate of Panzer Forces), and informed him that soldierly qualities manifested themselves 'in the moral qualities of holding out, in toughness and in tenacity.' Since in respect of Germany everything was at risk, the Germans had to hold out longer than the Allies: 'If we were to say, today, that we have had enough, we can go no further, then Germany will cease to exist.' To the end of the war, Hitler would not budge from this banal political-strategic concept. Next day the Hungarian Government in Opposition under General Miklòs took up arms against Germany, and the country was now at war with no fewer than 58 different nations.

On Boxing Day 1944, Guderian reappeared at FHQ to warn Hitler and the WFSt of the build-up of Soviet forces at the Vistula bridgehead around Baranov. Hitler granted him four additional divisions for the relief of Budapest but ignored the danger on the Vistula.

Hitler's New Year speech for 1945 was made from FHQ Adlerhorst. Five minutes after midnight on New Year's Day, he addressed the German people directly, stating that Germany would rise like a phoenix from the ashes and rubble of her cities and, despite all setbacks, would go on to win 'final victory'. He then gathered his 'inner circle' around him and predicted a great success for Germany in 1945. That day he received New Year's wishes in person from Göring, Keitel, Guderian, Jodl, Rudel and Bormann, and on 3 January from von Ribbentrop. In his *Neujahrstagesbefehl* (New Year's Order of the Day) to the *Wehrmacht*, he laid the blame for the setbacks of recent weeks squarely on Romania, Finland and Hungary, which had defected from the Axis alliance.

On 4 January 1945 Goebbels made a rare visit to FHQ, to advise Hitler on how his two New Year's speeches had been received. Describing the journey and his thoughts between the aerodrome and Ziegenberg, he made the following diary entry:

> We made a one-hour car drive through snow-covered terrain to the FHQ, which is tucked away from the whole wide world, hidden in a wood. One can be sure that, for their part, our enemies have no idea that the *Führer* is directing operations

from here; for, otherwise, they would have undoubtedly bombed the HQ. Even in the short while our car was driving along concealed country lanes, there was an air-raid warning and broad streams of enemy bombers droned above us. Thank heaven a layer of mist shielded us from the sky and allowed us to drive on unmolested. The FHQ is quite close to Frankfurt-am-Main. It makes an extraordinarily cosy impression and, most importantly, is well concealed. It is smaller than the FHQ in the East, so that the staff surrounding the *Führer* is smaller too. That will certainly be advantageous in terms of the work. The *Führer* and his staff are accommodated in very pleasant barracks, although the air-raid installations are not all they might be. But it is good that the *Führer* is now getting much more fresh air, although I do worry that, if the Anglo-American enemy discovers the existence of this HQ, the *Führer* will be in very great danger from their aircraft.

On 9 January 1945, Hitler's secretary Traudl Junge returned from a short break in Munich. After describing to Hitler during supper the effects of the heavy air raids on the city, he comforted her by saying that within a few weeks the nightmare would be at an end, for then the new jet fighter would have won back air supremacy over Germany.

The same day Guderian arrived back at Adlerhorst to warn Hitler, for the third time, of the imminent Red Army offensive in the East, explaining, with the help of maps he had brought with him, the manner in which the Russians had moved up. His visit was in vain, and he returned to his Zossen headquarters with the depressing rebuff that the East would have to look after itself and make do with what it had. Three days later, almost three million Russians broke through the German defences and advanced fifteen kilometres in twenty-four hours. Guderian telephoned Hitler, who was in the process of preparing his departure from Adlerhorst, pleading that he 'throw everything available into the East' if he wished to prevent a catastrophe. Hitler released the Sixth SS Panzer Army, though not to stem the Soviet advance but to defend Budapest.

FHQu-Kommandant Oberst Gustav Streve summoned the architect responsible for designing FHQ Wiesental, Franz Werr, to the situation conference of 14 January 1945 because Hitler required an explanation as to why his bunker had no emergency exit. Streve cautioned Werr that he could not hoodwink the *Führer*, who was 'the greatest master mason of all time'. Before the conference began, Werr was given the chance to speak to Hitler in the presence of several officers. He explained that there was no need for an emergency exit since, if the exit were blocked by rubble after an air raid, he would soon have hundreds of labourers on the job of clearing it. If the *Führer* insisted on having an emergency exit, this could be put in within a few days, although the noise level would be disturbing and sections cut out of the wall fabric might weaken the integrity of the structure. Hitler did insist on the change, and received a drawing for his approval. When Werr arrived two days later to begin the modification, he found that Hitler had already left.

At 1800 on 15 January 1945 Hitler left FHQ Adlerhorst for Hungen station, where his *Führersonderzug* was waiting. He returned to the *Reichskanzlei* at 1000 the next morning. The WFSt *Feldstaffel* did not arrive in Berlin until the 17th, the journey having been much interrupted by air-raid alerts. The WFSt's *Stellvertretend Chef* (Deputy Head), *General der Gebirgstruppe* August Winter, arrived with both the home and field staff at the Berlin-Zossen HQ Maybach II, while Keitel and Jodl were accommodated at Berlin-Dahlem from then until 20 April 1945.

Until the collapse of the German western defences in late March 1945, Schloss Ziegenberg functioned as the headquarters of *OB West*. *Generalfeldmarschall* Kesselring succeeded von Rundstedt on 9 March and arrived at the former FHQ Adlerhorst the following night. On 19 March the village and castle were bombed by US aircraft and the castle was set alight. Further attacks followed on 21 and 24 March, all intended to destroy the headquarters, and on the 27th Kesselring transferred to Fulda. At Wiesental the buildings of military use were torched, all that remained being ruins of blackened concrete. The US 76th Infantry Division reached Ziegenberg during the night of 30 March. British specialists identified the bunker north of the castle as Hitler's headquarters during the Battle of the Bulge. A correspondent attached to the US 80th Division described the installations thus:

> Each of Hitler's henchmen here had his own well-appointed apartment. In this Adlerhorst, as it is known to the Nazis, General von Rundstedt mapped out the plans for the Ardennes Offensive last winter. Adlerhorst is hewn artificially into the naked rock of the mountain and near to its peak, close to the ruin of the old Ziegenhain fortress. Along the hillside there is a stand of spruce, among which one finds some alpine-type chalets. The whole surroundings have a fairy-tale aura,

and one scarcely suspects being in the immediate vicinity of a *Führerhauptquartier* in which the great figures of the Third Reich went in and out and made important decisions. The accommodation of Hitler and his paladins was hewn into the outer rock face and worked into terracing laid out in such a manner that, looked at from the ground upwards, it appears to have been taken from the air.

Chapter 12

The Southward Migration of the High Command Staffs, 1945

THE expansion of Zossen by developing the incomplete Maybach II site commenced in 1942, and, although the location had not been planned as an FHQ, the advantages of having the nucleus in the immediate neighbourhood of OKH were obvious. In the early autumn of 1944, the *Feldstaffel des OKH* had begun urgent preparations to evacuate its headquarters north of Wolfschanze in the Steinort Forest (Mauerwald) and the Angerburg and Lotzen barracks by reducing them initially to the barest essentials. The intention was to concentrate all elements of the High Command into the bunkered areas at Zossen and its surrounding barracks. OKH had occupied the Zossen heqdquarters, only 40 kilometres from Berlin, from the outbreak of war, though since 1940 minus one field staff each from the operational and logistical sections which served at Hitler's far-flung FHQs.

'Zeppelin' and Maybach had remained in use throughout the war. The various FHQs drew on them for the OKH *Feldstaffeln* they needed for operational planning. The *Heimatstaffel* (Home Staff) stayed in the Bendlerstrasse. The exodus to Zossen began on the night of 29 March 1943, when the OKW complex on the Tirpitzufer was damaged by bombing. The aerial bombardment of the Reich capital became so intense that on 17 June 1943 Hitler ordered all military staffs out of central Berlin. The Wunsdorf barracks, which until then had been the domain of the Panzer crews, became home to the OKH *Heimatstaffel*. From mid-1944 elements of the OKH *Feldstaffel* began to evacuate *Führerhauptquartier* Wolfschanze for Zossen; next came a large part of the *Heerestransportwesen* (Army Transport Command), in mid-July the *Stab des Generalquartiermeisters* (Quartermaster-General's staff), in November the remainder of the OKH command posts and at the end of 1944 the *Stab des Inspekteurs der Panzertruppen* (Panzer Personnel Inspectorate's staff).

New bunkers were in place at Zossen/'Zeppelin' at the end of August 1944, and Maybach II—which included a small 'housing estate' of four-storey blockhouses, two storeys of which were below ground and all of which were connected by a circular subterranean gallery, for the use of *Führer* and his entourage—was finished at the turn of the year. It is to be assumed that this centralised FHQ did not find favour with Hitler, because at Zossen he would always be in the midst of senior Army officers, for whom his trust had been severely diminished following the attempted assassination of July 1944.

Martin Bormann spent a period at Zossen after the Ardennes offensive and appears to have been of the opinion that bunker-type blockhouses with two subterranean levels were safer than anything he had seen in Berlin, but he was unable to convince Hitler, who declined to use them, remarking that the blockhouses did not seem sturdy enough. (This argument was disproved by the merely superficial damage inflicted on the Zossen complex during the air raid of 16 March 1945.) Whatever the reasons behind his insistence upon Berlin, his adherence to the Reich capital was good for morale generally, and useful propaganda. Hitler's observation to Goebbels in mid-February that Berlin must be held under all circumstances indicates that, through his presence in the city, he wanted to stiffen the defenders' resistance to the utmost. This was a point he had argued at Wolfschanze in the autumn of 1944: everything was subordinated to holding Berlin.

After the Ardennes campaign, the WFSt *Feldstaffel* arrived on 17 January 1945 in Berlin, from where they made the short move to join Jodl's deputy and representative, *General der Gebirgstruppe* Winter, at Zossen on 16 January 1945, occupying Maybach II's bunker houses A13 to A15, which had been recently completed. Eight similar buildings, numbered 16 to 23, were those reserved for Hitler and his entourage as an FHQ but never occupied.

For the first time, at the end of January 1945 many Reich authorities and utilities applied to evacuate Berlin. Despite the obvious justification,

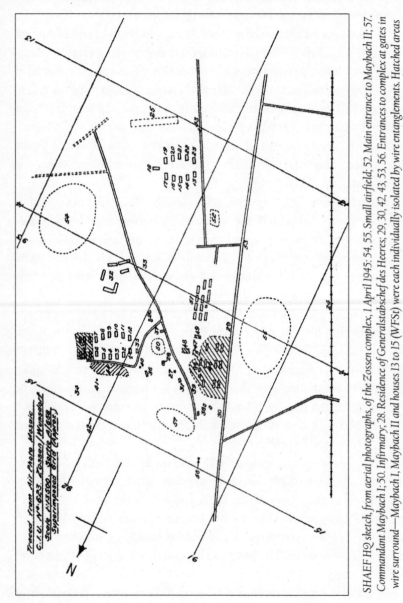

SHAEF HQ sketch, from aerial photographs, of the Zossen complex, 1 April 1945: 54, 55. Small airfield; 52. Main entrance to Maybach II; 57. Commandant Maybach I; 50. Infirmary; 28. Residence of Generalstabschef des Heeres; 29, 30, 42, 43, 53, 56. Entrances to complex at gates in wire surround—Maybach I, Maybach II and houses 13 to 15 (WFSt) were each individually isolated by wire entanglements. Hatched areas indicate infrastructure damaged or destroyed during the air raid of 15 March 1945.

they reaped the scorn of Dr Goebbels, who, as *Beauftragte für de totalen Kriegseinsatz* (Representative for Total War), succeeded in extracting from Hitler a prohibition on all such moves. although on 27 January *Reichswirtschaftsminister* (Reich Economy Minister) Funk obtained authority to relocate elsewhere 'the most important parts of the Reichsbank'. A short while later Goebbels recorded in his diaries that Hitler made the observation 'that a quite small staff ought to evacuate from Berlin from every important Government Ministry, perhaps to Oberhof in Thuringia, so that, if Berlin really does have to be fought for, the Reich Government will remain intact and still capable of ruling . . .'

Goebbels, who to all intents and purposes opposed these ideas, recognised the danger inherent in them. Since 1943, a large number of authorities and military headquarters had transferred at least out of Greater Berlin. if not to distant areas of the Reich unlikely to come under threat from the Soviets. In concert with Lammers and Bormann, Goebbels decided that a general exodus from the capital had to be prevented. In a *Runderlass* (directive) to the most senior departmental heads in mid-February 1945, he emphasised that it was their 'honourable duty' to press on with the management of affairs from Berlin and not leave the city unless it was absolutely unavoidable or for a purpose important to the war effort. Only 'fairly limited sections of certain senior staffs [may] transfer from the Reich capital . . . such small transfers are in no circumstances to be undertaken on the grounds of an apparent threat to the city by the Bolsheviks, but only in response to current and possibly future terror from the air.' Goebbels and Bormann had thus stipulated that to escape the bombing was the ultimate concession: if Berlin became drawn into the battle against the Russians or was besieged by them, one stayed put.

As regards the armed forces, Goebbels met them head-on and discovered that the exigiencies of propaganda came a distant second to military reality. The *Generalnachrichtenführer der Luftwaffe* (C-in-C Luftwaffe Signals) pointed out on 8 February that he thought it virtually impossible to provide any expansion of existing telephone facilities for an alternative location for the 1,500-strong *Hauptquartier der Luftwaffe*. As he was waiting for a decision of the *Generalstabschef*, equipment and personnel were being transferred provisionally to central Germany 'to get to work on it quickly' when the call came. As the *Luftwaffe* was in the process of preparing to move its *Oberkommando* to Bavaria and Thuringia on 13 February, Goebbels called them 'the *Fluchtwaffe*'—the Flight (i.e., Fleeing) Arm—but they ignored the insult.

The Army took much the same position. An order had been issued on 2 February that 'archives and valuable files not needed for day-to-day work' were to be transferred to storage at the infantry and artillery barracks at Bad Reichenhall near Berchtesgaden. On 12 February the *Generalstabschef* ordered space in barracks to be made available for front-troops and refugees, a pretext enabling him to transfer parts of the Zossen-Wunsdorf headquarters with effect from the following day. The staff was divided into two groups. Strictly command staff attached to the *Generalstabschef* would remain initially in Zossen; the other group 'taking with it as much material, equipment and luggage as possible', was then taken out by lorry out to southern Germany. This type of behaviour explains Goebbels' outrage at the beginning of March, when he learned that Keitel had readied 110 transport convoys for the evac-uation of the senior *Wehrmacht* officers and was allegedly looking to accommodate 50,000 people outside Greater Berlin. By the end of March and mid-April, respectively. the Army and *Luftwaffe* had accomplished what they set out to do and the evacuation transport programme was closed down. The major part of the various command staffs had been removed from the path of the Soviets, leaving only skeleton command staffs at Zossen and Wildpark Werder.

The maximum capacity of Zossen and Wunsdorf barracks is uncertain but, even after the principal headquarters staffs had begun to relocate to central and southern Germany in February 1945, there were 8,139 OKH personnel, including 811 *Wehrmacht* female auxiliaries, still there on 19 March. On 15 March 1945, in an attempt to knock out the command centre, a total of 675 USAAF bombers attacked Zossen/Wunsdorf. Accuracy was poor. The bunker complex was not seriously damaged and none of the concrete ceilings caved in. Several barrack huts at ground level were gutted and the telephone connections between Maybach I

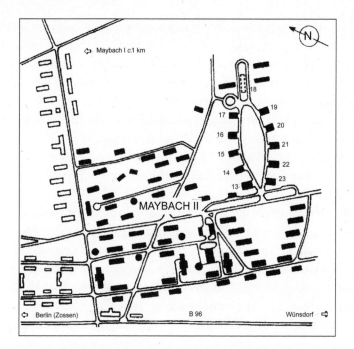

Layout of Maybach II (after Kampe). The housing intended for Hitler and his entourage are those buildings numbered 16 to 23.

and II were destroyed, although the damage was superficial and contact was restored within two hours. OKH and OKW went on working during the air-raid, and telephone traffic was not seriously interrupted. Nineteen 'sugar loaf' type air raid towers put up during the war also survived. In the evening situation conference of 23 March, Hitler described Zossen as 'unsafe' and the OKH structures generally as '*Schwindelbauten*' (jerry-built) because professional firms had not been used in their construction—a ridiculous objection if that was his true reason.

After the US bombing raid, the evacuation of the various command staffs from Zossen to southern Germany was accelerated. Although in the last weeks of the war ever more outward connections were severed, the *Kommandeur der Führer-Nachrichtenabteilung, Major* Josef Wolf, used a three-shift system to improvise or re-route wiring to maintain connections to OKH command levels.

The last *Generalstab des Heeres* situation conference was held in Maybach I's bunker-house A6 on 16 April 1945. The bunker for Hitler—should he have decided to use Maybach II as an FHQ, and on which 68,750 man-days had been expended since September 1944 (well over a third of the labour time estimated)—was eventually abandoned. The plans required no less than 18,000 cubic metres of concrete for the 1,180-square-metre structure. The reason given by Hitler to explain his disinclination to inhabit OKH '*Schwindelbauten*' is better explained by assuming that he might not have slept comfortably with senior OKH personnel as his neighbours.

The advance of the Third Soviet Guard Tank Army pushing north-wards towards Berlin through the Flemmingwiese marshes was so un-expectedly rapid that 'Zeppelin' had to be hurriedly evacuated on 20 April 1945, the bunkers falling more or less intact into the Red Army's hands. The dismantling process began within two months. All the tele-phone equipment—the most modern anywhere—was trucked out. Together with trunking exchanges and telex machines, the Russians also discovered a treasure trove of amplifiers, carrier-wave and AC telegraphy equipment and an emergency power unit the technical details of which were completely new to them. Later, large sections of the bunker complex were, with the agreement of the Western Allies, dynamited.

The *Oberkommando der Marine* (OKM, or Navy High Command) had continued to occupy its peacetime headquarters on the Tirpitzufer in Berlin after the outbreak of war. Air raids eventually forced a move to barracks at Eberswalde before it transferred to the fortified 'Koralle' near Bernau to the north-east of Berlin at the end of 1943. In late March 1945, 'Koralle' was abandoned in favour of 'Krokodil', which was probably the headquarters set up at Plön in Holstein.

From the outset, the *Oberkommando der Luftwaffe* (OKL, or *Luftwaffe* High Command) had attached only a comparatively small unit to FHQ, pre-ferring the mobility of the *Sonderzug*. The command unit in East Prussia in 1944 was stationed initially at Bartenstein, 50 kilometres north-west of Wolfschanze, and then in late August that year at Rosengarten, the former seat of the *Chef der Reichs- und der Parteikanzlei*, Dr Lammers, a few kilometres north-east of Wolfschanze. In early July 1944 OKL head-quarters had been removed from Goldap to Wildpark Werder near Pots-dam. The *Luftwaffe* field unit at FHQ remained until mid-November 1944, pulling out for good after assembling a *Volkssturmbataillon* to defend Göring's hunting lodges on the Romintener Heide. The *Luftwaffe* staff headquarters in Wildpark Werder, Kurfürst, was a central and protected site for a possible FHQ south-west of Berlin, and one with with good telecommunications, but it was abandoned save for a skeleton staff in late March 1945, by which time the threat to Berlin had worsened.

On the Obersalzberg in February 1945, female SS auxiliaries were taught how to operate the smoke-making apparatus. Himmler's idea that this unit would be better served by 'old forestry rangers, lumberjacks and resident farmers' was not taken up. In the situation conference of 23 March 1945 in Berlin, *Luftwaffenadjutant* von Below suggested that the smoke unit should be mothballed when Hitler was not in residence on the Obersalzberg, in order to save on acid consumption. Hitler replied, 'Yes, but we must be clear that we could lose everything. This is one of the last [FHQ] options we have.'

Bormann informed himself fully as to the progress of work on the new subterranean galleries on 17 March 1945. Then, according to Besymenski, on 27 March he discussed 'transport problems' with the *Chef der Heeres-rüstung* (Head of of Army Equipment) and *Chef des Heerestransportwesens* (Head of Army Transport), and on 9 April conferred with the *Gauleiter* of Tyrol, Jodl and Winter. If all this is correct, it would indicate that Bormann was the motivating force behind the transfer of FHQ to the Berchtesgaden area and may not have received Hitler's blessing in this respect.

OT senior management had been working since the autumn of 1944 on a project codenamed 'Lothar', which in January 1945 was renamed '*Sonderbauleitung Berchtesgaden*' (Special Construction Management Berch-tesgaden), and had as its purpose the expansion of the barracks at Strub and Bad Reichenhall. Amongst other land properties OKH had taken over Beseler, an OT woodland camp near Winkl station, expanded it and equipped it for OKH purposes. As a result of a controversy between the *FHQu-Kommandant* and the *Kommandant des Hauptquartiers des OKH* (OKH Headquarters Commandant), the latter had to step down and modify his intentions in the region. The OKL intended to locate its HQ at Wasserburg-am-Inn and in the Military Sports School at Berchtesgaden.

On 19 April 1945, more WFSt groups moved into Strub from Zossen, Jodl's deputy, Winter, arriving there on the 24th. On 20 April 1945 the operational parts of OKW assembled at Wannsee-Krampnitz to be divided into *Befehlsstelle Nord* (Command Centre North) and *Befehlsstelle Süd* (South), under Dönitz and Kesselring, respectively, the OKH *Führungsstab* continuing to occupy Zossen until the last moment. There was still time for Hitler to have repaired to the south of the Reich to be amongst WFSt and the *Generalstäbe* (general staffs) which had set up in the Hotel Schiffmeister at Königssee on 27 April. They were in all respects operational, but without Hitler they were hardly able to influence events.

In the final analysis, all the military staffs, with the exception of that of the *Kriegsmarine*, settled around Berchtesgaden and Bad Reichenhall 'in the closest proximity and all mixed up with countless other headquarters of every kind in the Reich. The loudest voice in favour of the FHQ redoubt here was that of Martin Bormann, but Hitler was not interested.

The last NSDAP *Ortsgruppe* (district group) in the Reich was founded on the Obersalzberg on 20 April 1945. Every seat in the *Theaterhalle* was taken by construction workers. Paul Giesler, *Gauleiter* of Upper Bavaria, told them that he was infusing new spirit and belief into 'the places of this holy mountain'. *Kreisleiter* Stredele bawled, 'A new miracle is coming! And that miracle will be Hitler himself!'

At 1700 on 24 April, by Hitler's order, Hermann Göring was arrested on the Obersalzberg by the SS Commandant. In a telex, Göring had arrogated to himself the succession to Hitler on the grounds that in an encircled Berlin the *Führer* was no longer able fully to command affairs. Hitler considered this to be 'treason against my person and the National Socialist cause'. Göring's arch-enemy Bormann managed to arrange for a death warrant to be prepared, but presumably it would have required

Hitler's signature for validity and so was never executed. *Reichsminister* Lammers had had knowledge of the signal and was placed under house arrest by *SS-Sturmbannführer* May until a commission of inquiry could arrive from Berlin. The chaotic state of the roads and railways guaranteed that this would take merely a couple of hours, and it appears that in the end the commissar never arrived. After being released from house arrest, Lammers left Berchtesgaden at the beginning of May for Zell-am-See in Austria with the WFSt.

On 25 April, USAAF aircraft bombed Obersalzberg. The warning came too late and the smoke-making apparatus was not in commission. The first aircraft came in over the Hoher Goll and knocked out the anti-aircraft batteries; the next wave dropped incendiaries and explosives. A total of 1,232 tonnes of bombs came down, leaving Obersalzberg in ruins. Building vehicles, equipment and tools were destroyed and the landscape was left pock-marked with huge craters, but the bunkers and galleries stood firm. Of the 3,500 people in the bombing zone, only six were killed. This air raid terminated all construction work on the Obersalzberg. Most of the workforce, nearly all of it foreign labour, was sent home. Children and care personnel left Berchtesgaden. *Frau* Bormann departed to South Tyrol with her family. Only Göring, who had taken shelter in the bunker of his house, elected to stay on the Obersalzberg.

At the urging of *Landrat* Jacob, leader of the Berchtesgaden municipality, the SS departed from the Obersalzberg immediately after the air raid. The RSD also dispersed. The notification of Hitler's death on 1 May was the signal for an outbreak of lawlessness and pillage by the local inhabitants. Georg Grethlein, the construction foreman, succeeded with difficulty in restoring law and order, having enlisted the assistance of the 430 German, Czech and Italian labourers remaining on site.

On 4 May the US 101st Airborne Division occupied Berchtesgaden, whilst French units took Obersalzberg without a fight at 1800 the same evening. A US soldier shot Georg Grethlein dead as he was administering first aid to his mortally wounded driver.

Chapter 13

The Last FHQ:
The *Reichskanzlei*

EVEN when expecting the Allied landings in Normandy. Hitler had not seen the need to transfer his FHQ westward, although in July 1944, once the Allies had actually put down roots, he did consider having a new headquarters on the Western Front, if possible in the Vosges. There are three reasons why it may be assumed that the idea was eventually abandoned: his reservation that the partially complete and 'generally ready' FHQ Brunhilde near Thionville in Lorraine was not proof against the heaviest bombs; the impossibility of having built at very short notice anywhere an FHQ which corresponded to his security requirements; and the deterioration of the situation in the East after the collapse of Army Group Centre.

On 20 June 1944, Speer reported to Hitler on work being carried out to existing FHQs and those under construction. Hitler noted that 28,000 labourers were engaged in the project as a whole. The document below, probably produced by the *Führer-Nachrichtenabteilung* between the end of August and mid-October 1944, shows that during that period there were four FHQs fully or generally at readiness as regards their tele-communications installations—Wolfschanze, Berchtesgaden, 'WO' (the codename for Felsennest at Rodert, near Munstereiffel) and Brunhilde (Diedenhofen). The fifth, Siegfried/Hagen near Munich, was at readiness for limited occupation. The sixth, Rudiger or Riese in Lower Silesia, was still under construction and would not be available until July 1945; the seventh, 'Amt 600' (Adlerhorst) had cables down but was otherwise not ready telephonically.

Speer was unable to give an answer in respect of the costs of construction until 22 September 1944, when he supplied a statement to the

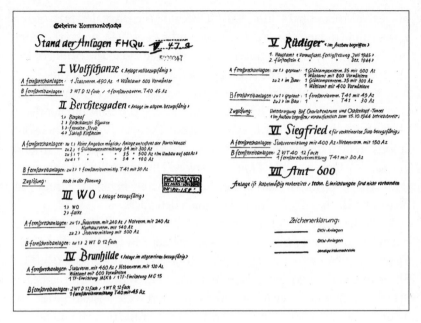

*The state of the telephone/telex network
at selected FHQs, 1944 (Bundesarchiv-Militararchiv WF01/10158).*

Wehrmacht ADC: 36 million *Reichsmark* for Wolfschanze, 13 million for Siegfried/Hagen and 130 million for Riese. The work at Zossen and 'Amt 600', for which the Army was responsible, fell outside his competence. Another document in the Allied archives is an intelligence report that states that at the end of 1944 there were finally five FHQ installations in existence that, after various preparations, could be used operationally—Adlerhorst, Felsennest, Berchtesgaden, Siegfried/Hagen and 'S-III'.* Wolfschanze had been abandoned, Riese, barring a miracle, would never be finished before the Soviets overran it, the other four were mentioned above, and there is a new addition to the list, 'S-III'. No other official document mentioning 'S-III' as an FHQ has ever been found.

On and off, Hitler had spent more time at Wolfschanze, his East Prussian headquarters, than anywhere else during the war. Following

* NA RG 165, Entry 79, 'P' file C.S./DIC (UK) Report SIR.1593, 1 April 1945 Sheet 3, Washington, College Park.

his arrival there on 24 June 1941, it became the pivotal centre of the European mainland theatre. In the second half of 1943, when the front line extended from Leningrad to Kiev and then along the banks of the Dnieper, or certainly at the latest by 1944, it was obvious that this FHQ, on account of its exposed geographical position and its peripheral location to the front, would be untenable in the long run. This did not deter Hitler from remaining there, even as late as October 1944, when Soviet troops brought the battle for the first time to Reich home territory around Goldap, scarcely seventy kilometres away. Hitler justified the tremendous risk by saying that his presence immediately behind the front put heart into the heavily oppressed German defenders.

With the exception of the *Reichskanzlei*, no FHQ was the subject of a major bombing raid while Hitler was in residence. By late 1944, the *Führer-Flakregiment* had grown in strength to fourteen heavy batteries, but its 8.8cm and 10.5cm weapons were not adequate to deal with the heavy attacks of the time: they had limited range and were unsuitable for use against low-flying aircraft. That anti-aircraft protection should not be neglected was proved by the attacks on Adlerhorst and Zossen south of Berlin in the spring of 1945.

The FHQ alternatives after Wolfschanze were the gigantic 'Riese' redoubt in the Eulengebirge, near Breslau in Lower Silesia, which was allegedly still under construction and nowhere near finished, if indeed it existed at all by that stage; the mysterious 'S-III'; Zossen, south of Berlin, which Hitler had condemned as '*Schwindelbauten*' and was the headquarters of the *Generalstab des Heeres*; and the two reserve FHQs in the south of Germany, Siegfried/Hagen near Munich and the Berchtesgaden/Bad Reichenhall/Salzburg complex based on the Obersalzberg. The last pair had adequate subterranean facilities, logistics and telecommunications for an FHQ, but to repair to either would have looked like a retreat. Accordingly, Hitler had no choice but to return to the *Reichskanzlei*, a move that, though having little else to recommend it, had propaganda value.

The Reich capital lacked a central command structure. If the *Reichskanzlei* could be called an FHQ, then it was a dysfunctional and

THE LAST FHQ: THE REICHSKANZLEI

disorganised one—not that this seemed to matter inordinately, for the leadership process had long been a stranger to all but the barest minimum staff work even though the collapsing fronts cried out for a rigorous resumption of proper control. The increasing scale of the destruction of Berlin from the air, and the restrictions on freedom of movement about the capital that this engendered, interfered with the work of a widely fragmented FHQ. Advance preparations for the eventuality of disaster had not been taken in hand. After his return from his failed Ardennes offensive, Hitler lived until about mid-February 1945 in his apartment in the *Alte Reichskanzlei* (Old Reich Chancellery) and 'after the place had become too dangerous' moved into the bunker below the gardens. Keitel and Jodl commuted daily from small bunkers at Berlin-Dahlem that had been built prewar on the instructions of a former *Chef OKW*. Berlin-Dahlem was where the OKH *Heimatstaffel* had its place of work: the quasi-ministerial OKW centres were scattered across Greater Berlin and the Reich generally.

It was from the Berlin bunker that Hitler broadcast for the last time to the German people in a recorded message, summoned the *Gauleiter* to himself also for the last time, and, on 11 March 1945, made his last visit to the front. In the words of his valet Linge, 'travelling across ploughland, field and meadow', Hitler drove to the Eastern Front between Wriezen and Seelow. Here the Ninth Army had a force of 50,500 men, only one-third of them fighting troops, to defend 138 kilometres of front. At Harnekop he called in at *Cl. Armeekorps* headquarters and also on 'some divisional headquarters'. He urged the assembled officers to motivate themselves once more for the coming battle. Hanns Schwarz, an *Offizier des Korps* (corps officer) described the events thus:

> We were advised that Hitler was coming. Staff officers from Army, Corps, Division and Regiment were assembled, the *Oberbefehlshaber* [*9. Armee*], *Generaloberst* Busse, amongst us. A small column of cars drove up. Hitler got out with an effort, bent, old. The unexpected took our breath away. His visit was unexpected, his physical appearance was unexpected. Was this the same man whom we had known and seen sometime, long in the past, before 20 July 1944? Then Hitler spoke, his body twisted, bent, with the one hand that still obeyed him grasping the other, weak. But his essence, his words, the look in his eyes—these were clear, measured and

had a serenity as if from afar, seeming to exceed the narrowness of his bodily limitations.

The *Lagebesprechungen* (situation conferences) continued on a regular basis until mid-March in the *Bundesratssaal* (Federal Council Chamber) of the *Alte Reichskanzlei* or in Hitler's study in the *Neue Reichskanzlei* (New Reich Chancellery). While the latter was the venue, there was enough room for all. From about the beginning of April, all military and political discussions were held in the bunker, and under extraordinarily restricted circumstances that were hardly called for by that stage. The so-called *Lageraum* (situation room) in the bunker was quite unfit for these in-variably long-drawn-out sessions with their many participants, since it had only fourteen square metres of floor space and an artificial air supply. The *Adjutant des Chefs des Generalstabs des Heeres* described the conditions thus:

> The people who came each day to discuss the military situation assembled in a very small conference room. It was about 3 by 4 metres. It was furnished with a bench along one wall, two or three chairs and a small table with two lamps to illuminate the map, which would be spread out. Everybody stood around this table, at which Hitler would be seated. The most elderly military men who took part regularly in the daily situation conferences were permitted to occupy the other chairs for a period because these conferences often lasted for hours. Everybody else had to stand, and that was an awful experience in this small room. Eighteen or twenty people were squashed together, and, despite the air-conditioning, the fug was very bad. And it was often a strain to keep one's attention on what was being said . . . The room was lit by a single bulb in the ceiling.

Bunker B207 had been ordered in 1942. It was probably under construction by 31 August that year, although the reference is ambiguous. The structural parts above ground had not been completed by 1944. It was not intended as an FHQ but as an air-raid cellar, and consequently was designed and built for temporary occupation only. The ground area measured 19.5 by 18.8 metres, and the concrete ceiling was 3.5 metres, and the outer walls 3.6 metres, thick. The foundation was eight metres below the garden surface and also below the water table, so that ground water had constantly to be pumped clear. The bunker had its own independent fresh-water and electricity supply.

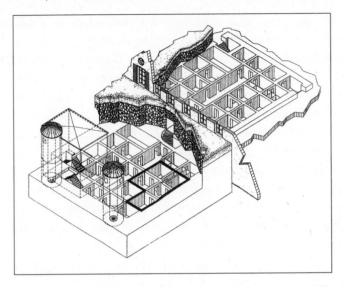

The bunker and ante-bunker below the Alte *and* Neue Reichskanzlei *(Old and New Reich Chancellery) buildings.*

There were two entrances, one from the *Reichskanzlei* garden through a large, rude concrete cube, from which one descended four landings to the work and accommodation floors, and one from the cellar of the Alte *Reichskanzlei* and the ante-bunker below large reception hall that had been built in 1936. In the spring of 1945, the ante-bunker housed the servants, and later it accommodated the Goebbels family, the food store and kitchens. The main bunker cost 1.35 million *Reichsmark*, five times the amount required for the ante-bunker.

The *Führerbunker*, two floors deeper than the ante-bunker, was reached by a stairwell into the central corridor. To the left and right were sixteen small rooms, most with a floor area of no more than 13 square metres. Here Hitler had a bedroom, a living room and a study, with a small hallway and a bathroom. Other rooms were occupied by Eva Braun, Goebbels, a doctor and Hitler's personal valet. The *Begleitkommando*— Hitler's personal bodyguard—had to make do with an ante-room and the gas-sluice compartment protecting the garden entrance. Two exterior cylindrical observation towers, one incomplete, served as air intakes.

In the functional areas were located a small telephone exchange, an 80-circuit telex room with one conference and six single telex machines, heating and air-conditioning units and the *Lageraum*. All the *Adjutanten* lived in the large cellar rooms below the *Neue Reichskanzlei*, while Keitel, Jodl and Guderian, the *Chef des Generalstabes des Heeres* (Chief of the Army General Staff), often spent many hours travelling in from their outlying posts.

On account of its small size and lack of telecommunications equipment—each bunker, including machinery and sanitary rooms, had a floor area of only 700 square metres—the complex was unsuitable for use an FHQ. The telephone exchange was inadequate even for the urgent traffic, and the *Führer-Nachrichtenabteilung* was obliged to improvise its expansion. One assumes that lines from the bunker went through junctions to OKH Bendlerstrasse, from where they linked to Zossen headquarters; this seems to be the only way FHQ could have accessed the secure *Wehrmacht* net.

Since at that time the *Führer-Nachrichtenabteilung* would not have been able to lay cables through shafts and underground trenches, the new connections were susceptible to damage and breakage; this was very noticeable in the final stages of the battle for Berlin. One solution was to bridge lines over radio and anti-aircraft towers, and towards the end of the war it was even accomplished using a barrage balloon at Rheinsberg. There was a 100W long-wave and medium-wave radio transmitter in the *Alte Reichskanzlei*, but this relied on an external aerial. During the evening of 22 April 1945, the men of the *Führer-Nachrichtenabteilung* disappeared without notice from the grounds of the *Reichskanzlei*. The rapidly deteriorating situation regarding communications was made worse by the variety of secret encryption equipment used by individual transmitting stations. Across the remaining areas of the Reich still held by Hitler, damage to the telephone infrastructure paralysed the trunk network.

Kurfürst, the headquarters of the *Führungsstab der Luftwaffe* (*Luftwaffe* Command Staff) in Wildpark Werder, was a central and protected site for an FHQ south-west of Berlin, and one with good telecommunications, but apparently Hitler was not made aware of Kurfürst by *Chefadjutant der Wehrmacht* Burgdorf or *Luftwaffenadjutant* von Below until late March 1945, by which time the threat to Berlin was worsening and the *Luftwaffe* had abandoned Wildpark Werder save for a skeleton staff. Remarking that the bunkers there 'had until now been kept completely secret from me', on 23 March 1945 he dismissed this last attempt of his 'inner circle' to find more tolerable conditions for his work as leader than were available in the *Reichskanzlei*. He showed as little enthusiasm for Berchtesgaden/Bad Reichenhall, whither the greater body of the higher command staffs had relocated by April, when Keitel recommended it to him that month 'in accordance with instructions received'.

Between October 1944 and 9 March 1945, Hitler appears to have ordered an existing location to be expanded to accommodate a new FHQ. As with 'S-III', only one official document bears witness to it. The vaguely worded communiqué was drafted by Burgdorf and informed the *Wehrmacht* arms of service and *Aussenministerium* (Foreign Ministry) that the *Reichsführer-SS* had the development—which was at Ohrdruf, in the Harz mountains of central Germany—in hand.

When Hitler, on his 56th birthday, 20 April 1945, decided to remain in Berlin, all plans for a new FHQ anywhere became obsolete. To justify his decision, at his last situation conference of 25 April he explained that there would be no point in 'sitting in the south, for there I would have neither army nor influence. I would simply be there with my staff.' The option for him to escape by air remained available until the Red Army overran Berlin-Gatow airport. The *Regierungsflugstaffel* (Government Flight) consisted of at first one, and later several, Focke-Wulf FW 200 Condor passenger aircraft, to which, in the autumn of 1944, one four-engined Junkers Ju 290, a large number of three-engined Junkers Ju 52s and some unspecified light aircraft were added. In the last days of the war, the readiness of the *Regierungsflugstaffel* had increased to forty aircraft—thirteen FW 200s, three Ju 290s, a few He 111s and an indeterminate number of Ju 52s and light aircraft, some of which were on permanent stand-by both at Berlin-Gatow and, according to Hitler's pilot Baur, also at Rechlin, the test airfield west of Neustrelitz, to evacuate the *Führer* and his entourage.

From 20 April, while Keitel and Jodl were leaving Greater Berlin for the OKW headquarters at Neustadt in Holstein, Hitler spent the last ten days of his life in the bunker of the *Neue Reichskanzlei* in the bosom of the *Sperrkreis I* intimates he tolerated and the Goebbels household. On 21 April *Grossadmiral* Dönitz transferred from Berlin to the new *Befehlsstelle Nord* in the *Marine-Nachrichtenabteilung* (Naval Signals Command) barracks at Plön ('Krokodil') and there took command of all *Wehrmacht* troops in the northern half of Germany. In the evening of 30 April, it was at Plön that he received the notification from Bormann in Berlin that Hitler had appointed him, Dönitz, to be his successor in place of *Reichsmarschall* Göring. Goebbels and Bormann did not inform Dönitz that Hitler was dead until 1 May, when they also told him that the office of *Reichspräsident* had been transmitted to him in Hitler's last will and testament, and with it supreme command of the *Wehrmacht*. Goebbels was *Reichskanzler* (Reich Chancellor).

Domarus points out that the 'transmission' of the office of *Reichspräsident* to Dönitz was not within Hitler's gift and formally unconstitutional, and that, equally formally, Dönitz was not authorised under German law to exercise the prerogative of supreme command of the *Wehrmacht*. However, few machinations since 1934 had been constitutional, elections were not possible, and all parties, friendly and hostile, recognized Dönitz as the successor to Hitler's offices after Goebbels' suicide. In his first *Tagesbefehl* that same day, Dönitz notified the *Wehrmacht* of recent events and declared:

> I assume supreme command of all arms of the German *Wehrmacht* with the intention to continue the struggle against the Bolsheviks for as long as it takes to save the fighting men and the hundreds of thousands of families in eastern Germany from slavery or liquidation. I am obliged to continue the war against Britain and the United States only insofar and as long as they obstruct me in the prosecution of the struggle against the Bolsheviks.

Because of the Allied thrust against Hamburg, Dönitz transferred his headquarters to the Marineschule (Naval College) at Murwik on 2 May. There he learned of the partial surrender of German troops in Italy, which had been negotiated without Hitler's consent. On 4 May he issued an order to end the U-boat war and for all attacking U-boats to return to port, and ordered all German forces in the Netherlands, Denmark and north-western Germany to cease hostilities against the Western Allies at 0800 on 5 May. The general surrender document was signed at Rheims at 0230 on 7 May and came into effect at one minute past midnight on 9 May, by which time Dönitz had arrived at Karlshorst to repeat the procedure before the Soviet commander-in-chief at sixteen minutes after midnight.

Dönitz continued to be recognised as supreme commander of the *Wehrmacht* until 23 May 1945, when together with the temporary *Reichsregierung* (government), he was arrested by British forces.

Chapter 14

The Greatest FHQ: Riese

O N 11 September 1943, Hitler's *Chefadjutant der Wehrmacht*, *General-major* Rudolf Schmundt, placed the order for the great redoubt known as 'Riese' (Giant). The plans were discussed four days later by *Rüstungsminister* Speer, *Leiter der OT* Xaver Dorsch and *Oberbauleiter* Leo Müller at OT House, Moysee, near FHQ Wolfschanze. Riese's geographical location was less exposed than that of Wolfschanze and more central for the defensive operation into which the Eastern Front was degenerating. The critical areas to protect had been identified as the oilfields of Hungary and the Vienna Basin, the Bay of Danzig and the industrial region of Upper Silesia.

On 1 November 1943, work was begun south east of Bad Charlotten-brunn in the Eulengebirge mountains, along a 36-kilometre ridge of gneiss running north-west to south-east between the valleys of Schweidnitz and the eastern Neisse. This central mountainous region of Lower Silesia, with its dense woods and ravines, was to be the location for a dispersed group of subterranean, bomb-proof establishments consolidated into one great *Führerhauptquartier*. Dorsch mentioned under interrogation in 1946 a figure of 20,000 places, but the official report of *Chefbaumeister der Führer-hauptquartieranlagen* (FHQ Project Leader) Siegfried Schmelcher, issued on 17 November 1944, puts the figure at 27,244 made up as follows:

Flak personnel:	6,640
FHQ:	752, plus 1,858 security and 5,832 unspecified personnel within a radius of 25 kilometres
OKH:	2,523 members of the *Generalstab des Heeres* plus 983 *Generalquartiermeister* and 2,079 others in the

	immediate environs and 1,903 unspecified within a radius of 25 kilometres
OKL:	Göring plus 2,004, including the *Führungsstab der Luftwaffe* and *Generalstab der Luftwaffe*, all in the immediate environs
SS	229 *Reichsführer-SS* staff plus 1,541 in the immediate environs
Reichsaussen-minister	300

With the assumed exception of the *Adjutant* to Hitler, the *Kriegsmarine* was not represented.

A subterranean military-industrial complex was to be built in the Eulengebirge at the same time, and when completed this would be the second largest underground factory after Mittelbau-Dora in the Harz. It is not, however, known what was going to be produced there. According to Weinmann, it seems that on the Wolfsberg, two kilometres west of Wustewaltersdorf, concentration-camp inmates worked on the construction of an underground plant allegedly for munitions or aircraft assembly between May 1944 and March 1945. It remains to be determined whether this is correct or whether the true purpose has been deliberately concealed. The 27,000-capacity of the new FHQ, the devouring of resources and the financial extravagance during the fifth year of a disastrous war all point to a clear extension of the HQ beyond a formal military command function.

The first bunkers were dug in the Schirgenschanke, west of the town of Dorfbach. On 10 November 1943, Schmelcher and Müller went over the plans with Hitler's *Luftwaffenadjutant*, von Below. On 17 December 1943, von Below met Dorsch and Müller at Rastenburg for more talks on the required changes of locality. Müller took the opportunity to revise progress on the building programme.

Because of the shortage of construction workers, on 6 April 1944 Hitler ordered that the '*Reichsführer-SS* should make up the shortfall'. This resulted in Hungarian Jews being transported to the site over the ensuing weeks. On 9 May 1944, Speer complained to Keitel in a telex that 'only 50,000 to 60,000 of the Jews brought to Germany by the SS are able to work. As regards the remainder (about 200,000), these are old people, children and the sick and so on, who cannot be used as manual labour for the type of bunker-work envisaged.'

At some time between April and June 1944, OT was ordered to deploy its industrial workforce at Riese. According to Dorsch's testimony after the war, at the end of 1943 Speer awarded the building contract to Hauptausschuss Bau, one of his numerous cartels, but progress under the codename 'Industriegemeinschaft Schlesien' was unsatisfactory and OT, which had not been employed as of itself on a project in the Reich previously during the war was obliged to take over the job at an enforced pace. According to Garba, a letter dated 22 April 1944 from the Gesund-heitsamt Reichenberg (Reichenberg Health Department) to the Regier-ungspräsidium (Breslau Praesidium) suggests that OT had already moved in during April 1944, the date when the first concentration-camp inmates were put to work at Riese.

In contrast to its record in constructing concrete bunkers, Organis-ation Todt had no expertise in creating subterranean galleries, and in mid-July Speer set up within the OT office a special department for underground workings. Duwe was the *Oberbaudirektor* and Dr Kress the *Chefingenieur*, the latter assuming the responsibility for establishing the fitness of locations, running the engineering offices and finding solutions to technical problems to do with underground workings, machinery and equipment. By virtue of an OKW order of 30 May 1941 known as 'Sonder-elbe', the mining firms involved could obtain exemption from military service for miners of conscriptable age, or if necessary their recall from the front.

The firms retained ownership of drills and boring equipment. The technique of gallery construction used was to caulk the freshly bored walls with 30 to 60 centimetres of concrete plastered over with cement containing a rubber compound. A 25cm-thick facing of stonework was added for the finish. Ground water passed through filters in the concrete mantle to drainage canals for expulsion to the exterior.

The gallery entrances had thick steel doors for protection against bombs. In general, a straight passage of stairway led from the entrance to a point where the overhead cover was from 30 to 50 metres thick. Here there would be a shock wall to absorb blast, and behind it a gas baffle. The passage then became a central corridor, with rooms leading off at either side.

On 20 June 1944, Speer updated Hitler regarding the plans. It has to be assumed that designs and blueprints were used for the purpose, but not a single one has survived. As a result of this conversation, only 'Block I' and four sections of 'Block II' were to be taken on at first. The development of Schloss Fürstenstein was ordered to be so accelerated that the castle would be ready for occupation if possible on or about 1 November 1944. Hitler took the opportunity to stress that he wanted 'the interior furnishings of the bunker to be of the simplest kind' and to 'omit the wood trimmings'. Speer said that the bomb-proofing work and living quarters would not be ready until August 1945.

Fürstenstein had been the seat of the Princes of Pless, and in 1940 the 275-hectare estate had been taken by the Reich into compulsory administration; by 1943 the Breslau *Reichsbahn* directorate had moved there for safety. The SS-*Reichssicherheitshauptamt* (RSHA, or Head Office for Reich Security) was also using the castle as an archive under the cover-name 'Brabant I'. In 1944 OT took over the building and began substantial conversion work to turn the Schloss into a Government guest-house. A description of what was entailed appeared in 1954 in an article by the castle custodian, *Herr* Fichte, and published in the *Neue Züricher Zeitung*. Fichte alleged that Speer had 35 architects working there. He also described how the courtyard in front of the main porch had been taken up to excavate a 50-metre deep shaft for a car-lift. He was only able to guess at the purpose to which the various castle rooms were to be put. Hitler's suite was to consist of the 'Gobelinzimmer' (Tapestry Room) and the 'Italienisch Room' (Italian Room) and would have a lift to the underground bunker system. The 'Krumme Saal' (Crooked Hall) was to be used as a banqueting hall, while the dining rooms for the entourage were to be the 'Kaiserzimmern'. From the terrace there was an entrance leading to the underground galleries, the latter 950 metres in length and 3,200 square metres in terms of floor space and offering adequate protection against air raids. From a study of the room usage plan now filed at the Bundesarchiv, it seems probable that the majority of rooms were intended primarily for the *Reichsaussenminister* and his staff, who would number 300. Hitler would have an apartment of several rooms suitable for entertaining visitors of State, together with three flats and twenty single rooms for his closest intimates. Göring would have four rooms. It was also planned to accommodate wireless, Press, *Reichssicherheitsdienst* (RSD, or Reich Security Service) and logistics. The suggestion by Koch that the planned arrangements for Hitler at Fürstenstein was similar to those at Schloss Klessheim near Salzburg seems confirmed by the inclusion of rooms for Hitler's *Hausintendant* (housekeeper) Artur Kannenberg and his family.

To carry out the work on Riese, the OT head office set up a new management team under senior architect Meyer. It operated from offices at Bad Charlottenbrunn with a branch at nearby Tannhausen. The plans for Riese were drawn up by Professor Herbert Rimpl, whose Berlin office oversaw all building projects for the armaments industry costing over 1 million *Reichsmark*. On Speer's orders, it was also responsible for working out designs for the siting underground of industrial plants and factories. The four major companies involved at Riese were Gustav Dubener and Heinrich Butzer of Berlin, and Huta and Philipp Holzmann of Breslau. The 25-man OT planning staff had their studio in the head office of the Breslau textile firm Schmelz near the Schirgenschanke. Supplies were stockpiled nearby in the disused Wustewaltersdorf textile factory. Initially, 1,000 OT labourers began the work at Riese. When, in June 1944, at Polsnitz near the foot of Schloss Fürstenstein, an outside working party from Gross-Rosen concentration camp, joined the workforce, the total number of personnel employed was 2,000.

On 19 July 1944, OT management held a conference at Rastenburg with a view to transferring firms from there to Riese. In addition to the workers supplied by the four principal builders, at the end of August 1944 another 800 personnel attached to OT went from Rastenburg to

Riese. After the Warsaw Uprising, which ended on 2 October 1944 with the capitulation of the ghetto, on Hitler's express order Keitel authorised that at least 100,000 of those taken captive were to be put to work on the 'most urgent construction projects', including Riese. *Oberbauleiter* Müller remained on site during the last three months of 1944, and occasionally from then until 19 February 1945. Schmelcher also visited from time to time, and on 28 September 1944 brought '*das endgültige Bauprogramm*' (the definitive building programme). When Xaver Dorsch came to Bad Charlottenbrunn on 28 January 1945 to gain an impression of the work, the temperature was −23° Centigrade. The appropriation for Riese was 130 million *Reichsmark*, four times as much as for FHQ Wolfschanze and ten times the budget for Siegfried/Hagen at Pullach.

For the planned completion date in August 1945, the OT management had calculated that 6.3 million days' work would be required. This almost unimaginable figure could only be achieved using an army of labourers working three shifts round the clock. Their number rose from 1,000 in December 1943 to 5,000 in April 1944, and to 1,500 in July 1944. In August that year the pressure to have something ready for occupation increased. On Jodl's instruction, the surface work was put back so as to bring on the subterranean borings, 'in order that the staff there is able to work efficiently and at the same time live in acceptable quarters.' Labourers not required at Riese were to be 'used at Berchtesgaden and Zossen on the new bunker systems'.

In October 1944, the number of workers engaged at Riese rose to 19,000, and reached its maximum, 23,000, at the end of the year. These figures included a large number of inmates from concentration camps at Gross-Rosen, for whom more than a dozen work camps, two of them for women, were set up in the vicinity of the construction sites. Of the 12,000 people who, at one time or another, toiled on the Riese project from Gross-Rosen, 4,900 died as a result of the working conditions. As in all comparable cases, however, the statistics for concentration-camp prisoners vary. The first forced-labour camps had opened in November 1943. By November 1944 3.4 million days' work had been expended on the project, which was now 55 per cent complete; 2.8 million days remained, but the worsening military situation ensured that no prospect existed for the satisfactory conclusion of the venture.

The enormous scale of this project defies the imagination. If a permanent workforce of 1,000 men had been used, the construction would have taken seventeen years. For the twelve months from November 1943, the average labour force on site was 9,500.

A total of 359,100 cubic metres of concrete—sufficient to erect a pyramid nearly 450 feet to its apex from a base the size of a professional soccer pitch—was planned for the fabric of the bunkers and subterranean galleries. In the 600 work days set aside from start to finish, this meant the daily mixing, transportation and working of 598 cubic metres of concrete, requiring the regular supply of sand, cement, gravel and scrap metal fragments in large quantities to the site for mixing with water. Riese was in the mountains, and in order to get there and back trucks needed fuel and the occasional repair. The spoil had to be taken up and ferried out to storage dumps. Riese required more than twice the concrete used at FHQ Wolfschanze.

The total floor area would have been 191,232 square metres, equivalent to 1,618 villas each with a ground area of 10 by 12 metres. Of this total, 99,030 square metres was barracks, blockhouses and specialist structures (51 per cent), 44,802 square metres fortified houses such as barracks with concrete cladding (23), 40,160 square metres of subterranean galleries (12) and 10,240 square metres of bunkers and bunkered gallery entrances (5, equivalent in the example to 81 villas). Hitler was to have 5,240 square metres and the OKH 5,000. OKH had the greater proportion of the galleries, 16,750 square metres (42 per cent of 21 per cent); OKL would have 13,000 square metres (32 of 21) and the FHQ 6,250 (15.6 of 21); *Reichsführer-SS* would have 3,600 (9 of 21) and the *Reichsaussenministerium* 560 (1.4 of 21). The distribution of 44,802 square metres of floor space in reinforced housing (23 per cent of the total) was to be 16,802 square metres for the *Reichsaussenministerium* (37.5 per cent), 12,000 for the OKH (26.8), 7,000 for the FHQ (15.6), 6,000 for the OKL (13.4) and 3,000 for the *Reichsführer-SS* (6.7). Almost 100,000 square metres for allocation to barracks (51 per cent of the total area) was to be apportioned

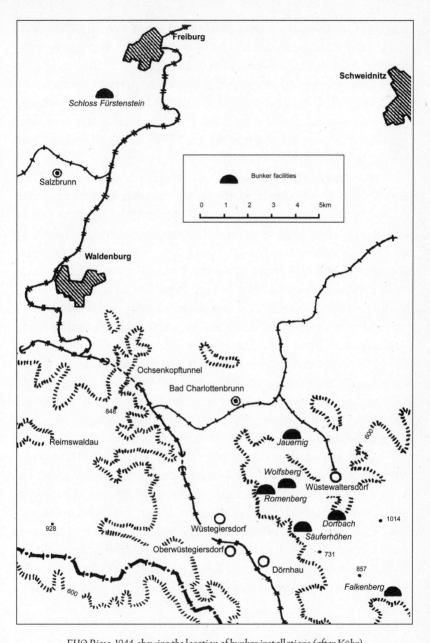

FHQ Riese, 1944, showing the location of bunker installations (after Kühn).

thus: OKH 37,000 square metres, FHQ 18,750, *Reichsführer-SS* 19,000, OKL 16,000, and *Reichsaussenministerium* 8,280, the total corresponding to more than 300 standard barrack huts of medium size.

The Riese project was abandoned once the Red Army had broken into Silesia; only a few days beforehand, the labour force had been working intensively on underground galleries and casemates. A section of the camp complex was shut down in February 1945, and the remainder was overrun by the Red Army in early May 1945.

No blueprint of the FHQ or military complex here appears to have survived the war. The suspicion that the real reason behind the existence of Riese is being deliberately concealed even decades after the war is reinforced by contradictory statements between the diary entries of Leo Müller and the memoir of Nicolaus von Below, who published his auto-biography in 1980. The latter stated that he saw the installations under construction for the first time in September or October 1944, when 'hardly anything more than the foundations were visible'. Von Below, who, as Hitler's *Luftwaffenadjutant*, had been given the responsibility for reporting on all aspects relating to FHQs, alleged that 'this undertaking [Riese] was considered to be completely superfluous' and to all intents and purposes 'the works were abandoned quite soon'. This statement is obviously untrue, since the many thousands of labourers accommodated in the work camp for the major part of the building project were not liberated by the Soviets until May 1945. It seems impossible, in view of the *FHQu-Kommandant's Kriegstagebuch* entry of 24 August 1944, that von Below was unaware that Jodl had ordered a change in the work schedules at Riese so as to be able to concentrate on completing some habitable underground accommodation for staff. Furthermore, *Rüstungsminister* Speer states on page 547 of his memoirs, *Erinnerungen*, that by the autumn of 1944 more concrete had been used for Riese than was available for air-raid shelters across the entire Reich, and at 150,000,000 *Reichsmark* the cost of the project had already exceeded budget almost a year before completion.

Research since 1945 has confirmed the existence of several distinct sites of varying dimensions:

1. For the *Sonderzug*, a bomb-proof siding was to have been engineered into the 1.6-kilometre-long Ochsenkopf tunnel between Waldenburg and Bad Charlottenbrunn. It seems confirmed that towards the end of the war one track of the two-way stretch in the tunnel was closed to general traffic, but a special siding would have required building measures comparable to those at 'W 3' in France. It is possible that track was laid for the purpose near Dornhau station, since a permanent-way party from the Gross-Rosen concentration camp was working there.

2. Dorfbach was a small, subterranean installation of 2,500 square metres near Schirgenschanke. Five hundred metres of galleries have been discovered. There were three entrances, of which two were provided with guard rooms and defences against unauthorised access. Some 15 per cent of the installation was already concreted when the work was given up.

3. Jauernig (Oberdorf) was abandoned in its early stages. Of the six galleries, two were still accessible after the war. Some 500 metres of borings had produced a floor surface of 1,500 square metres.

4. Sauferhohen had two entrances with completed armoured machine-gun positions by the time work stopped. Two horizontal galleries totalling 1,700 metres in length were linked by four transverse tunnels, presumably for work or accommodation, providing a total floor area of 6,200 square metres. The complex was 48 metres below ground and was connected to buildings at the surface by a six-metre-wide lift shaft.

5. Ramenberg had three entrances, one of which can still be negotiated. The galleries are 700 metres in length and the excavations extend over 1,800 square metres. On the hill above, work on concrete buildings had been started.

The central mountainous area in which Riese stood had a good natural protection but was remote from the centres of telecommunication. By mid-1944, the supply of raw materials had become so difficult that the demand for new telephone cables could no longer be met. Bottlenecks also existed in other areas of supply. At the end of the war enormous amounts of material for the erection of surface structures were found stored on site.

Chapter 15

S-III: Reality or Bluff?

NO other FHQ has quite fired the imagination of the German media to the same extent as the installation presumed to be 'S-III' in the Harz mountains of Thuringia and possibly begun in late 1944. S-III merits only an observation in the margin of MacDonald's standard history *The Last Offensive*, together with Allen, Dyer, Koyen, Mick, Toland, Ziemke, amongst others, CIOS and other reports from intelligence sources make no mention of it. When they arrived in the Ohrdruf area in the spring of 1945, US forces found nothing that they might have immediately associated with the special FHQ-type infrastructure to be expected. The inference that the US National Archives must therefore be holding back relevant information cannot be considered well-founded.

The US XX Corps was assuming a partial evacuation of OKW and military command centres to Thuringia but in the event only managed to capture one prominent Nazi, the former *Landwirtschaftsminister* (Agriculture Minister) Darré, who had been relieved of office in 1942. Although *OB West* had spent a period at Friedrichroda with his staff, he had removed his headquarters to safety at Blankenburg/Harz in good time.

General Patton, C-in-C US Third Army, argued vehemently for a thrust in the Gotha–Arnstadt–Ohrdruf area and obtained the reluctant consent of General Eisenhower, Supreme Commander Allied Forces, to make this thrust. The move prevented any chance of an effective defence by the jumble of German Army units at the gates of Thuringia, but the US source material makes it clear that the attack north of Eisenach was based on the statement of an officer attached to the *Stab des Chefs der Wehrmachtnachrichtenverbindungen* (Staff of the Chief of *Wehrmacht* Signals).

Patton's strategy to keep the steamroller going from the Rhine into northern Hesse and from there into central Germany was to score points against Eisenhower, not to discover a *Führerhauptquartier*. Although the US 4th Armored Division found indications of German activities aimed at transferring all major military headquarters to western Thuringia, there was no evidence and, as the official divisional journal related, 'the intended move was probably discontinued at an early stage'. US War Diary entries give the impression that neither US fighting troops, nor military authorities, nor intelligence agencies succeeded in finding traces of anything significant pointing to the existence of an FHQ. There are a large number of journal entries gleaned from prisoners-of-war, civilians and forced labourers regarding the existence of an FHQ, but accounts from these oral sources proved fictitious. All the US forces found here were some subterranean assembly plants for armaments material and one gallery complex still under construction.

Having regard to the situation in the East, which had begun to deteriorate rapidly in the late summer of 1943, and to their expectation of Allied landings in the West in the spring of 1944, it seems perfectly reasonable that the Germans would have given some thought to finding a site for a centrally placed FHQ which would be ready for occupation at the appropriate time. This would be especially true if recourse was to be had in the East to the 'bulwark ideology', whereby the mass of one's forces would be deployed there. Work on the first predominantly underground FHQ Riese had begun in the autumn of 1943 but failed to progress at the required rate because of the difficult problems with raw materials and the collapse of Army Group Centre in mid-1944, which ended any prospect of completing the project.

For a possible heavy involvement in France—Hitler had emphasised on more than one occasion that a successful Allied invasion of Europe meant the end for the Reich—he had in 'W 2' a suitable, well-built FHQ, but, probably because he was brought under pressure between two fronts at the same time, this was never used as such in the long term.

Regardless of whatever possibilities might have existed in Greater Berlin, consideration had to be given to the question of an absolutely central situation for the last FHQ. From a military point of view, Obersalzberg had almost everything to commend it, and, accordingly, a special OT management team, 'Lothar', moved in and soon had erected in Berchtesgaden a bunker with a seven-metre thick roof, below which the WFSt *Feldstaffel*, parts of the OKH and a central telephone exchange could be accommodated in safety. Judging by the long-term preparations made by the *Chef des OKH* to transfer there from Zossen, there can be no doubt but that the military had decided on the move; in mid-February, Jodl was expecting to be briefed about which section of OKH ought to be transferred there; in April Keitel reported to Hitler the possibility of transferring FHQ to Berchtesgaden 'as envisaged in accordance with orders'; and Hans Baur, Hitler's pilot, reported that the major part of the Government's duty flight-crews had moved there.

One person who was apparently reluctant to set up headquarters at Obersalzberg was Adolf Hitler. *Rüstungsminister* Speer mentioned in his autobiography that, during the construction of Riese, Hitler had also authorised the building of something similar in Thuringia, although Speer had been left in the dark and did not know where it was. Hitler's *Luftwaffenadjutant*, von Below, went to the Harz in January 1945 and declared in his memoirs that he had been shown the location for the new FHQ on the *Truppenübungsplatz* (Army Training Ground) at Ohrdruf.

General der Nachrichtentruppe Albert Praun, *Chef der Wehrmachtnachrichtenverbindungen*, was of the opinion that the *Reichsführer-SS* had taken the decision on his own responsibility to expand an underground headquarters in the Ohrdruf area with the intention of offering it to Hitler to celebrate his 56th birthday as an alternative to the Berlin bunker. Himmler had been *Befehlshaber des Ersatzheeres* (C-in-C Reserve Army) since 20 July 1944 and had the jurisdiction to do so, but it could have misfired badly and was more likely Himmler's little joke. The *Inspektor für das KZ-Wesen* (Inspector of Concentration Camps) and former *Kommandant des KZ Auschwitz*, Rudolf Höss, had also heard this story, and he repeated it in his deposition. A further variation was supplied by *Chef des Amtes Bau-OT* Xaver Dorsch in an affidavit in 1947, when he maintained that *Gruppenführer* Kammler, head of SS construction work, had suggested to Hitler

Adjutantur der Wehrmacht
beim Führer

Br.B.Nr. 340/45 g.Kdos.

F.H.Qu., den 9.3.45

10 Ausfertigungen

3. Ausfertigung.

6 Abschriften v. 3. Ausf.
s.Verteiler.

Auf Befehl des Führers hat Reichsführer-// im Raume Ohrdruf den Ausbau einer neuen Unterkunft FHQu übernommen. Mit der Durchführung ist //-Gruppenführer Kammler beauftragt worden.

Auf Grund der gemäß Führerentscheid vorzubereitenden und teilweise durchzuführenden Verlegung des FHQu's und anderer Dienststellen in diesen Raum ist eine Neuregelung der örtlichen Leitung und Lenkung von baulichen und unterkunftsmäßigen Fragen erforderlich.

Im Einvernehmen mit //-Gruppenführer Kammler wird für alle auftretenden Bau- und Unterkunftsfragen sowie für Sonderzugabstellungen als dessen Vertreter der dem Chefadjutanten der Wehrmacht beim Führer unterstehende

Oberst S t r e v e , Kommandant Führerhauptquartier bestimmt.

Die zuständigen örtlichen Dienststellen im Raume Ohrdruf

        a) Arbeitsstab Oberst Streve (Major Budnick)
        b) Bauleitung //-Gruppenführer Kammler (Hptstuf, Grosch.)

haben Weisung, an sie herantretende Anforderungen nur nach Genehmigung durch Oberst Streve durchzuführen.

gez. B u r g d o r f
General der Infanterie.

F.d.R.d.A.

Ozm.

Verteiler:
1.) OKW (WZ)
2.) ObdE , Chef des Stabes
3.) O K H (GZ)
4.) ObdM, Adjutantur Großadmiral
5.) Stabsamt Reichsmarschall
6.) Chef GenSt Luftwaffe
7.) RAM, Adjutantur

nachrichtlich:
//-Gruppenführer Kammler
Oberst Streve, Kommandant FHQu.

1.Abschrift von	3.Ausfertigung:		Adjtr Chef Gen St d H			
2. "	" 3.	"	"	Adjtr Chef Führgs Gr i GenStdH		
3. "	" 3.	"	"	Chef Trspw		
4. "	" 3.	"	"	Chef H N W		
5. "	" 3.	"	"	Kdt. H.Qu. O K H		
6. "	" 3.	"	"	Sonderstab Z		

G Z - Ia -
Nr. 246/45g.K.

U.
mit der Bitte um Kenntnisnahme.

Major i.G.

Communiqué from the Wehrmacht Adjutantur regarding an FHQ in the Ohrdruf area.
Source: Bundesarchiv-Militararchiv RH2/306, Bl.96 (OKH).

that 'instead of Riese being built by OT, he should have a new underground headquarters built in Thuringia as soon as possible.'

It seems to be confirmed that Hitler was either not always aware of FHQs in the process of construction or at least was not kept informed as to their progress. The point has been discussed earlier in this volume.

The only German primary document extant concerning the Ohrdruf FHQ is the communiqué from the *Adjutantur der Wehrmacht* at FHQ Berlin dated 9 March 1945, a copy of which is reproduced here. It was drafted by *General der Infanterie* Burgdorf, *Chefadjutant der Wehrmacht*, but signed by a senior paymaster. This might indicate that Burgdorf preferred not to sign the document for some reason. However, having another officer sign for and on behalf of Burgdorf is not necessarily significant. The important fact is that the document was accredited and definitely circulated. The distribution list shows seven recipients, these being various offices of the three branches of service and the *Reichsaussenminister* (RAM). Speer is not listed as a recipient. The opening paragraph reads: 'By order of the *Führer*, *Reichsführer-SS* has taken over the expansion of a new FHQ accommodation in the Ohrdruf area. *SS-Gruppenführer* Kammler has been given the responsibility for carrying it out. The significant word is 'expansion', which must be interpreted to mean that the underlying structure was already in existence when the document was written. The text continues:

> By reason of the need to prepare and partially carry out the transfer of FHQ and other military offices into the area according to the *Führer*'s decision, a rearrangement of the control and direction of questions concerning construction and accommodation locally is necessary. By agreement with *SS-Gruppenführer* Kammler, *Oberst* Streve, *FHQu-Kommandant* and the subordinate representative of the *Chefadjutant der Wehrmacht* with the *Führer*, is responsible for dealing with all construction and accommodation questions which may arise and also for arranging for sidings for the *Sonderzug*.
>
> The competent local military offices in the Ohrdruf area,
>
> (a) Work staff *Oberst* Streve (*Major* Budnick) [and]
> (b) Construction Management *SS-Gruppenführer* Kammler (*Hauptsturmführer* Grosch),
>
> have instructions to act on requests made to them only after approval by *Oberst* Streve.

As to the nature and extent of the Harz FHQ, there are no sources. At Ohrdruf there was an underground telephone centre known as 'Amt 10' (Department 10). The unit was checked over by *General der Nachrichten-truppe* Albert Praun, *Chef des Wehrmacht-Nachrichtenverbindungswesens*, in early 1945; adequate telephone connections were an indispensable pre-condition for an FHQ. The plans for 'Amt 10' were first drawn up in 1934, when it was considered a viable alternative to Zossen. It became operational in the autumn of 1938. This exchange had the inestimable advantage not only of being in the geographical centre of the Reich, but also of being linked up to the most important telephone trunk lines and subsidiary routings. This supports the theory that, somewhere in the immediate vicinity of 'Amt 10', an infrastructure might have existed for an FHQ.

Following the results of the search by OT for a suitable location in the Harz area, the organisation might have recommended additionally the underground assembly shops begun by Kammler at Woffleben and Appenrode in the southern Harz, but these were never considered. Kammler was also in charge of the project known as 'S-III' at Jonastal, ten kilometres from Ohrdruf, where 10,000 concentration-camp inmates had been working on an underground gallery complex since late 1944.

The Harz FHQ has been dubbed 'S-III', but the subterranean instal-lations at Jonastal do not resemble the pattern of former FHQs as regards layout and size, and whether this could have been the location is left open. As far as OKW was concerned, the Harz FHQ had the cover-name 'Olga', which from 1936 had also been the cover name for Ohrdruf.

One assumes that the rapidly deteriorating military situation might have motivated a last-ditch project in Thuringia, but such a site has never been identified, and certainly no bunkers exist. *Truppenubungsplatz Ohrdruf* could have been converted into an extensive compound with barracks centred over the 'Amt 10' underground telephone exchange, and at Eisenach there was a Morse station, but the necessary expansion was apparently never taken in hand.

As regards the *Adjutantur der Wehrmacht*'s communiqué of 9 March 1945, there are a number of unanswered questions about this document and this author is preparing a special publication dealing with his investigations. On the matter of the Ohrdruf FHQ as a whole, the lack of an adequate documentary resource leaves us to interpret and construct a theory based on the contradictory reports about the events occurring there in early 1945. The roles of Himmler and Kammler, and probably also that of Burgdorf, therefore require further investigation.

Appendices

APPENDIX I
DIARY OF HITLER'S WARTIME HEADQUARTERS

The dates below have been extracted from various official War Diaries as well as memoirs and other publications. They reflect *approximately* the days of arrival and departure for a particular stay (an example of a disputed date is Hitler's first arrival at Wolfschanze: the FHQ War Diary records 24 June 1941, Hitler's *Luftwaffenadjutant* recalls, in his memoirs that is was 'the evening of the 23rd', while Zoller noted that it was 22 June 1941. Hitler liked his train and made a number of long excursions in it from Forst Gorlitz. In June 1942, for example, he made a sixteen-day tour covering 3,365 kilometres and travelling from Wolfschanze to Berlin, Munich, Linz and St Valentin and back, broken by a nine-day stopover at the Berghof. Periods of residences at the *Reichskanzlei* are not listed until Hitler's occupation became permanent with effect from November 1944, but it may generally be assumed that these occurred during the gaps that appear in the dates listed below..

1939

Führersonderzüg	Bad Polzin east of Stettin	3–4 September
	Gross-Born, Pommerania	5–8 September
	Ilnau, Upper Silesia	9–11 September
	Gogolin, near Oppeln	12–17 September
	Goddentow, near Danzig	18 September
	Casino Hotel Zoppot	18–25 September

1940

Felsennest	Rodert, Munstereiffel	10 May–5 June
Wolfsschlucht 1	Brûly-de-Pesche, Belgium	6–25 June
Tannenberg	Kniebis, Black Forest	26 June–6 July
Berghof	Obersalzberg, Bavaria	10–14 July, 26 July–3 August, 8–12 August, 17–29 August, 4–8 October, 16–20 October, 16–19 November, 27 November–2 December, 13–16 December, 28–31 December

1941

| Berghof | Obersalzberg, Bavaria | 1–27 January, 7 February–14 March |
| *Führersonderzug* | Mönichkirchen, Austria | 11–25 April |

Berghof	Obersalzberg, Bavaria	9 May–11 June
Wolfschanze	Rastenburg, East Prussia	24 June–27 August
Askania South	Krosno, Poland	27–28 August
Wolfschanze	Rastenburg, East Prussia	28 August–31 December

1942

Wolfschanze	Rastenburg, East Prussia	1 January–11 June
Berghof	Obersalzberg, Bavaria	11 June–20 June
Wolfschanze	Rastenburg, East Prussia	20 June–15 July
Wehrwolf	Vinnitsa, Ukraine	16 July–31 October
Wolfschanze	Rastenburg, East Prussia	1–5 November
Berghof	Obersalzberg, Bavaria	12–22 November
Wolfschanze	Rastenburg, East Prussia	23 November–31 December

1943

Wolfschanze	Rastenburg, East Prussia	1 January–18 February (?)
Wehrwolf	Vinnitsa, Ukraine	18 February–13 March
Wolfschanze	Rastenburg, East Prussia	13–21 March
Berghof	Obersalzberg, Bavaria	22 March–2 May
Berghof	Obersalzberg, Bavaria	21 May–30 June
Wolfschanze	Rastenburg, East Prussia	29 June–26 August
Wehrwolf	Vinnitsa, Ukraine	27 August
Wolfschanze	Rastenburg, East Prussia	27 August–7 November
Berghof	Obersalzberg, Bavaria	8–15 November
Wolfschanze	Rastenburg, East Prussia	16 November–31 December

1944

Wolfschanze	Rastenburg, East Prussia	1 January–23 February (?)
Berghof	Obersalzberg, Bavaria	24 February–16 June
Wolfsschlucht II	Margival, France	17 June
Berghof	Obersalzberg, Bavaria	18 June–8 July
Wolfschanze	Rastenburg, East Prussia	9 July
Berghof	Obersalzberg, Bavaria	10–14 July
Wolfschanze	Rastenburg, East Prussia	16 July–20 November
Berlin	New Reich Chancellery	20 November–9 December
Adlerhorst	Bad Nauheim, Hesse	10–31 December

1945

Adlerhorst	Bad Nauheim, Hesse	1–15 January
Berlin	*Neue Reichskanzlei*	16 January–30 April

APPENDIX II
POST-WAR REFLECTIONS

Even in the closing weeks of the war, Organisation Todt had orders to look for other suitable sites for FHQ building in central Germany and the border region with Austria. At this juncture, the Reich leaders were expecting the country to be further compressed by the Allies and that existing installations and projects would be lost. On 7 April 1945, *Chefbaumeister der Führerhauptquartieranlagen* Siegfried Schmelcher submitted his top-secret OT report listing eight areas which seemed promising. Five of these were subsequently discarded on account of their situation or other difficulties of a technical nature. There remained four possibilities—the underground gallery complexes at Niedersachswerfen, Bad Berka and Ebensee, and the Obersalzberg and its surrounding area.

At Niedersachswerfen, the SS was supervising the assembly of A-4 (V-2) rockets in the expanded Dora-Mittelbau underground factory. The greater part of the galleries in the Kohnstein mountain were used for this purpose. In the Himmelberg to the north of it, SS-*Gruppenführer* Kammler, Himmler's *Beauftragte für bautechnische Sonderaurgaben* (Representative for Special Technical Construction Projects), had begun to supervise the boring two long tunnels for missile assembly, the 130,000-square metre 'B3a' in the western part of the mountain near Woffleben and the 100,000-square metre 'B3b' in the northern part near Appenrode. Germans and foreign volunteer labour were lodged in a camp between Woffleben and Bischofferode, while the 12,000 or so prisoners of war and concentration-camp inmates were accommodated at Ellrich, Harzungen and Bischofferode.

At the beginning of 1945, when 'B3a' was 25 per cent complete and 'B3b' had just been started, the work was abandoned in favour of an underground project at Jonastal about seven miles from Ohrdruf in the Harz. Some 10,000 concentration-camp inmates were put to work on gallery construction. That this project was codenamed 'S-III' seems to confirm that it formed part of the general FHQ complex at Ohrdruf. The sketches correspond to the design of SS subterranean factories found elsewhere.

If Niedersachswerfen had been chosen as an FHQ, OT would have encountered serious difficulties creating the 120,000 square metres of surface area that would have been necessary for an underground development of 50,000 square metres. The tunnels faced a valley under heavy industrial development, and few suitable places existed for the erection of further large numbers of camouflaged blockhouses and barracks huts; there were already enough of these around Dora-Mittelbau.

At Bad Berka, there was an underground factory of the *Geilenberg-Programm*, which had been abandoned by the SS. This project had prescribed that, with effect from June 1944, industrial enterprises important for the war effort, especially the synthetic oil industry, were to be relocated underground. When the work at Bad Berka was abandoned in April 1944, 8,000 square metres of the required 32,000 square metres had been dug out, which meant that, for an FHQ, a further 42,000 square metres remained to be excavated. As the requirement for the entire FHQ totalled 170,000 square metres, another 120,000 square metres ground area for surface structures needed to be prepared. This would have caused similar difficulties at Bad Berka as had been apparent at Niedersachswerfen, besides which new communications centres would have had to be installed, and this could not have been achieved having regard to the war situation and the shortage of raw materials.

At Ebensee there was an SS-run flying-bomb and rocket assembly plant. OT agreed to incorporate the former Geilenberg labourers into their workforce if the Reich authorities approved the change of purpose. On 17 April 1944, however, Hitler had forbidden the location of headquarters in the Salzburg Gau or the Traunstein, Reichenhall or Berchtesgaden districts and had ordered the abandonment of existing headquarters structures at whatever stage of completion they happened to be. Moreover, in February 1945 Bormann forbade 'the family members of leading NSDAP personalities and of the State' to establish themselves in the districts.

In addition to the four possible locations cited above, in the spring of 1945 OT carried out land surveys and trial drillings at Salzkammergut and in the Tyrol. Who ordered these is not known, but nothing came of any of them. What is significant is that OT was still bothering about plans for new FHQ redoubts a mere month before total defeat. The end of the war was in sight, and these were no more than phantom projects. Whether there, or at Niedersachswerfen, Bad Berka, Ebensee or Berchtesgaden, the shortage of materials and time put an end to the FHQ programme.

On entering the Siegfried/Hagen FHQ complex near Munich for the first time at the end of April 1945, US forces observed an absence of war damage, although the site had been ravaged by looters. The communications installation had been taken apart, but all other utilities were functioning. From a survey of the building plans drawn up by the architectural design firm Moll and found on site, the Commission of Investigation held at Siegfried between 21 and 23 May 1945 concluded that it was 'a safe place' where one could have survived for a long period. The fitting-out of the rooms was 'modern and first class'. This may have been the motivation for its occupation by US forces and later their military government. In October 1947, the intelligence agency 'Organisation Gehlen', the predecessor of the Federal German Intelligence Service, took over the complex, which remains in operational use as an headquarters to this day.

After spending a period early in 1945 in sidings at Berlin-Tempelhof, the *Führersonderzug* was brought to a point south of Zell-am-See near Bruck in Austria. At the beginning of April 1945, the Chef des *Wehrmacht-Nachrichtenverbindungswesens, General der Nachrichtentruppe* Albert Praun, examined the railway tunnel near Gotteszell in the Bayrischer Wald for its suitability to instal telecommunications equipment for a possible future FHQ using the *Führersonderzug*. In the tunnel, he had, as a precaution, prepared connections to the *Reichspost* trunk line. Nothing came of it all, since Hitler remained in Berlin.

It is reported that in April 1945 the *Führersonderzug* was positioned at the southern end of the Tauern tunnel near Mallnitz and used for a short while as a command centre by Army Group South's *Chef des Stabes*. On 1 May, the train was brought to Saalfelden and the locomotives were dynamited. The coaches were coupled up with Himmler's train, *Steiermark*, to form two separate trains, *Brandenburg I* and *Brandenburg II*, which, according to Dietrich 'fell into the hands of the Americans after numerous attacks by dive-bombers'.

US Secretary of State James F. Byrnes used a coach of the *Führersonderzug* on a journey from Berlin to Stuttgart in September 1946. In 1952 the newly appointed US High Commissioner for Germany, Walter J, Donn, arrived in Göring's slate-grey *Sonderzug* at Bonn-Mehlem.

In the 1950s, all the *Sonderzüge* of former prominent Nazis were transferred into the ownership of the Deutsche Bundesbahn. As to their subsequent whereabouts, there are many rumours. Hitler's dining car was allegedly still in use in 1973 and *Bundespräsident* Theodor Heuss is said to have made long-term use of the sleeping car, while *Kanzler* Adenauer used a train made up from a selection of *Sonderzug* coaches.

The Zossen complex south of Berlin appears to have been so robust, or was so lightly dynamited by the Soviet Army, that it survived sufficiently for its infrastructure to be occupied as the headquarters of GSTD (Soviet Fighting Forces Group in Germany) and later WGT (West Group Troops). After the reunification of Germany, the Red Army withdrew in 1994.

In summer 1946, the Wiesental bunkers of FHQ Adlerhorst were blown up and the land was taken over by displaced persons for a settlement. In 1960 the *Bundeswehr* took possession of the parcel north-west of the castle and converted two former bunkers into a depot. The land, with the large garage east of Ziegenberg castle, remained in US hands until 1992. In contrast to Ziegenberg, Kransberg suffered no war damage and the castle was used as an Allied interrogation centre for two years. Numerous prominent Nazi leaders and the industrial and technical élite of the Third Reich passed through here. After reverting to German ownership, the Kransberg complex was put to various uses by the German military after the war before being returned to private ownership in 1994.

When US forces were approaching Rodert in 1945, German engineers destroyed the structures on the height above the village and burned down the wooden housing. In 1974 the roadway from the village to the site was dug up, so that today the location of the former 'most beautiful' FHQ, Felsennest, is difficult to identify without recourse to a military survey map.

In 1955, the NATO Europe-Centre Headquarters was established at the former FHQ 'W2'. When General de Gaulle brought France out of NATO in 1963 and the NATO headquarters was transferred to Brussels, the Margival complex was left vacant for several years. In 1969 the French VI Corps set up a training centre for commandos there, and in the early 1990s the 67th Infantry Regiment had its quarters in the bunkers. 'W2', used only two days in the role for which it had been constructed, is the only FHQ whose bunkers are more or less in the same condition as when they were abandoned by the *Wehrmacht* over fifty years ago. The original fittings have gone and nothing remains of the wooden buildings, and the bunkers are either in disrepair or overgrown with brushwood and thicket.

Askania Mitte, ready in early summer 1941, was never used by Hitler, although on 28 August 1941 the *Frontgruppe* of the *Führer-Begleitbataillon* occupied it during the visit to the Eastern Front by Hitler and Mussolini, who stayed overnight at Askania Süd. On 23 June 1944, 2,800 square metres of tubular shed at Askania Mitte II were taken over by Bruim GmbH, Warsaw, for the production of weapons components under the cover-name 'Goldamsel'.

In 1949, in accordance with Directive No 50 of the Allied Control Committee, Obersalzberg passed into the ownership of the *Freistaat Bayern* (Bavarian Free State), subject to American right of use. The 1952–3 SPD government had a number of ruined structures destroyed and afforested much of the open land to discourage sightseers. American forces used Obersalzberg as a recreation centre based around the rebuilt Platterhof. In 1996 they relinquished their rights in the area and in 1999 a documentation centre was opened on the site of the former *Gasthaus*.

Bibliography

Published Sources (including Documents and Theses)

Absolon, Rudolf (ed.), *Die Wehrmacht im Dritten Reich*, Vols 5 and 6 (Schriften des Bundesarchivs 16, V and VI) (Boppard-am-Rhein 1988, 1995)

Allgemeine Heeresmitteilungen, *Jahrgänge*, 1939–45

Amtliche Nachrichten für die Oberkommandos der Wehrmacht, des Heeres und der Kriegsmarine, *Jahrgänge*, 1940–4

Archiv der Gegenwart, *Nachdruck von Keesings Archiv der Gegenwart*, Series I (Bonn *et al.*, 1962)

Boelcke, Willi A., *Deutschlands Rüstung im Zweiten Weltkrieg: Hitlers Konferenzen mit Albert Speer, 1942–1945* (Frankfurt/Main, 1969)

Böhm, Klaus, *Die Organisation Todt im Einsatz, 1939–1945, dargestellt nach Kriegsschauplatzen aufgrund der Feldpostnummern* (sourced to *Geschichte der Organisation Todt*, Vols 1–3; ed. von Hedwig Singer) (Osnabrück, 1987)

Domarus, Max, *Hitler: Reden und Proklamationen, 1932–1945*, 2 vols (Neustadt/Aisch, 1962, 1963; Wiesbaden, 1973)

Fröhlich, Elke (ed.), *Die Tagebucher von Joseph Goebbels*, 15 vols (Munich, New Providence, London, 1995)

Halder, Franz, *Kriegstagebuch: Tagliche Aufzeichnungen des Chefs des Generalstabes des Heeres, 1939–1942* (rev. Hans-Adolf Jacobsen), 3 vols (Stuttgart, 1962–1964); trans. as *The Halder War Diary, 1939–1942*, eds Charles Burdick and Hans-Adolf Jacobsen (London, 1988)

Heiber, Helmut (ed.), *Hitlers Lagebesprechungen: Die Protokollfragmente seiner militärischen Konferenzen* (Stuttgart, 1962)

Heeresverordnungsblatt, Parts A–C, years 1939 et seq.

Hubatsch, Walther (ed.), *Hitlers Weisungen für die Kriegführung, 1939–1945: Dokumente des Oberkommandos der Wehrmacht* (Frankfurt/Main, 1962)

Jany, Curt, *Geschichte der Preussischen Armee vom 15. Jahrhundert bis 1914*, reprint of 2nd edn of 4 vols (Osnabrück, 1967)

Jochmann, Werner (ed.), *Adolf Hitler: Monologe im Führerhauptquartier, 1941–1944. Die Aufzeichnungen Heinrich Heims* (Hamburg, 1980)

Kannapin, Norbert, *Die deutsche Feldpostübersicht, 1939–1945*, 3 vols (Osnabrück, 1980–2)

Reichsarchiv, *Der Weltkrieg 1914–1918. Vol. 1: Kriegsrüstung und Kriegswirtschaft* (Berlin, 1930)

Reichsgesetzblatt für das Deutsche Reich. Parts I and II: Years 1933–45

Schott, Franz Josef, *Der Wehrmachtführungsstab im Führerhauptquartier, 1939–1945* (thesis) (Bonn, 1980)

Schramm, Percy Ernst (ed.), *Kriegstagebuch des Oberkommandos der Wehrmacht (Wehrmachtführungsstab)*, 8 vols (Sonderausgabe Herrsching, 1982)

Singer, Hedwig (ed.), *Quellen zur Geschichte der Organisation Todt. Vol. 4: Handbook of the Organisation Todt* (reprinted London, March 1945; Osnabrück 1992)

Trevor-Roper, Hugh, *The Bormann Letters: The Private Correspondence between Martin Bormann and His Wife from January 1943 to April 1945* (London, 1954)

Weinmann, Martin (ed.), *Das nationalsozialistische Lagersystem (CCP)* (Frankfurt/Main, 1980)

Reference Books, Bibliographies, Handbooks

Boberach, Heinz (ed.), *Inventar archivalischer Quellen des NS-Staates: Die Dberlieferung von Bestanden und Einrichtungen des Reiches, der Länder und der NSDAP*, 2 vols (Munich, 1991, 1995)

—— *Ämter – Abkürzungen – Aktionen des NS-Staates: Handbuch für die Benutzung von Quellen der nationalsozialistischen Zeit* (Munich, 1997)

Buck, Gerhard, 'Das Führerhauptquartier: Seine parstellung in der deutschen Literatur', *Jahresbibliographie der Bibliothek für Zeitgeschichte*, 38 (1966), pp. 549–66

—— 'Der Wehrmachtführungsstab im Oberkommando der Wehrmacht', *Jahresbibliographie der Bibliothek für Zeitgeschichte*, 45 (1973), pp. 407–54

Fischer, Helmut J., *Hitlers Apparat: Namen, Ämter, Kompetenzen. Eine Strukturanalyse des 3. Reiches* (Kiel, 1988)

Henke, Josef, *Persönlicher Stab Reichsführer-SS* (Findbücher zu Bestanden des Bundesarchivs. 57), 2 vols (Koblenz, 1997)

Hillgrüber, Andreas; and Hümmelchen, Gerhard, *Chronik des Zweiten Weltkrieges: Kalendarium militärischer und politischer Ereignisse, 1939–1945* (Konigstein, Düsseldorf, 1978)

Hummel, Alfred, *Das Beton-ABC* (Berlin, 1959)

Keilig, Wolfgang (ed.), *Rangliste des deutschen Heeres, 1944–45* (Bad Nauheim, 1955)

—— (ed.), *Das deutsche Heer: Gliederung, Einsatz, Stellenbesetzung*, 3 vols (loose-leaf edn) (Bad Nauheim, 1956 et seq.)

Lohmann, Walter; and Hildebrand, Hans H., *Die deutsche Kriegsmarine 1939-1945* (loose-leaf edn) (Bad Nauheim, 1956 et seq.)

Loos, Werner, *Oberkommando des Heeres/Generalstab des Heeres* (Findbücher zu Bestanden des Bundesarchivs. 33), 4 vols (Koblenz, 1988)

Podzun, Hans-Henning (ed.), *Das Deutsche Heer, 1939: Gliederung Standorte, Stellenbesetzung und Verzeichnis sämtlicher Offiziere am 3.1.1939* (Bad Nauheim, 1953)

Stockhorst, Erich, *Fünftausend Kopfe: Wer war was im Dritten Reich* (Velbert-Kettwig, 1967)

Tessin, Georg, *Verbände der deutschen Wehrmacht und Waffen-SS im Zweiten Weltkrieg*, 17 vols (Osnabrück, 1977–96)

Verlande, Gregor; and Wolfram, Werner, *Reichskanzlei* (Findbücher zu Beständen des Bundesarchivs, 13), 4 vols (Koblenz, 1984)

Wichert, Hans Walter, *Decknamenverzeichnis deutscher unterirdischer Bauten des Zweiten Weltkrieges* (Marsberg, 1994)

Further Reading

Allen, Robert S., *Lucky Forward: The History of Patton's Third Army* (New York, 1947)

Baur, Hans, *Mit Mächtigen zwischen Himmel und Erde* (Preussisch Oldendorf, 1971)

Beierl, Florian, *Projekt Kehlstein: Historischer Rückblick auf Hitlers legendare 'Alpenfestung'* (Berchtesgaden, 1991)

Below, Nicolaus von, *Als Hitlers Adjutant, 1937–1945* (Mainz, 1980); trans. as *At Hitler's Side: The Memoirs of Hitler's Luftwaffe Adjutant, 1937–1945* (London, 2001)

Besymenski, Lew, *Die letzten Notizen von Martin Bormann: Ein Dokument und sein Verfasser* (Stuttgart, 1974)

Boldt, Gerhard, *Hitler: Die letzten 10 Tage* (Frankfurt/Main, Berlin, 1973)

Boog, Horst, *Die deutsche Luftwaffenführung: Führungsprobleme, Spitzengliederung, Generalstabsausbildung* (Stuttgart, 1982)

Bracher, K. D. (ed.), *Deutschland 1933–1945: Neue Studien zur nationalsozialistischen Herrschaft* (*Schriftenreihe Bundeszentrale für politische Bildung*, Vol. 314) (Bonn, 1993)

Brunzel, Ulrich, *Hitlers Geheimobjekte in Thüringen* (Zella-Mehlis/Meiningen, 1997)

Buck, Gerhard, *Das Führerhauptquartier, 1939–1945: Zeitgeschichte im Bild* (Leoni, 1983)

────── 'Führerhauptquartier Tannenberg', *Deutsches Soldatenjahrbuch*, year 19 (Munich, 1971)

Bücheler, Heinrich, *Hoepner: Ein deutsches Soldatenschicksal des XX. Jahrhunderts* (Herford, 1980)

Bullock, Alan, *Hitler: A Study in Tyranny* (London, 1952); trans. as *Hitler: Eine Studie über Tyrannei* (Düsseldorf, 1953)

Busch, Eckart, *Der Oberbefehl: Seine rechtliche Struktur in Preussen und Deutschland seit 1848* (Militärgeschichtliche Studien, 5, ed. vom Militärgeschichtlichen Forschungsamt) (Boppard-am-Rhein, 1967)

Carsten, Francis L., *Reichswehr und Politik, 1918–1933* (Cologne, Berlin, 1965)

Clarke, Bruce Cooper, *The Command, Control and Communications National System of Germany during World War II* (Menlo Park, 1963)

Cramer, Peter; Zeigert, Dieter, et al., *Truppenübungsplatz Ohrdruf* (Zella-Mehlis/Meiningen, 1997)

Cron, Hermann, *Geschichte des deutschen Heeres im Weltkriege 1914–1918*, reprinted edn, 1937 (Osnabrück, 1990)

Crone, Wilhelm, *Achtung! Hier Grosses Hauptquartier: Erschautes und Erlauschtes aus der deutschen Kriegszentrale* (Leipzig, 1935)

Demeter, Karl, *Das deutsche Offizierskorps in Gesellschaft und Staat, 1650–1945* (Frankfurt/Main, 1962)

Demps, Laurenz, *Berlin-Wilhelmstrasse: Eine Topographie preussisch-deutscher Macht* (Berlin, 1994)

Dietrich, Otto, *12 Jahre mit Hitler* (Munich, 1955)

────── *Auf den Strassen des Sieges: Erlebnisse mit dem Führer in Polen* (Munich, 1939)

Dost, Paul, *Der rote Teppich: Geschichte der Staatszüge und Salonwagen* (Stuttgart, 1965)

Dullfer, Jost, 'Überlegungen von Kriegsmarine und Heer zur Wehrmachtspitzengliederung und zur Führung der Wehrmacht im Kriege im Februar/Marz 1938', *Militärgeschichtliche Mitteilungen*, 1/1971

Durth, Werner, *Deutsche Architekten: Biographische Verflechtungen, 1900–1970* (Munich, 1992)

Dyer, George, *XII Corps: Spearhead of Patton's Third Army* (Baton Rouge, 1947)

Enders, Gerhard, 'Die ehemaligen deutschen Militärarchive und das Schicksal der deutschen Militärakten nach 1945', *Zft. für Militärgeschichte*, 8 (1969), pp. 559, 608

Enke, Paul, *Bernsteinzimmer-Report* (East Berlin, 1987)

Erfuth, Waldemar, *Die Geschichte des deutschen Generalstabes von 1918–1945* (Göttingen, Berlin, Frankfurt/Main, 1960)

Exner, Gunther, *Hitlers zweite Reichskanzlei* (Cologne, 1999)

Fest, Joachim, *Hitler: Eine Biographie* (Frankfurt/Main, Berlin, Vienna, 1973); trans. as *Hitler* (London, 1974)

Feuersenger, Marianne, *Mein Kriegstagebuch: Zwischen Führerhauptquartier und Berliner Wirklichkeit* (Freiburg et al., 1982)

Frank, Bernhard, *Der Obersalzberg im Mittelpunkt des Weltgeschehens* (Berchtesgaden, 1991)

Franz-Willing, Georg, *Die Reichskanzlei, 1933-1945: Rolle und Bedeutung unter der Regierung Hitler* (Tübingen, 1984)

Frei, Norbert, *Der Führerstaat: Nationalsozialistische Herrschaft, 1933–45* (Munich, 1977)

Freund, Florian, *Arbeitslager Zement: Das Konzentrationslager Ebensee und die Raketenrustung* (Vienna, 1989)

Frevert, Ute (ed.), *Militär und Gesellschaft im 19. und 20. Jahrhundert* (Stuttgart, 1997)

Fucker, Karl, *Ein Leben im Spiegel der Jagd: Im grünen und im grauen Rock* (Wiener Neustadt, 1993)

Garba, Dariusz, *Riese: Das Rätsel um Hitlers Hauptquartier in Niederschlesien* (Zella-Mehlis 2000)

Gaspard, Eugène; and Hohengarten, André, 'Anlage Brunhilde: Un "FHQu" Quartier Général d'Hitler à Angevillers en Moselle', *Revue Lorraine Populaire*, 57 (1984), pp. 30ff.

Gehlen, Reinhard, *Der Dienst: Erinnerungen, 1942–1971* (Mainz, Wiesbaden, 1971); trans. as *The Gehlen Memoirs* (London, 1972)

Geiss, Josef, *Obersalzberg: Die Geschichte eines Berges* (Berchtesgaden, 1972)

Gordon, Harold J., *Die Reichswehr und die Weimarer Republik, 1919–1926*, Frankfurt/Main, 1959)

Gorlitz, Walter (ed.), *Generalfeldmarschall Keitel: Verbrecher oder Offizier? Erinnerungen, Briefe, Dokumente des Chefs OKW* (Göttingen, Berlin, Frankfurt/Main, 1961)

—— *Geschichte des deutschen Generalstabes von 1650–1945* (Augsburg, 1997)

Grall, Jeanne, *1940–1944: Le Mur de l'Atlantique en Images* (Brussels, 1978)

Greiner, Helmuth, *Die oberste Wehrmachtführung, 1939–1943* (Wiesbaden, 1951)

Grether, Michael; and Kampe, Hans Georg, *Deckname 'Hansa': Die Bunker im geplanten Hauptquartier des OKH in Giessen* (Berlin, 1997)

Groehler, Olaf, *Die Neue Reichskanzlei: Das Ende* (Berlin, 1995)

Gross, Manfred, *Der Westwall zwischen Niederrhein und Schnee-Eifel* (Cologne, 1982)

Guderian, Heinz, *Erinnerungen eines Soldaten* (Heidelberg, 1951); trans. as *Panzer Leader* (London, 1952)

Halder, Franz, *Hitler als Feldherr* (Munich, 1949)

Hallig, Christian, *Festung Alpen: Hitlers letzter Wahn* (Freiburg, 1989)

Hartlaub, Felix, *Im Sperrkreis: Aufzeichnungen aus dem Zweiten Weltkrieg* (Frankfurt/Main, 1984)

Hartmann, Max, *Die Verwandlung eines Berges unter Martin Bormann, 1936–1945: Ein Augenzeuge berichtet: 'Meine zehn Jahre auf dem Obersalzberg'* (Berchtesgaden, 1989)

Hautefeuille, Roland, *Constructions spéciales* (Paris, 1985)

Hepp, Michael, 'Falschung und Wahrheit: Albert Speer und der "Sklavenstaat" ', *Mitteilungen der Dokumentationsstelle zur NS-Sozialpolitik*, 1 (1985), Book 3, pp. 1–69

Herbert, Ulrich; Orth, Karin; and Dieckmann, Christoph (eds), *Die nationalsozialistischen Konzentrationslager*, 2 vols (Göttingen, 1998)

Hermann, Carl Hans, *Deutsche Militärgeschichte: Eine Einführung* (Frankfurt/Main, 1966)

Heusinger, Adolf, *Befehl im Widerstreit: Schicksalsstunden der deutschen Armee, 1923–1945* (Tübingen, Stuttgart, 1957)

Hillgruber, Andreas, *Hitlers Strategie Politik und Kriegführung, 1940–1941* (Munich, 1982)

—— *Staatsmänner und Diplomaten bei Hitler*, 2 vols (Frankfurt, 1967, 1970)

Hoffmann, Heinrich, *Mit Hitler in Polen* (Berlin, 1939)

—— *Mit Hitler im Westen* (Berlin, 1940)

Hoffmann, Karl Otto, *Geschichte der Luftnachrichtentruppe*, 3 vols (Neckargemünd, 1965 et seq.)

Hoffmann, Peter, *Die Sicherheit des Diktators: Hitlers Leibwachen, Schutzmassnahmen, Residenzen, Hauptquartiere* (Munich, Zürich, 1975)

—— *Widerstand – Staatsstreich – Attentat: Der Kampf der Opposition gegen Hitler* (Munich, 1985)

Hossbach, Friedrich, *Die Entwicklung des Oberbefehls über das Heer in Brandenburg, Preussen und im Deutschen Reich von 1655–1945* (Würzburg, 1964)

Hubatsch, Walther, 'Grosses Hauptquartier 1914/18: Zur Geschichte einer deutschen Führungseinrichtung', *Ostdeutsche Wissenschaft: Jahrbuch des Ostdeutschen Kulturrates*, V (1958), pp. 422, 461

Joachimsthaler, Anton, *Hitlers Ende: Legenden und Dokumente* (Augsburg, 1999)

Jodl, Luise, *Jenseits des Endes: Der Weg des Generalobersten Jodl* (Munich, 1987)

Kaiser, Gerhard, *Sperrgebiet: Die geheimen Kommandozentralen in Wünsdorf seit 1871* (Berlin, 1993)

Kampe, Hans Georg, *Die Heeresnachrichtentruppen der Wehrmacht 1935–1945* (Bad Nauheim, 1994)

—— 'Streng geheim! Die Bunkeranlage von Zossen: Baugeschichte und Nutzung durch Wehrmacht und Sowjetarmee 1937-1994', *Waffen-Arsenal special*, Vol. 13 (1995)

—— *Zossen-Wünsdorf: Die letzten Kriegswochen im Hauptquartier des OKH* (Berlin, 1997)

———— *Deckname 'Zeppelin': Die Bunker im Hauptquartier des Oberkommandos des Heeres in Zossen* (Berlin, 1997)

———— *Nachrichtentruppe des Heeres und Deutsche Reichspost: Militärisches und staatliches Nachrichtenwesen in Deutschland, 1830–1945* (Waldesruh-bei-Berlin, 1999)

Knopf, Volker; and Martens Stefan, *Görings Reich: Selbstinszenierungen in Carinhall* (Berlin, 1999)

Koch, W. John, *Schloss Fürstenstein: Erinnerungen an einen schlesischen Adelssitz – Eine Bilddokumentation* (Würzburg, 1989)

Kotze, Hildegard von (ed.), *Heeresadjutant bei Hitler, 1938–1945: Aufzeichnungen des Majors Engel* (Schriftenreihe der Vierteljahrshefte für Zeitgeschichte, 29) (Stuttgart, 1974)

Koyen, Kenneth, *The Fourth Armored Division from the Beach to Bavaria* (Munich, 1946)

Krier, Leon (ed.), *Albert Speer: Architecture, 1932–1942* (Brussels, n.d.)

Kruszyinski, Piotr, *Die unterirdischen Bauten im Eulengebirge und auf Schloss Fürstenstein*, ed. Panstwowe Muzeum (extracts trans. by Jan Krebs) (Gross-Rosen, 1989)

Kühn, Hans-Jürgen, 'Die vergessenen Führerhauptquartiere: Unvollendete Befehlszentren in Schlesien und Thüringen', *IBA-Informationen*, No. 22, July 1993, ed. Association for the Study of Fortifications of the Two World Wars; also *Militärgeschichte*, NF 2 (1993), pp. 21–5

Lakowski, Richard, *Seelow 1945: Die Entscheidungsschlacht an der Oder* (Berlin, 1996)

Lang, Jochen von, *Der Sekretar: Martin Bormann – Der Mann, der Hitler beherrschte* (Stuttgart, 1977)

Lange, Eitel, *Der Reichsmarschall im Kriege: Ein Bericht in Wort und Bild* (Stuttgart, 1950)

Lammers, Hans Heinrich, 'Die Reichskanzlei im Kriege: Entwicklung, Aufgaben, Abgrenzung', *Das Reich*, No. 5, 30 January 1944, p. 3

Laternser, Hans, *Verteidigung deutscher Soldaten: Plädoyers vor alliierten Gerichten* (Bonn, 1950)

Leber, Annedore; and Moltke, Freya Gräfin, *Für und Wider: Entscheidungen in Deutschland, 1918–1945* (Berlin, Frankfurt/Main, 1961)

Leyen, Ferdinand Prinz von der, *Rückblick zum Mauerwald: Vier Kriegsjahre im OKH* (Munich, 1965)

Linge, Heinz, *Bis zum Untergang: Als Chef des Persönlichen Dienstes bei Hitler* (ed. Werner Maser) (Munich, Berlin, 1980)

Longerich, Peter, *Hitlers Stellvertreter: Führung und Kontrolle des Staatsapparates durch den Stab Hess und die Partei-Kanzlei Bormann* (Munich et al., 1992)

Lossberg, Bernhard von, *Im Wehrmachtführungsstab* (Hamburg, 1949)

MacDonald, Charles Brown, *The Last Offensive* (Washington, 1973)

Mai, Gunther, *Das Ende des Kaiserreichs: Politik und Kriegführung im I. Weltkrieg* (Munich, 1997)

Margry, Karel, 'Nordhausen', *After the Battle*, 101 (1998)

Martens, Stefan, *Hermann Göring: Erster Paladin und zweiter Mann im Dritten Reich* (Sigmaringen, 1993)

Maser, Werner, *Adolf Hitler: Legende – Mythos – Wirklichkeit* (Munich, 1971); trans. as *Hitler* (London, 1973)

———— (ed.), *Wilhelm Keitel: Mein Leben – Pflichterfüllung bis zum Untergang: Hitlers Generalfeldmarschall und Chef des Oberkommandos der Wehrmacht in Selbstzeugnissen* (Berlin, 1998)

Masson, Philippe, *Die deutsche Armee: Geschichte der Wehrmacht, 1935–1945* (Munich, 1995)

Metzel, Konrad, 'Ein fliegendes Hauptquartier', *Wehrtechnische Monatshefte*, September 1935, pp. 417ff.

Michalka, Wolfgang (ed.), *Der Zweite Weltkrieg: Analysen, Grundzüge, Forschungsbilanz* (Munich, Zürich, 1989)

Mick Allan, H., *With the 102th Infantry Division through Germany* (Washington, 1947)

Militärgeschichtliches Forschungsamt (ed.), *Deutsche Militargeschichte, 1648–1939*, 6 vols (Herrsching, 1983)

———— *Das Deutsche Reich und der Zweite Weltkrieg*, Vols 1, 2, 4, 6 (Stuttgart, 1979 et seq.)

Mueller-Hillebrandt, Burkhart, *Das Heer, 1933–1945*, 3 vols (Darmstadt, 1954, 1955, 1969)

Muller, Klaus-Jürgen, *Das Heer und Hitler: Armee und nationalsozialistisches Regime, 1933–1940* (Stuttgart, 1969)

———— *Armee Politik und Gesellschaft in Deutschland, 1933–1945* (Paderborn, 1986)

———— (ed.), *Armee und Drittes Reich* (Paderborn, 1989)

Muller, Klaus-Jürgen; and Opitz, Eckardt (eds.), *Militär und Militärismus in der Weimarer Republik* (Düsseldorf, 1978)

Müller, Rudolf; and Ueberschar, Gerd R., *Kriegsende 1945: Die Zerstörung des Deutschen Reiches* (Frankfurt/Main, 1994)

Neitzel, Sönke, *Die deutschen U-Bootbunker und Bunkerwerften* (Koblenz, 1991)

Neul, Josef, *Adolf Hitler und der Obersalzberg: Eine Dokumentation in Wort und Bild* (Rosenheim, 1997)

Neumärker, Uwe; Conrad, Robert; and Woywodt, Cord, *Wolfschanze: Hitlers Machtzentrale im Zweiten Weltkrieg* (Berlin, 1999)

Nowarra, Heinz J., *Die deutsche Luftrüstung, 1933–1945* (Bonn, n.d.)

O'Donnell, James; and Bahnsen, Uwe, *Die Katakombe: Das Ende der Reichskanzlei* (Stuttgart, 1975)

Operation Foxley: The British Plan to Kill Hitler, ed. Public Record Office (London, 1998)

Ose, Dieter, *Entscheidung im Westen 1944: Der Oberbefehlshaber West und die Abwehr der alliierten Invasion* (Beitrage zur Militär- und Kriegsgeschichte, ed. Militärgeschichtlichen Forschungsamt, Vol. 22) (Stuttgart, 1982)

o.V., *Obersalzberg: Bilddokumentation* (Berchtesgaden, 1983)

Padfield, Peter, *Dönitz, The Last Führer: Portrait of a Nazi War Leader* (London, 1984); trans. as *Dönitz: Des Teufels Admiral* (Berlin et al., 1984)

Patton, George S., *War as I Knew It* (London, 1948); trans as *Krieg: wie ich ihn erlebte* (Bern, 1950)

Picker, Henry; and Hoffmann, Heinrich, (ed. von Lang, Jochen von), *Hitlers Tischgespräche im Bild* (Oldenburg, Hamburg, 1969)

Poeppel, Hans; Preussen, Prinz Wilhelm-Karl von; and Hase, Karl-Günther von, *Die Soldaten der Wehrmacht* (Munich, 1999)

Pohl, Manfred, *Philipp Holzmann: Geschichte eines Bauunternehmens, 1849 bis 1999* (Munich, 1999)

Poreszag, Karsten, *Geheime Kommandosache: Geschichte der 'V-Waffen' und geheimen Militäraktionen des Zweiten Weltkrieges an Lahn, Dill und im Westerwald* (Wetzlar, 1996)

Praun, Albert, *Soldat in der Telegraphen- und Nachrichtentruppe* (Würzburg, 1965)

———— 'Nachrichtentruppe und Führung', *Wehrwissenschaftliche Rundschau* (1952), pp. 226–35, 297–302

Raiber, Richard, *The Führerhauptquartiere: Guide to Hitler's Headquarters* ('After the Battle', 19) (Stratford, 1977)

Rauchensteiner, Manfred, 'Die "Alpenfestung" ', *Truppendienst* (1973), pp. 238ff., 325ff.

Remdt, Gerhard; and Wermusch, Günter, *Ratsel, Jonastal: Die Geschichte des letzten Führerhauptquartiers* (Berlin, 1992)

Ritter, Gerhard, *Staatskunst und Kriegshandwerk: Das Problem des 'Militarismus' in Deutschland, 1740–1945*, 4 vols (Munich, 1954–68)

Rohde, *Das deutsche Wehrmachttransportwesen im Zweiten Weltkrieg* (Stuttgart, 1971)

Rhode, Pierre; and Sünkel, Werner, *Wolfsschlucht 2: Autopsie eines Führerhauptquartiers* (Leinburg, 1993)

Rodney, Minnot, *Top Secret: Hitlers Alpenfestung – Tatsachenbericht über einen Mythos* (Reinbek, 1967)

Rupp, Kurt, *Das ehemalige Führerhauptquartier 'Adlerhorst' mit den Bunkeranlagen in Langenhain-Ziegenberg* (Ober-Mörlen, 1997)

Salewski, Miehael, *Die deutsehe Seekriegsleitung, 1935–1945*, 3 vols (Frankfurt/Main, 1970–5)

Sandner, Harald, 'Wo war Hitler. Die vollstandige Chronologie der Aufenthaltsorte und Reisen Adolf Hitlers vom 1.1.1933 bis zum 30.4.1945', IfZ, Ha 01-84

Schaffing, Ferdinand, et al., *Der Obersalzberg: Brennpunkt der Zeitgesehiehte* (Munich, Vienna, 1985)

Schamfuss, Axel, 'Deutsche Fernverbindungen in Frankreich', *Museum für historische Wehrtechnik*, 3/1994

Schlie, Ulrieh (ed.), *Albert Speer: Alles, was ich weiss. Aus unbekannten Geheimdienstprotokollen vom Sommer 1945* (Munich, 1999)

Schmelcher, Siegfried, 'Der Ausbau der Plassenburg', *Der Deutsche Baumeister*, Year 1, Book 4

Schmidt, Paul, *Statist auf diplomatischer Bühne* (Bonn, 1949)

Schramm, Percy Ernst, *Hitler als militärischer Führer: Erkenntnisse und Erfahrungen aus dem Kriegstagebuch des Oberkommandos der Wehrmacht* (Bonn, 1965)

Schroeder, Christa, *Er war mein Chef: Aus dem Nachlass der Sekretärin von Adolf Hitler* (Munich, 1985)

Schulz, Alfons, *Drei Jahre in der Nachrichtenzentrale des Führerhauptquartiers* (Stein am Rhein, 1996)

Schwarz, Hanns, *Brennpunkt FHQu: Mensehen und Massstäbe im Führerhaupt-quartier* (Buenos Aires, 1950)

Seidler, Franz W., *Die Organisation Todt: Bauen für Staat und Wehrmacht* (Bonn, 1998)

────── *Frauen zu den Waffen? Marketenderinnen, Helferinnen, Soldatinnen* (Bonn, 1998)

────── *Deutscher Volkssturm: Das letzte Aufgebot, 1944/45* (Munich, 1989)

────── *Fritz Todt: Baumeister des Dritten Reiches* (Munich, 1986)

Sommerfeldt, Martin H., *Das Oberkommando der Wehrmacht gibt bekannt* (Frankfurt/Main, 1952)

Sonnleithner, Franz, *Als Diplomat im 'Führerhauptquartier': Aus dem Nachlass, mit einem Vorwort von Reinhard Spitzy* (Munich, Vienna, 1989)

Spaeter, Helmuth, *Die Geschichte des Panzerkorps Grossdeutschland*, 3 vols (Duisburg, 1958)

Speer, Albert, *Erinnerungen* (Frankfurt/Main, Berlin, 1993)

────── *Der Sklavenstaat: Meine Auseinandersetzungen mit der SS* (Stuttgart, 1981); trans. as *The Slave State: Heinrich Himmler's Masterplan for SS Supremacy* (London, 1981)

Speidel, Hans, *Invasion 1944: Ein Beitrag zu Rommels und des Reiches Schicksal* (Tübingen et al., 1952)

Sünkel, Werner, 'Führerhauptquartier Wolfsschlucht 3', ed. *Museum für historische Wehrtechnik*, Mitteilungen für Freunde und Förderer 38 (Rothenbach, 1993)

Sünkel, Werner; Rack, Rudolf; and Rhode, Pierre, *Adlerhorst: Autopsie eines Führerhauptquartiers* (Leinburg, 1998)

Szynkowski, Jerzy, *Reiseführer Wolfschanze* (Leer, 1990)

Szynkowski, Jerzy; and Wünsche, Georg S., *Das Führerhauptquartier (FHQu) Wolfschanze* (Ketrzyn/ Rastenburg, 1998)

Thaer, Albrecht von, *Generalstabsdienst an der Front und in der OHL: Aus Briefen und Tagebuchaufzeich-nungen 1915–1919* (Abhandlungen der Akademie der Wissenschaften in Göttingen, 3rd series, No. 40, (Göttingen, 1958)

Thiele, Fritz, *Zur Geschichte der Nachrichtentruppe* (Berlin, 1925)

Toland, John, *The Last Hundred Days* (New York, 1966); trans. as *Das Finale: Die letzten Hundert Tage* (Bergisch-Gladbach, 1978)

────── *Adolf Hitler* (Leicester, 1976); trans. as *Adolf Hitler* (Bergisch Gladbach, 1977)

Uhlich, Werner, *Deutsche Decknamen des Zweiten Weltkrieges* (Berg-am-See, 1987)

Vat, Dan van der, *Der gute Nazi: Albert Speers Leben und Lügen* (Berlin, 1997)

Volker, Heinz, 'Zur 50jährigen Geschichte der Führungsorganisation der deutschen Luftwaffe', *Jahrbuch der Luftwaffe*, Book 3 (Darmstadt, 1966), pp. 118–123

Vormann, Nikolaus von, 'Erinnerungen des Verbindungsoffiziers des Heeres beim Obersten Befehlshaber der Wehrmacht 27.8.–22.9.1939', ItZ, F 34/1-2

Warlimont, Walter, *Im Hauptquartier der deutschen Wehrmacht, 1939–1945: Grundlagen – Formen – Gestalten* (Frankfurt/Main, 1962); trans. as *Inside Hitler's Headquarters, 1939–1945* (London, 1964)

Wein, Friedrich, *Die Luftverteidigungszone des Westwalls bei Freudenstadt*, (Waldachtal, 1995)

Wendt, Bernd-Jürgen, *Grossdeutschland: Aussenpolitik und Kriegsvorbereitung des Hitler-Regimes* (Munich, 1987)

Wiedemann, Fritz, *Der Mann, der Feldherr werden wollte* (Velbert/Kettwig, 1964)

Wien, Otto, *Ein Leben und viermal Deutschland: Erinnerungen aus Siebzig Lebensjahren 1906–1976* (Düsseldorf, 1978)

Wildhagen, Karl-Heinz (ed.), *Erich Fellgiebel: Meister operativer Nachrichtenverbindungen. Ein Beitrag zur Geschichte der Nachrichtentruppe* (Wennigsen, 1970)

Wollstein, Günter, *Theobald von Bethmann-Hollweg: Letzter Erbe Bismarcks, erstes Opfer der Dolchstosslegende* (Göttingen, Zürich, 1995)

Wolters, Rudolf, *Albert Speer* (Oldenburg, 1943)

Wulf, Joseph, *Martin Bormann: Hitlers Schatten* (Gütersloh 1962)

Zduniak, Jan; and Ziegler, Klaus-Jürgen, *Wolfschanze und Hitlers andere Kriegshauptquartiere: Seltene Bilddokumente* (Karolewo, 1999)

Zeigert, Dieter, 'Irrlichter im Jonastal: Ratsel um eine Bauruine' (MS, 1995)

—— 'Aus der Geschichte des Truppentibungsplatzes Ohrdruf', in Cramer, Peter, et al., *Truppentibungsplatz Ohrdruf* (Zella-Mehlis, 1997)

—— *Militärbauten in Thüringen* (Arbeitshefte des Thüringischen Landesamtes für Denkmalpflege, 1/1998) (Bad Homburg, Leipzig, 1997)

Ziemke, Earl Frederick, *The US Army in the Occupation of Germany, 1944–1946* (Washington, 1975)

Zoller, Albert, *Hitler privat: Erlebnisbericht seiner Geheimsekretärin* (Düsseldorf, 1949)

Index

Gerland, Luis, 146
German Press Agency, 41
Gibraltar, 82
Giesler, Professor Hermann, 72, 159, 182
Giesler, Paul, 206
Gigurtu, Ion (Romanian President), 81
Goebbels, Joseph, 74, 78, 107, 199, 213; and visits to FHQ, 194–5; opposes evacuation of Berlin, 201–2; becomes *Reichskanzler*, 216
Goldap, 102, 174, 205, 210
'Goldap' group, 101
Göring, Hermann, 25ff., 42, 43, 63ff., 72, 77, 87, 94, 97, 106, 115, 116, 123, 154, 159, 171, 174, 190, 194, 205, 216, 219, 222; and altercation with Hitler, 193; arrest of, 206; stays at Berchtesgaden, 207
Grandes, General Munoz, 111, 123
Grethlein, Georg, 79, 207
Grosch, *Hauptsturmführer*, 233
'Grossdeutschland' infantry regiment, 30, 39, 42; *Führer-Begleitbataillon*, 56
Grosse Hauptquartier, 15–17, 18
Guderian, *Generaloberst* Heinz, 171, 214; visits FHQ Adlerhorst, 193, 194, 195

H

Hagen, FHQ (Siegfried), 209, 223; construction of, 181–2; layout of, 182–6
Halder, *General der Artillerie* Franz, 25, 41, 44, 58, 60, 70, 107, 113; and disagreement with Hitler, 118
Halle Army Signals School, 30
Hartlaub, Professor, 24, 114
'Haus Wachenfeld', 78
Heerespersonalamt, 163
Heerestransportwesen (Army Transport Command), 198
Hegewald, 116–17
Heimatfront (Home Front), 157
Heimatstaffel (Home Staff), 198, 211
Heinemann, *Generalleutnant* Erich, 170
Heinrich, 28, 62, 87, 158, 190
Henne, *Einsatzleiter*, 59
'Herbststurm' (Autumn Storm), 82
Hess, Rudolf, 39, 72, 96, 181; flight of, 88
Hewel, Ambassador, 95
Hewel, Walther, 21, 111
Heydrich, Reinhard, 105
Himmler, Heinrich, 25ff., 39, 43, 53, 62, 84, 87, 98, 105, 107, 110, 124, 145, 158, 160, 168, 172, 175, 190, 193, 205, 231, 235; attendance at FHQ of, 95
Hirsch, Wilhelm, 190
Hoehne, *SS-Obersturmbannführer* Dr, 159
Hoffmann, Heinrich (photographer), 21, 61, 62
Horthy, Count (Hungarian regent), 87
Höss, Rudolf, 231
Hube, *Generaloberst* Hans, 168
Huntzinger, *Général*, 72

I

'inner circle', Hitler's, 38, 75, 10, 170, 194, 215, 216
'Inselsprung', 180

J

Jacob, *Landrat*, 207
Jacob, *General der Pionere* Friedrich, 180
Jagen, 141, 35
Jauernig (Oberdorf), 227

Jews, 122, 219, 220
Jodl, *Generaloberst* Alfred, 21ff., 54, 61, 67, 69, 73ff., 81, 86, 103ff., 110, 153, 163, 169, 179, 188, 192ff., 206, 211, 214, 216, 223, 226, 231; influence of, 64–5; and argument with Hitler over Caucasus, 119; draws up anti-paratroop plan, 172, 174
Joint Intelligence Objectives Agency, 182
Jonestal, 234; *see also* 'S-III'
July Bomb Plot, 173–5
Junge, Traudl, 195

K

'K', Project, 190
Kammler, *Gruppenführer* Hans, 231ff.
Kampe, Hans Georg, 20
Kannenberg, Artur, 222
Karlshorst, 217
Kassel, 76
'Kehlsteinhaus', 77, 78
Keitel, *Generalfeldmarschall* Wilhelm, 18, 21, 24, 27, 38, 43, 53, 54, 61ff., 72, 81, 82, 86, 103ff., 111, 162, 163, 168, 193ff., 202, 211, 214ff., 220, 223, 231
Kesselring, *Generalfeldmarschall* Albert, 154, 196, 206
Klaushohe, 159
'Kleine Reichskanzlei' (Little Reich Chancellery), 81
Kleist, von, 156
Klessheim, Schloss, 154, 167, 169, 222
Kluge, *Generalfeldmarschall* Günther von, 40, 69, 117, 118, 154
'Kolonne F' (Convoy F), 29
Kommando 'Führerreise', 29
'Koralle', 204
Kraftwagenkolonne (Hitler's motorcade), 62, 157; composition of, 30, 40
Krampnitz Cavalry School, 30
Kransberg, 50, 55, 188, 190
Kransberg, Schloss, 50ff., 188–90
Kress, Dr, 220
Kriegsmarine, 25, 28, 84, 206, 219
'Krokodil', 216
Küchler, *General der Artillerie* Georg von, 43, 112, 118
Kuhnell, *Baurat*, 51, 55
Kurfürst, suitability as FHQ of, 214
Kursk offensive, *see* 'Zitadelle', Operation

L

labour force, *see* workforce
Lagebesprechungen (situation conferences), 212
'Lager K' (Camp K), 51
Lammers, *Reichsminister* Dr Hans Heinrich, 21, 22, 28, 43, 62, 81, 95, 105, 116, 157, 201, 204; arrest of, 207
Landhausstil, 54
Laval, Pierre (French President), 82, 85, 123, 154
Leningrad, 151, 210
Leopold III of Belgium, 82, 83
Linge, Heinz, 39, 106, 193, 211
List, *Generalfeldmarschall* Wilhelm, 109, 118; dismissal of, 119
Lohr, *Generaloberst* Alexander, 105
'Lothar', 205, 231
Luftnachrichtenabteilung, 176
Luftverteidigungszone West (Air Defence Zone West), 46, 50, 58, 73
Luftwaffe, 20, 25, 28, 31, 41, 44, 50, 59, 64ff., 75, 88, 89, 94, 102, 152, 169, 174, 187, 202, 205, 215
Luftwaffe Reserve-Festungs Flakabteilung, 321, 56
Luftwaffenadjutantur, 77

253